27.⁰⁰ 9/13 U

MANCHU

LIA

Changchun

Mukden

Peking

Tientsin

Yenan

Yalu River

...tok

NORTH
KOREA

Pyongyang

Dairen
Port Arthur

Seoul

SOUTH
KOREA

Tsingtao

Nanking

Woosung
Shanghai
CHUSAN
ISLANDS

Hankow

Yangtze River

Chengtu

Chungking

MATSU

Taipei

TAIWAN
(FORMOSA)

QUEMOY

Canton

PESCADORES

engtze

Nanning

HONG KONG

ORTH
ETNAM

HAINAN ISLAND

DIVIDED COUNSEL

DIVIDED COUNSEL

The Anglo-American Response to Communist Victory in China

EDWIN W. MARTIN

THE UNIVERSITY PRESS OF KENTUCKY

Copyright © 1986 by The University Press of Kentucky

Scholarly publisher for the Commonwealth,
serving Bellarmine College, Berea College, Centre
College of Kentucky, Eastern Kentucky University,
The Filson Club, Georgetown College, Kentucky
Historical Society, Kentucky State University,
Morehead State University, Murray State University,
Northern Kentucky University, Transylvania University,
University of Kentucky, University of Louisville,
and Western Kentucky University.

Editorial and Sales Offices: Lexington, Kentucky 40506-0024

Library of Congress Cataloging-in-Publication Data

Martin, Edwin W.
    Divided counsel.

    Bibliography: p.
    Includes index.
    1. United States—Foreign relations—China.
2. China—Foreign relations—United States. 3. Great
Britain—Foreign relations—China. 4. China—Foreign
relations—Great Britain. 5. China—History—Civil
War, 1945-1949. 6. United States—Foreign relations—
Taiwan. 7. Taiwan—Foreign relations—United States.
8. Great Britain—Forign relations—Taiwan.
9. Taiwan—Forign relations—Great Britain. I. Title.
E183.8.C5M36   1986   327.73051   86-1708
ISBN 0-8131-1591-4

E
183
.8
.C5
m36
1986
c.1

dh

To Emma Rose

UWEC McIntyre Library
DISCARDED
NOV X X 1986
EAU CLAIRE, WI

Contents_____

Part III. IMPACT OF THE KOREAN WAR

Part IV. SUMMING UP

Illustrations follow page 116

Preface

When I began research for this book, my intention was to describe how the United States had responded in China to the Communist triumph there, for this story, I thought, had not been adequately dealt with in the existing literature on Sino-American relations. I had long noted, for example, that otherwise knowledgeable people were often unaware that the United States had sought for months to maintain an official presence in areas of China that had come under Communist control and that American representatives had tried in vain to discuss specific problems with Communist officials both before and after the establishment of the People's Republic of China.

As part of my book, I planned to describe the role played by the British in representing American interests in China after American officials were withdrawn in the spring of 1950. However, upon examination of British diplomatic documents, I decided to change the scope of the book and to devote major attention to Sino-British relations. Detailed comparison of how the British Foreign Office responded to Communist policies in China with the way the Department of State responded to them enabled me to look at the evolution of Sino-American relations in this period from a new perspective. The British chose policy alternatives that the United States might have chosen but did not. Yet American politics did not play as important a role in Anglo-American differences as has been popularly supposed. How and why U.S. and U.K. policies toward China diverged are the principal questions pursued in this book.

Most of the book is devoted to describing the evolution of British and American policies from late 1948 to early 1951. Since for years after the spring of 1951 there was little significant change in these policies, especially American policy, the book might logically have ended at this point. I have added two chapters dealing with developments in 1953-1954 because of the significant changes in Peking's policies toward the United Kingdom and the United States manifested at the Geneva Conference. Had these policy changes occurred before, instead of after, the Korean War, the course of Sino-British and Sino-American relations might have been a good deal smoother.

Acknowledgments ───────

I am grateful to the American Philosophical Society for a grant from the Penrose Fund, enabling me to travel to the United Kingdom to do research at the Public Record Office, to Professor Trevor May of Hertfordshire College for his helpful letters of introduction, and to the Record Office for courteous assistance. At the National Archives my research was ably and cheerfully facilitated by Sally Marks.

I am especially indebted to Ralph N. Clough, now at the Johns Hopkins University School of Advanced International Studies, for his incisive comments and suggestions while the manuscript was in preparation. I am also grateful to Catherine Forman for her patient and careful work through several drafts of the manuscript, and to Robert Aylward for providing me with valuable source material. To Gladys Hubbard Swift, I owe thanks for granting me access to her father's letters and oral history tapes, and for permission to quote from them. I wish also to thank Philip Fugh, Philip Manhard, and William N. Stokes for the benefit of their experienced views.

Note on Romanization _____

Since January 1, 1979, foreign language publications of the People's Republic of China, and most foreign publications, have used the *pinyin* system of Romanization. However, in order to be consistent with the documents excerpted in it, this study uses the Wade-Giles system for the names of persons and the Postal Atlas system for place names. There are a few exceptions in cases where the usual Romanization of a well-known name deviated from the Wade-Giles system: for example, Chiang Kai-shek is used rather than Chiang Chieh-shih.

For those readers who are more familiar with *pinyin* than with the Wade-Giles and Postal Atlas systems, a list follows of *pinyin* equivalents of important Chinese personal and place names appearing in the text, except for the names of Nationalist officials.

Names of Persons		*Names of Places*	
Text	*Pinyin*	*Text*	*Pinyin*
Chang Han-fu	Zhang Hanfu	Canton	Guangzhou
Chou En-lai	Zhou Enlai	Chengtu	Chengdu
Chu Teh	Zhu De	Chungking	Chongqing
Huan Hsiang	Huan Xiang	Dairen	Dalian
Huang Hua	Huang Hua	Hankow	Wuhan
Kao Kang	Gao Gang	Mukden	Shenyang
Li Chi-shen	Li Jishen	Nanking	Nanjing
Lin Piao	Lin Biao	Peiping/Peking*	Beiping/Beijing
Liu Shao-ch'i	Liu Shaoqi	Port Arthur	Lushun
Mao Tse-tung	Mao Zedong	Tientsin	Tianjin
Nieh Jung-chen	Nie Rongzhen	Tihwa (Urumchi)	Urumqi
Wang Ping-nan	Wang Bingnan	Tsingtao	Qingdao
Yeh Chien-ying	Ye Jianying		

_____

* Peking is used in the text for the period after October 1, 1949.

Part I
Staying Put

1

Responses to a Parade of Victories

The closing weeks of the year 1948 saw a series of stunning Communist military triumphs in China. Completing their conquest of Manchuria in November, Communist armies swept south to threaten the great cities of Tientsin and Peiping on the north China plain, both of which they took early in the new year. Meanwhile, in the battles of the Huai-Hai campaign in east China, Communist forces "600,000 strong," according to their own account, "wiped out" more than half a million Chinese government troops, subjecting China's capital, Nanking, to a "direct threat by the People's Liberation Army."[1]

In the midst of this parade of military victories, Communist party Chairman Mao Tse-tung proclaimed in his 1949 New Year's message to the Chinese people that the "Chinese reactionaries" and "the aggressive forces of U.S. imperialism" now realized that "the country-wide victory of the Chinese People's War of Liberation [could] no longer be prevented by purely military struggle." Precisely for this reason, they were placing more and more importance on "political struggle," which meant "using the existing Kuomintang government for their 'peace' plot." But Mao was in no mood for peace negotiations. "The question now facing the Chinese people," he declared, "is whether to carry the revolution through to the end or abandon it half-way. . . . Only by completely destroying the Chinese reactionaries and expelling the aggressive forces of U.S. imperialism can China gain independence, democracy and peace."[2]

A year earlier, in a report to the Central Committee of the Chinese Communist party (CCP), Mao had announced that a turning point had been reached in the worldwide struggle of the "democratic forces headed by the Soviet Union" against the "imperialist and anti-democratic forces," and that the "strength of the world anti-imperialist camp" had surpassed that of the "imperialist camp." The Central Committee not only endorsed Mao's report but resolved that the "Chinese people's revolutionary war" should be carried forward "uninterruptedly to complete victory, and that the enemy should not be allowed to use stalling tactics [peace negotiations] to gain time for rest and reorganization."[3] Thus Mao's 1949 New Year's message reflected the CCP's determination, now given powerful effect by its recent battlefield victories, to pursue its revolutionary objectives without thought of conciliation or compromise.

British and American policymakers could hardly ignore the dramatic manifestations of rising Communist power in China, and they made plans, as best they could, to adapt their policies to the changing scene. On December 13, 1948, the British cabinet considered a Foreign Office memorandum dealing with the problem of "what action is open to us to counter the spread of Communism in China and from China to adjacent territories in the Far East." The cabinet concluded that the only power that could take counteraction in China was the United States, but that it was unlikely that such action would be taken and extremely doubtful whether it would be effective.[4] These cabinet views were reflected in a policy paper that the British embassy in Washington gave the Department of State on January 11, 1949. According to this paper, only the United States was in a position to "contribute financial, material or military resources for counter-action against the Chinese Communists in China." The United Kingdom's best hope in China lay "in keeping a foot in the door . . . stay[ing] where we are, to have *de facto* relations with the Chinese Communists in so far as these are unavoidable, and to investigate the possibilities of trade."[5]

A U.S. National Security Council paper (NSC 34/1), coincidentally dated January 11, expressed the American objective in China as the development "by the Chinese themselves of a unified, stable and independent China, friendly to the U.S." Clearly, however, there did not seem to be much prospect that any Chinese group would fulfill this objective: the Chinese government was not expected to be around much longer and the Communists were not friendly. In these circumstances the immediate U.S. objective, according to the NSC, was "to prevent China from becoming an adjunct of Soviet power." The cold war between the United States and the Soviet Union had, of course, long since broken out in earnest. When NSC 34/1 was prepared, the Berlin blockade had been in full swing for some months.

The NSC did not say precisely how the United States would try to keep China from becoming an adjunct of Sovie power, but it recommended that the United States should make plans and preparations to exploit opportunities, "while maintaining flexibility and avoiding irrevocable commitments to any one course of action or to any one faction." Another important proviso of the NSC paper was that the

United States should "regard efforts with respect to China as of lower priority than efforts in other areas where the benefits to U.S. security are more immediately commensurate with expenditure of U.S. resources."[6]

The political impact of the Communists' military triumphs on the Chinese government was, of course, enormous. The already waning public confidence in President Chiang Kai-shek's leadership was further eroded, while support for those in the government who favored a negotiated settlement of the war grew rapidly. In a personal telegram to Secretary of State George Marshall on December 21, 1948, Dr. John Leighton Stuart, the China-born missionary educator who had been the United States ambassador to China since mid-1946, commented on "how completely Chiang had lost public confidence" and "how widespread is desire he retire," a sentiment "shared by most officials of all ranks in Government."[7] Just a month after Stuart's message to Marshall, Chiang finally announced his retirement, leaving the task of negotiating a peace settlement to his principal political rival within the Kuomintang, Vice-President Li Tsung-jen.

Li's prospects of salvaging anything for the government from negotiations with the Communists were hardly bright in the wake of the latter's successes on the battlefield. Moreover, the CCP's eight conditions for undertaking peace talks, which had been broadcast by the Communist-controlled North Shensi radio on January 14, gave little ground for encouragement. At the head of the list of conditions was "strict punishment of war criminals," among whom was Chiang Kai-shek himself. The U.S. embassy called the CCP's terms "something closely approximating unconditional surrender," pointing out, "Most immediate and irreconcilable divergence now is that Kmt wants armistice before beginning peace talks while CCP will not cease fire prior to Kmt capitulation to CCP peace terms."[8]

Despite the poor prospects for a negotiated peace, Acting President Li decided to send a delegation to Peiping, and the Communists agreed to receive it, but under conditions that, in the embassy's view, left "no scope for bargaining." The embassy believed Li was now faced with a choice between "complete capitulation and continued resistance" and that he would choose resistance.[9] Li did choose resistance eventually, but only after his peace delegation had spent three fruitless months in Peiping. In the end, Li's resistance was to prove equally fruitless.

2

Consulates Carry On

A key element in the American and British response to the Communist triumph in Manchuria and north China was to stay put. To this end, the United States kept its consulate open in Mukden when the People's Liberation Army captured that industrially important Manchurian city on November 1, 1948, and it followed the same policy in Tientsin and Peiping when those cities fell to the Communist armies. The Department of State assumed that American business and philanthropic organizations would stay on in China under the Communists. It even encouraged their key personnel to remain, assuring them that in case of emergency they would be given the same consideration as U.S. consular personnel, who were staying on. The department evidently hoped that its policy of maintaining "all the present Foreign Service establishments in China even though the tide of civil war should pass over them" would encourage those private citizens to remain whose presence in China was essential for the continued functioning of American institutions.[1] At the same time, however, nonessential Americans were periodically warned of the dangers of staying in China and advised to leave.

The decision of the United States, British, and other governments to keep their consulates open in cities taken by the Communists was quite in line with usual diplomatic practice, but the decision that faced them with respect to their embassies was politically more sensitive. On January 26, 1949, Ambassador Stuart and other diplomatic mission chiefs in Nanking received a formal note from the Ministry of Foreign Affairs announcing the removal of the Chinese government to Canton and asking diplomatic missions to follow the government there.[2] As Ambassador Stuart later noted in his autobiography, "The government naturally wanted the Diplomatic Body to remove to Canton and thus help to maintain its own prestige. Technically we all were accredited to it and properly should follow it to the 'temporary capital.' "[3]

In view of the threat to Nanking posed by the Communists' victories in the Huai-Hai campaign, the Foreign Ministry's request did not come as a surprise. Ambassador Stuart and his colleagues of the North Atlantic Group had, in fact, been discussing such a possibility for some time.[4] At a meeting on January 19, they had unanimously agreed to recommend to their governments that, should the Chinese government actually move to Canton, each ambassador would send a senior officer of his staff, possibly accompanied by others, to maintain contact, preserving the position of the ambassador himself for future consideration.[5] This decision was in line with the State Department's contingency plan drawn up the previous month.[6] Nevertheless, the whole question was reviewed once again in Washington before the department's plan to keep Ambassador Stuart in Nanking was reaffirmed.

The rationale for this decision was spelled out in a memorandum from Walton Butterworth, director of the Office of Far Eastern Affairs, to Acting Secretary of State Robert Lovett.[7] According to Butterworth, the majority of American businessmen and missionaries in China would soon be in Communist areas. If Ambassador Stuart were withdrawn from Nanking, it would look as though the United States intended to continue aid to the Chinese Nationalists, making the position of Americans in Communist areas untenable. "If the U.S. is to afford any protection to or promote U.S. interests in these areas," Butterworth explained, "it must have official representation which can get in touch with the central governing authorities of the area."[8]

Butterworth acknowledged that some congressional quarters and newspapers would be highly critical of a decision not to direct Ambassador Stuart to follow the Chinese government to Canton, but he maintained these circles were not aware of the hopelessness of the military situation. He cited a statement by General David G. Barr, director of the Joint U.S. Military Advisory Group in China, to the effect that the Nationalist government could maintain a foothold in southern China only with unlimited U.S. assistance, including the immediate deployment of American armed forces. Barr emphatically discouraged such a course, and in any case, the U.S. government was not prepared to go this far to save the Chinese government. Only two alternatives remained: complete U.S. withdrawal from China or an effort to influence the final outcome in a way that would salvage as much as possible of American interests there.[9] Keeping Ambassador Stuart in Nanking would serve the latter purpose.

President Truman approved the State Department's recommendation that Stuart remain in Nanking, on the understanding that he carry out his instructions in concert with the North Atlantic Group.[10] Nearly three months were to elapse, however, before the Communists captured Nanking and put to the test the wisdom of the decision of the United States and its allies to leave their ambassadors there.

Meanwhile, the Communists served notice in the cities they had occupied that they were not going to play the diplomatic game by the international rules practiced in the West if it did not suit them. For about two weeks or so after their capture of Mukden on November 1, 1948, they did seem to be playing by these rules. Thus on November 5 the new mayor of Mukden, Chu Chi-wen, summoned the British, French, and American consuls general to his office in their official capacities and promised that he would issue identity cards to consular personnel and identification pennants for consular motor vehicles.[11] Four days later the mayor made return calls on the consuls, again in their official capacities. In the meantime the American consul general, Angus Ward, had received "several communications from local authorites" addressed either to him "as Consul General or to the office as the American Consulate General." This led Ward to conclude: "It was obviously the intention of the Communist authorities at the time to recognize us and permit us to function as an official United States Government establishment."[12]

The treatment accorded the foreign consulates in Mukden was so exemplary that the State Department cited it to allay the fears of Americans in other cities in the path of the Communist armies.[13] But this treatment did not last for long. As William N. Stokes, at the time American vice consul in Mukden, subsequently recalled:

A notification dated November 14, addressed to the *"former* American Consul" (similar letters were sent to the "former" French and British Consuls), demanded that all foreign residents surrender within 48 hours all radio "stations" in their possession. Consul General Ward requested an interview with the mayor to discuss the notification, but no reply was received from the municipality, despite repeated inquiries. . . . Mr. Ward then informed the garrison commander (who had originated the letter) that more than 48 hours might be required for a reply, inasmuch as the United States Government as the owner of the equipment would have to be consulted; he nevertheless promised to expedite a response. The commander rejected this approach. . . .

Instructions from Washington had no time to arrive because of the makeshift communications and coding facilities then available. Promptly at the appointed hour, evidently in possession of explicit instructions, the Communist command in Mukden surrounded the American Consulate General with troops, cut off its electricity and water, and placed the entire establishment under incommunicado house arrest.[14]

In this way the new authorities in Mukden ended abruptly and unilaterally American hopes that U.S. consular officials could establish working relations with them. For their part, the American personnel of the consulate, all of whom had volunteered to remain in Mukden, had looked forward with some excitement to manning the first U.S. consulate in Chinese Communist-controlled territory. As for Consul General Ward, who had been instructed by the State Department to initiate a dialogue with local Communist officials, he had made an honest, and what at first seemed a promising effort to do so.[15]

For some time the State Department was not aware of what had happened to the American consulate in Mukden; it believed that the consulate was merely being forbidden to transmit messages. Thus on December 2, the department instructed U.S. Consul General George D. Hopper in Hong Kong to have a member of his staff inform Chinese Communist representatives in Hong Kong of the situation in Mukden and ask if they could arrange to have a message transmitted to Ward.[16] This effort proved fruitless.[17] The department tried again on March 2, instructing Consul General Edmund Clubb in Peiping to seek an interview with the "highest Comm authority available" to convey a message on behalf of the U.S. government concerning the "continuing absence of communications from Mukden and persistent rumors Comm restrictions on staff." Clubb was to point out that "international custom has sanctioned continued exercise by resident foreign consuls of their legitimate and proper functions within their consular districts even during periods of non-recognition" between governments. He was to acknowledge that military and administrative exigencies understandably might interrupt communications with the U.S. Consulate General temporarily. Nevertheless, he was to emphasize, the U.S. government was seriously concerned by the "extraordinarily long period" that had passed without communication of any kind from the consulate general and by the "persistent though unconfirmed reports of confinement of U.S. consular personnel to their residential quarters."[18]

Clubb delivered the message to a petty official at the Peiping Foreign Nationals Office, who took it and returned forty-five minutes later with a person understood to be the responsible official of that office, "one Li Li-hua." Li said the sense of the message was understood, and Clubb should take it back with him; Li could not say whether action would be taken, since the authority of his office and of the municipal government was limited to Peiping, nor could he give any assurances of an early reply.[19] Li's caution was wise, since no reply was ever given to this message of such obvious importance to the United States.

The same message the State Department had instructed Clubb to deliver to the highest available Communist authority in Peiping was also telegraphed to the American consul general in Hong Kong for delivery to the senior Chinese Communist party official there. However, American officials in Hong Kong were no more successful than was Clubb in Peiping in making contact with senior Communist officials. Since the senior Communist in Hong Kong would not meet the American consul general, because of "the absence of recognition," the message was delivered by Vice-Consul Richard Service to Chiao Mu, the Hong Kong representative of the New China News Agency (NCNA), with the request that he deliver it to the most senior local Communist. Chiao Mu returned the message to Service four days later with a personal note saying, "Very sorry that I cannot forward such a message."[20]

Shortly therafter, Britain's Foreign Office, which had also become concerned by the absence of communications from the British consulate in Mukden, sought to contact the Communists in Hong Kong on the matter through an official of the Hong Kong Government. But the governor of Hong Kong demurred on the grounds that he did not want to "confer some degree of official recognition [on] any Chinese Communists at present time." Furthermore, he did not wish to open himself to a snub such as was given the U.S. vice-consul by Chiao Mu.[21] The Foreign Office was "inclined to agree with the Governor that for us to make an approach through Hong Kong now would merely invite another snub." Instead, it instructed the British ambassador in Nanking to send letters to the British consular officers in Mukden and Tientsin "by open post," so that they "would at any rate become aware of our attitude."[22]

Meanwhile, the British ambassador in Nanking had reported that the American embassy regarded the instructions to Clubb to take up the Mukden problem with the Communist authorities in Peiping as a "last attempt." If the position of the U.S. consulate in Mukden were not improved, it would be withdrawn. Peter Scarlett, head of the Far Eastern Department at the Foreign Office (though he had had no Far Eastern experience), was somewhat surprised by this report. The British had been talking to the State Department about the possibility of bringing pressure on the Communists to "treat our Consuls with normal decency," but he had not previously heard that the instructions to Clubb were to be a last attempt. Scarlett could "not see what good they can hope to get out of moving their Consul General [Angus Ward] from Mukden." He had understood that "Mr. Ward was deliberately chosen as being a man who would weather a seige if necessary and that the Consulate General had been provisioned for at least a year."[23]

A similar reaction came from Malcolm MacDonald, the British commissioner-general for Southeast Asia, headquartered in Singapore. In a telegram to the Foreign Office dated March 17, he expressed the hope that the State Department could be induced not to withdraw the U.S. consul general from Mukden, since this withdrawal would merely play into Communist hands. In his view, Communist policy was "clearly designed to render our Consular establishments useless and thereby to bring about their removal." MacDonald said he wanted to avoid "any crack in the solidarity front" presented by the Western allies.[24]

Commenting on MacDonald's suggestion, Patrick Coates, the China desk officer at the Foreign Office, thought it was "doubtful whether the State Department would take any notice of a request from us that they should leave their man in Mukden." It was "more in the cards," he felt, that the department would press the Foreign Office "to withdraw His Majesty's Consul General at once." Peter Scarlett, Coates's boss, agreed.[25]

However, when these comments were penned in the Foreign Office, the State Department had not yet decided to withdraw from Mukden, let alone to ask the British to do so. In Peiping, Consul General Clubb was still opposed to withdrawal. Mukden was valuable to the United States as an observation post in Manchuria, a strategic area for Soviet expansion.[26] Of course, neither Clubb nor the Foreign Office was then aware of how useless the U.S. consulate in Mukden had become, but they would soon be enlightened. On March 30 the British embassy in Nanking received a communication from British Consul General Walter Graham in Mukden, the first since November, reporting that the U.S. consulate general there had "ceased to exist" and that the British and French consuls were "quite unable to protect nationals though their presence does support morale."[27] When the Foreign Office received this report, Coates commented that the Communists' behavior "has been more disgraceful than we had known, and this information will no doubt add to the already existing U.S. desire for strong action."[28]

Although consulates in other cities captured by the People's Liberation Army did not suffer the fate of those in Mukden, authorities in these cities quickly made it plain that they did not agree with the traditional view that consular officers had a right to perform their functions without regard to the questions of recognition or diplomatic relations between national governments. The Communists' view was that in the absence of recognition or diplomatic relations, consular officials were merely private persons not entitled to carry out official functions.[29] Thus, though they made repeated attempts to do so, British, American, and other consular officials were unable to take up matters of urgent concern to their governments with the appropriate Communist officials.

Their predicament, and the basis for their frustration, is cogently explained in the following extracts from a telegraphic version of a joint letter sent April 12 by the North Atlantic consuls in Peiping to Mayor Yeh Chien-ying, a senior CCP official.

We have during two months since occupation this town by Chinese Communist Army been without those usual contacts with local authorities which would make it possible for us to take up direct with those authorities outstanding official matters of importance and our several attempts to establish such contacts through medium of Alien Affairs Office have been fruitless.

. . . it is noted that only explanation which has been received from local administrative organs for refusing to deal with Peiping Consular establishments in normal way is that Chinese Communist side is without diplomatic relations. We would emphasize at this point that we are assured that Consular function by international law and practice while having to do with such matters as promotion of trade and intercourse and with such affairs of mutual interest as assistance and protection of nationals residing abroad is quite without reference to recognition between states which matter is subject for action by national governments.[30]

This joint communication was, typically, returned to the consuls unanswered.[31] The Communists did not budge from a policy that had effectively shut off what might have become a highly useful channel of communication between the United States, British, and other Western governments and the local authorities. Peiping by this time had become the headquarters of the CCP as well as of the People's Liberation Army. Mao Tse-tung, chairman of the Central Committee of the CCP and chairman of the People's Revolutionary Military Commission, and Chu Teh, commander in chief of the PLA, along with other high-ranking Communist officials, including Chou En-lai, had been living in Peiping since March 25.[32] Although the highest ranking Communist officials might not have been expected to deal directly with foreign consuls, their presence ensured that authoritative policy guidance was immediately available to lesser officials who could have done so had they been permitted.

At the Foreign Office, Coates was reminded of the situation in early nineteenth-century imperial China, when the inability of foreigners to obtain access to officials made it "impossible ever to settle, or even discuss, any problem." In a minute dated April 29, he went on to observe that had the British been able to maintain "day to day contact with the Communists," the *Amethyst* incident might have been averted.[33]

The "*Amethyst* incident" had occured on April 20, when PLA artillery fire heavily damaged the British frigate *Amethyst*, which was proceeding up the Yangtze River from Shanghai to Nanking to relieve the British destroyer *Consort* on station there. Further British casualties occurred when Communist gunfire drove off three British warships, including *Consort*, coming to *Amethyst*'s rescue. British pride was wounded, Chinese pride bolstered. As Ambassador Stuart later noted in his autobiography: "I could sense an undertone of national pride among other Chinese in this achievement. Commercial and naval ships of foreign countries, principally British, had long sailed up and down this mighty river at their own unbridled will, but now at last they had been bravely challenged and routed."[34] The Communists, of course, were able to make excellent antiimperialist propaganda out of the affair. For example, an NCNA editorial of April 25 declared: "The British imperialists must understand that China is no longer the China of 1926 when British naval vessels bombarded Wanhsien in Szechuan province. She is no longer the China of the days when Great Britain and the United States jointly bombarded Nanking. The Yangtze River now belongs to the Chinese people and the People's Liberation Army and no longer belongs to the servile and weak-kneed traitors. . . . The aggressive military forces of Britain must be withdrawn from China."[35]

Coates's speculation that the tragic *Amethyst* affair might have been averted by day-to-day contact between Communist officials and British consular officers (presumably in Tientsin or Peiping) may go too far, but his point about the impossibility of dealing with problems if they cannot be discussed is well taken. The Communists insisted they could not undertake any discussions with foreign powers in the absence of diplomatic relations, but of course, no diplomatic relations could be established with the Communist authorities, who, British Foreign Secretary Ernest Bevin pointed out, "do not claim to have set up a government of national character." Bevin continued in answer to a parliamentary question, "We had hoped that our representatives in China would be able to maintain day-to-day contact with their authorities for the solution of common problems. Unfortunately, all such contacts have been declined."[36] Because they refused to discuss problems with foreign consular or diplomatic officials,[37] the Communists must bear primary responsibility for the misunderstandings and frustrations that beset their relations with the foreign community at this time.

3

The Soviet Union and the CCP

In sharp contrast to Britain and the United States, the Soviet Union espoused the Chinese Communist view of the status of consuls. It closed its consulates in cities taken by the PLA on the ground that no diplomatic relations existed with the Chinese Communists.[1] Presumably for the same reason, the Soviet ambassador did not remain in Nanking when the Chinese Communists occupied the erstwhile capital. These Soviet moves, far from displaying coolness toward the Chinese Communists, as some have supposed,[2] manifested a common view with them as to proper diplomatic conduct—a view that probably derived from the Soviet Union in the first place. Certainly the Chinese Communist policy of refusing any meaningful contact with Western consular personnel served what might safely be presumed to have been a Soviet objective—the exacerbation of Sino-Western relations.

Be this as it may, both American and British diplomats, in the first few months of 1949, noted increasing praise for the CCP in Soviet media while the Chinese Communist media seemed to be stepping up support of the Soviet Union and denunciation of the United States. For example, on February 3 the American embassy in Moscow called the attention of the State Department to two articles containing the "first recent Soviet editorial comment on the China situation," which furnished "clear evidence of the solid alignment" of the Kremlin with the CCP. The embassy saw evidence in these articles that the Kremlin's line on the Chinese situation had finally been issued and that the "recent evasion of this topic" was now ended. One of the articles described the

Chinese Communists as the most loyal, consistent, selfless strugglers for peace and democratic rights.[3]

In Nanking the British embassy reported that an NCNA editorial of March 18 "religiously adopts a regular Communist pattern of accusing U.S. of being imperialist warmongers on one hand and of idealizing motives and actions of Soviet Union on the other." The editorial claimed that the Soviet Union had brought about the Japanese surrender, and it praised the Sino-Soviet Treaty of 1945 and the friendship of the Soviet Union in the Chinese people's struggle against imperialism. In the Foreign Office, Coates noted, "This is the best material with which the Communists have supplied us for some time to demonstrate . . . . that General Mao Tse-tung continues to adopt an orthodox attitude."[4]

The American embassy in Nanking agreed that the NCNA editorial confirmed the CCP's full support of the Soviet Union. The embassy reported that the editorial, which had been broadcast by the North Shensi radio, advanced the CCP's "satellite foreign policy still further" than Mao had done in his Cominform journal article of November 1, 1948, or Liu Shao-ch'i had done in his essay "Internationalism and Nationalism."[5] The embassy pointed out that the United States was the sole object of attack in the broadcast, which rationalized the Soviet occupation of Port Arthur and Dairen as "blows against American imperialism."[6]

Ambassador Stuart, in recording his personal reaction in his diary entry of March 19, linked the broadcast to the North Atlantic Pact.

This was an eventful day.
1. The text of the North Atlantic Pact was announced with its evidence of an epochal change in USA policy to join in resistance to aggression declared in advance.
2. North Shensi Broadcast announced its unequivocal support of USSR and Stalin—its anti-American purpose. Lies, misrepresentations in defense of former—hatred of latter—probably synchronized with (1) under Moscow direction.[7]

On April 4, the day the North Atlantic Pact was signed, a "solemn declaration," signed on behalf of the CCP by Chairman Mao, was issued by "all democratic parties of Liberated China" asserting that if the Atlantic Pact led to war against Russia, they would help her resist aggression.[8] At the Foreign Office, Guy Burgess noted: "Peking, the seat of the CCP, was immediate in broadcasting the CCP's advance support for the USSR in the event of war with the Atlantic Powers."

Unlike similar statements by Maurice Thorez and Palmiro Togliatti on behalf of the French and Italian Communist parties, Burgess pointed out, the Chinese statement was not hedged about with conditions.[9]

Coates reflected the Far Eastern Department's view of Chinese Communist orthodoxy when he commented on an article by Peter Fleming in the *Times* of April 22. "The writer attaches, I think, too little importance to the rigorous orthodoxy of recent Communist announcements in China, of which the attacks on Tito and the Atlantic Powers have been only the most outstanding examples; . . . on the 18th April our Embassy at Nanking reported . . . that 'the Communists have suddenly and noticeably intensified their professions of allegiance to the U.S.S.R. and recent actions indicate practical application of Soviet Communist dogma.' "[10] This view of the CCP's orthodoxy was not confined to the Far Eastern Department of the Foreign Office. On February 3 the Research Department had issued a long memorandum that stressed the CCP's allegiance to the Moscow line, and argued that even if he wished to do so, which was highly doubtful, it was unlikely that Mao would be able to turn against the Soviet Union. After summarizing Mao's report to the Central Committee of the CCP of December 25, 1947, the memorandum continued:

Six months later further evidence of subservience to Moscow was provided in the denunciation issued by the Chinese Communists of Tito and the Communist Party of Yugoslavia in phraseology totally un-Chinese. And then, as if the writing on the wall were not already sufficiently clear, on 1st November, 1947 [*sic*], Mao Tze-tung dotted the i's and crossed the t's of what may be expected by a Communist dominated China. An article under Mao's signature, entitled *Revolutionary Forces of the World Rally to Combat Imperialist Aggression,* setting out the lines on which the Communist Party intend to proceed when they come into power, but couched in equally un-Chinese phraseology, appeared in the Cominform Journal published in Bucharest.[11]

Contributing to the growing British and American perceptions of CCP-Soviet harmony in the early months of 1949 was the surfacing on April 1 in Dairen of a CCP branch organization that had been closely collaborating with the Soviet military authorities there in administering the city. Paul Paddock, the American consul in Dairen at the time, reported the events of that day. "The local brand of the CCP officially emerges from underground and announces it is subordinate to the Northeast Bureau (Manchuria) of the CCP. Various front agencies have changed their names or admitted Communist connections. Until today the Chinese Nationalist and Russian flags had flown over public buildings together as a token of Russia's 'correct' policy. Now the Chinese Communist flag replaces the Nationalist flag. Parades of various front organizations, government employees, factory workers and police are held in honor of the official emergence of the CCP."[12] Paddock could not understand "why Russia turned over civil administration of Kwantung to the Chinese Communists, first tentatively in 1946 and then definitely reaffirming it in 1949." He notes: "In the beginning, Russia did worry about possible Chinese Nationalist interference and about world opinion. Yet, it set up the 1946 predecessor of the Kwantung administration presumably for political advantages of the moment with the Chinese Communists. Russia thereby let the Chinese Communists staff the civil administration, which in 1949, for the first time, was publicly displayed."[13]

Not only was there close Soviet-CCP collaboration in Kwantung in civil administration, but also in economic development. Thus, in a speech reported by NCNA on April 17, 1949, Ou-yang Ching, secretary of the Dairen–Port Arthur Section of the CCP, discussed the progress made by jointly operated Soviet-Chinese companies "thanks to the active assistance of the Soviet Military Headquarters."[14] In a series of articles on his visit to Dairen–Port Arthur in early June, Shanghai *Sin Wan Jih Pao* correspondent Chang Pai reported that by October 1947 "some of the Sino-Soviet jointly operated factories had already begun to resume operations" and that now "after two years of experience the efficiency in production in Sino-Soviet jointly operated factories had increased." In early 1950 another Chinese journalist confirmed Chang Pai's date, writing, "In October, 1947, the Chinese Communist Party called upon the people of Dairen and Port Arthur to build up their cities' industrial production, judiciously patterning their efforts upon the experience of the Soviet Union."[15]

The Soviet Union was in occupation of Dairen and Port Arthur, of course, under the terms of a treaty signed by the Chinese (Nationalist) government and the Soviet government on August 14, 1945. This treaty, which restored to the Soviet Union some of the special rights and privileges in Manchuria that Russia had enjoyed under the czar, embodied, as Coates noted in a Foreign Office minute dated March 26, "as arrant a piece of imperialist aggression against China as has ever been perpetrated."[16] Nevertheless, the CCP media consistently praised it, whereas it denounced treaties negotiated by the Chinese Nationalists in 1943, under the terms of which the United States and the United Kingdom gave up the last vestiges of the special rights and privileges they had acquired in the era of "unequal treaties."

4

British and American Policies

While the CCP and the USSR drew closer, British and American policies toward China began to diverge. Initially, the United States and the United Kingdom had adopted policies on trade with the Chinese Communists that were quite compatible. In Washington the National Security Council had examined the alternatives of imposing sanctions on trade with the Chinese Communists or allowing such trade. The first alternative called for the mobilization of the "political and economic power of the western world to combat openly, through intimidation and direct pressure, a Chinese Communist regime." Such a policy would have been designed "either (a) to force the Chinese Communists, by the threat of application of severe economic restrictions, to resist Kremlin pressure and adopt domestic and foreign policies acceptable to the United States, or (b) to isolate China completely from Japan and the western world in an attempt to bring about the overthrow or collapse of the Chinese Communist regime." The council rejected this alternative because it was "difficult to see how the necessary degree of concerted action could be obtained from all western nations so as to make effective the imposition of severe restrictions or embargoes on trade with China."[1] The United Kingdom in particular was expected to oppose such a policy, for Britain had much larger investments in China than did the United States, and the economic position of Hong Kong depended on an active entrepôt trade with the Chinese mainland. Moreover, British firms had "expressed frequently their intention to continue doing business under a Chinese Communist regime," and the British embassy had indicated to the Department of State that its "primary concern" was to protect British interests in China and the position of Hong Kong.[2]

Other arguments in the NSC against a policy of economic pressure are also worth noting, since they largely explain why this policy, which the United States later adopted, failed. It was noted that China's relative economic self-sufficiency and low level of consumption would reduce the effectiveness of economic restrictions and embargoes. Imposition of such restrictions by foreign powers would also enable the Communists to pose as defenders of Chinese national interests against foreign persecutors. Restrictions would impede the reestablishment of Japanese trade with Manchuria and China, thereby prolonging Japan's economic dependence on the United States. What most concerned the NSC, however, was the fear that trade sanctions might drive a Chinese Communist regime into a position of complete subservience to the Soviet Union, thus frustrating the very policy they were designed to serve, that is, to "prevent China from becoming an adjunct of Soviet power."[3]

In view of these objections to a policy of economic pressure, the NSC, with the approval of President Truman, elected to permit, under essential security safeguards, a restoration of ordinary economic relations between China, on the one hand, and Japan and the Western world, on the other. Security would be safeguarded by a system of controls that would screen exports to China to prevent the Chinese from reexporting important industrial, transportation, and communications supplies and equipment to the USSR and eastern Europe. The NSC also decided that the United States should use its economic position "to intensify any conflicts" that might appear between the Chinese Communists and the USSR "and to increase the importance to China of trade with Japan and the west."[4]

In discussions with the British on China trade policy March 21, American officials explained that the United States planned to extend to China the so-called R-procedure export controls that now applied only to Europe. Under this system all exports to Europe had to be covered by export licenses, which gave the U.S. Commerce Department a chance to approve or deny licenses based on strategic considerations.[5]

British views on trade policy were set forth on a memorandum dated March 23, one of a series of memorandums on China policy that the British embassy in Washington had been presenting to the Department of State since January 11. Acknowledging that in the long term Chinese Communist policy would be "the expropriation and expulsion of foreign interests," the British assumed that "in the initial period economic difficulties will be so great that the Communists will perforce move slowly towards these goals, and accordingly they may be disposed to tolerate foreign interests for a time." Moreover, the British believed that the "probable results of any attempt to bring economic pressure to bear during the first phase would be to expedite the coming of the second phase."[6]

American officials denied that they were contemplating bringing economic pressure against the Chinese Communists in the form of sanctions. On April 7 Butterworth pointed out to Hubert Graves, counselor of the British Embassy, that although the United States wanted "sufficient control to prevent military supplies or certain strategic materials reaching the Chinese Communists and to guard against stockpiling or trans-shipment to the USSR," the Americans did not want "to engage in economic warfare with the Chinese Communists."[7] Nevertheless the British perception was that the Americans would pull the trigger of the economic weapon sooner than they would. Thus, in a letter to Peter Scarlett on April 11, Graves said he had told Butterworth that "HMG had come to the conclusion that their armoury of economic weapons should not be resorted to until we were forced, by Communist malfeasance, into taking positive action." Graves felt that the British approach differed from that suggested by the Americans "in that we timed our countermeasures for a later date."[8]

While Anglo-American discussions were taking place in Washington on trade policy, the Department of State was receiving suggestions from the field that economic pressures be used to induce the Communist authorities to permit U.S. consulates to carry out their normal functions. For example, as early as February, Consul General John M. Cabot in Shanghai had informed the department that in view of the apparent refusal of the Communist authorities in Tientsin and Mukden to have anything to do with the consulates there in the absence of recognition, he considered it "vital we should have most effective possible means force them deal with us in Shanghai after they take city." Cabot suggested that the United States could tell the Communists that "no import or export trade between Shanghai and U.S. will be permitted except from recommendation from this consulate that it should." Like most westerners in China at that time, who tended to exaggerate the Chinese Communists' economic vulnerability, Cabot said such a step "would practically force" the Communists to deal with the consulates.[9]

However, the use of economic pressure to gain Chinese Communist recognition of consular status was in the end rejected by the State Department. A memorandum from the secretary of state to the executive secretary of the NSC dated April 14 declared that such pressure "would be tactically undesirable at this time and inconsistent with the policy set forth in NSC 41." The memorandum held that "The exercise of consular functions . . . should be sought on its own merits" and noted that consular posts had been instructed to certify invoices upon request.[10]

Emerging differences between Britain and the United States on policy toward Formosa (as the island of Taiwan was then usually called in the West) were more fundamental than their differences on trade policy. Both governments wanted trade with Communist-controlled areas of China to continue, and both saw the necessity of instituting some controls on this trade. Their differences principally revolved around the timing and the extent of trade controls. In the case of Formosa, however, their differences boiled down to whether to regard Formosa as just another Chinese province destined to fall to the Communists—the British view—or to place it in a special category and seek to deny it to the Communists—the policy adopted by the United States.

American policy seems to have been influenced by several considerations. Most important of these was the view of the Joint Chiefs of Staff that Formosa, and the adjacent Pescadores Islands, were of great strategic importance to the United States. Another consideration was that the legal status of the islands was unclear. Japan had surrendered Formosa and the Pescadores to China at the end of World War II, in keeping with promises made in the Cairo Declaration of 1943, but it could be argued that in the absence of a treaty of peace between China and Japan, legal transfer of sovereignty to China had not yet taken place. Of more political substance than this consideration was the existence of an independence movement on Formosa and the manifestations of widespread anti-Chinese government feeling among the Formosan population. Thus Washington could envisage denying Formosa to the Communists by separating it from China.[11]

A divergence in attitude toward Formosa had developed not only between the United States and the United Kingdom but also within the United States government between the State and the Defense departments. Agreeing that "any overt military commitment in Formosa would be unwise at this time," the Joint Chiefs of Staff recommended, in a memorandum submitted to the secretary of defense on February 10, "the stationing of minor numbers of fleet units at a suitable Formosan port or ports, with such shore activity associated therewith as may be necessary for maintenance and air communication and for the recreation of personnel." The JCS admitted that this course might cause diplomatic difficulties and risks but thought the threat to U.S. security "implicit in Communist domination of Formosa" to be worth the incurrence of these risks and costs.[12]

The Department of State opposed the JCS recommendation, however, reaffirming "its consistent position" that such a course would be "not only diplomatically disadvantageous but also, and far more importantly, a heavy political liability for us." A show of military force, the State Department contended, "would have serious political repercussions throughout China; it might create an irredentist issue just at the time we may wish to exploit Soviet action in Manchuria and Sinkiang." The State Department's view prevailed in the NSC, which decided that units of the fleet "should not now be stationed at or off Formosan ports in support of the political and economic measures" the United States was taking to deny Formosa to the Communists.[13]

The State Department acknowledged that force might eventually have to be used to accomplish the U.S. objective in Formosa but did not want it to be applied unilaterally. As Secretary Dean G. Acheson explained to the NSC: "At some date in the future, we may conclude that it is impossible to accomplish our aim by present measures and shall then recommend reexamination of the problem . . . . If we are to intervene militarily on the island, we shall, in all probability, do so in concert with like-minded powers, preferably using UN mechanisms and with the proclaimed intention of satisfying the legitimate demands of the indigenous Formosans for self-determination either under a UN trusteeship or through independence."[14]

While the State Department was keeping an eye on the potential utility of a Formosan independence movement as an instrument for denying Formosa to the Communists, the instrument more readily at hand was the Nationalist government and its armed forces on the island. Confronted with the victorious advance of the Communist armies in northeast China in late 1948, President Chiang Kai-shek had begun to stockpile military equipment and other assets on Formosa. On January 8, 1949, for example, Ambassador Stuart had reported to the State Department: "Generalissimo moving large quantities gold, silver, other mobile assets to Taiwan and is apparently planning to make it an island fortress from which to continue the fight against Communism. Appointment of Chen Cheng and Chiang Ching-kuo as Governor and Kmt Chief respectively of Taiwan, together with transfer of air force headquarters, navy and industry to island, all confirm this intent."[15] Though Washington had virtually written off the Nationalists as an effective resistance force on the mainland, their prospects appeared better for defending Formosa, at least in the short run. Thus, on March 22, British ambassador to the United States Sir Oliver Franks reported as the present view of the State Department that "the U.S. position in the Pacific would be better safeguarded, even if only on a temporary basis, by the National Government's retention of administration of the island." Franks also noted that, speaking informally, the director of the Office of Far Eastern Affairs (Butterworth) had said the subject of Formosa might have to be brought to the attention of the United Nations, and the latter might arrange a plebiscite on a possible U.S. trusteeship. At present, however, there was "no crystallization of U.S. options on the future of the island."[16]

In the Foreign Office, Patrick Coates reviewed Franks's report (and the memorandum of the State Department accompanying it). In Coates's view, the absence of a considered U.S. policy made it "all the more likely that the State Department will conceive ill-advised and hasty *ad hoc* measures to deal with certain aspects of the China situation."[17]

5
Ambassador Stuart's Initiative

Emerging Anglo-American differences on Formosa did not prevent the United States and Britain, and other members of the Atlantic Group, from reaffirming in April their common decision of the previous January to keep their ambassadors in Nanking after Communist occupation. Although Chinese government ministries, including the Foreign Ministry, had moved to Canton in February, Acting President Li Tsung-jen had remained in Nanking to pursue peace negotiations with the Communists. By early April, however, hope seemed dimmer than ever that these negotiations would bear fruit or that the Communists, poised on the northern banks of the Yangtze River, would refrain much longer from attacking Nanking.

Under these circumstances the British embassy in Washington on April 9 presented a memorandum to the State Department reiterating the British position that it was "of great importance that a common front should be maintained in regard to the question of the locale of our representation in China." As the British saw it, the abandonment of Nanking would be likely to jeopardize chances of "establishing satisfactory relations with a communist dominated China," to abandon commercial interests in areas already overrun by the communists, and to risk putting British consulates in an intolerable position.[1]

The State Department agreed that diplomatic mission chiefs of the United States and other countries of the Atlantic Group should remain in Nanking, and so informed Ambassador Stuart in a message that crossed one he had sent to Washington making the same recommendation.[2] Stuart noted in his diary April 13: "News of Dept. decision replying to our Embassy message, confirmed previous one I stay Nanking—I am much pleased."[3]

Britain and the United States had basically the same reasons for keeping their ambassadors in Nanking after its capture by the Communists, but Ambassador Stuart's unique qualifications provided a special reason why he should remain there. Butterworth had pointed out in his memorandum of January 26 that Stuart, who was born in China and spoke Chinese "with great fluency," had a wide acquaintance in Chinese political circles. Moreover, as former President of Yenching University, "approximately fifty percent of whose graduates were reportedly in the Communist camp," Stuart occupied "the traditional position of the teacher vis-à-vis the pupil in his relationships with many Chinese."[4] Stuart himself believed that this relationship would help him get through to the Communist leaders. One of his Asian colleagues, Indian Ambassador K.M. Panikkar, was rather skeptical on this point, however. He described Stuart as a "man of great mortal rectitude and unusual simplicity of life, . . .who was perpetually surprised by the villainy of the world." Stuart's "one weakness" was his inclination "to rely too much on his own judgment of Chinese character, which he idealized in some respects." "He used to tell me," Panikkar recalls, "that the relationship of teacher and student was one of the basic conceptions of Chinese ethics, his own position as the teacher of many of the younger communist leaders would help to shape their policy in favour of the West!"[5]

The British were at least as eager to keep their ambassador in Nanking as were the Americans, but Sir Ralph Stevenson did not have the unusual qualifications of his American colleague. His previous experience did not include service in China, and he had no longstanding personal connections to exploit in the cause of enhancing Sino-British relations. Moreover, unlike Stuart, he saw little point in trying to influence the Communist leadership. Stevenson's attitude is illustrated in his reply to a suggestion from British Consul General Robert Urquhart in Shanghai that an effort be made to arrange a peaceful handover of that city to the Communists. In Sir Ralph's view "our fruitless efforts over a long period . . . [to] establish *de facto* relations with the Communists preclude any prospect of direct contact whereby it might be possible to influence them." Even if such contact could be established, Stevenson thought, it was "too much to hope, in view of their recent attitude, that the Chinese Communists would at this stage listen to reason in response to any foreign approach, official or unofficial, or in deference to public opinion abroad."[6]

Reflecting his belief in the special value of personal relationships in China, Stuart thought he might be able to influence Communist leaders if he were able to talk to them. Accordingly, on March 10 he had sent a long dispatch to Secretary of State Dean Acheson suggesting that he be authorized to approach the Communist leaders "not only as an official representative of the American Government but as one who through long residence here is known to have constantly stood for Chinese national independence and democratic progress as well as for closer American-Chinese relations primarily for the benefits these would bring to the Chinese people." Stuart hoped that however much the Communists might identify him with "bellicose American imperialism," his previous activities and personal acquaintance with many of them "would not be entirely disregarded."[7] Though Stuart acknowledged that it might be "naively visionary to imagine that I or anyone else can influence the Chinese Communist Party to a more broadly tolerant policy," he was convinced, "in view of the fateful issues at stake," that the attempt was "abundantly worth the effort."[8]

In his message to Acheson, Stuart rested his hopes that he might be able to influence the Communist leadership on his belief that their anti-American sentiment was based not only on ideological conviction and animosity arising from American aid to the Nationalists but also on inordinate suspicion of non-Communists and genuine misapprehension about American intentions. If the misapprehension "could be removed or to some extent reduced," he wrote, "it would prepare the way for a settlement of the remaining problems." To reduce their fears Stuart proposed to tell the Communist leaders "in friendly discussions" that the United States had always been China's friend and had consistently supported its independence, that the United States recognized the right of the Chinese to choose their own form of government, and that it would be advantageous to both China and the United States to clear away mutual suspicions and to cooperate for the common good.[9]

There is no reason to doubt that Stuart sincerely wished to find a way to work with the Communists; but the teacher was prepared to chastise his former students and expel them if they proved to be recalcitrant and wayward. Thus he wanted to warn the Communist leaders with whom he would talk that if they brought not genuine liberty and new democracy to China but a form of despotism on the Russian model, the United States might "feel called upon to assist any nucleus of organized opposition" and to "use every available resource we possess to restore real liberation to the Chinese people." In making this recommendation to the secretary of state, Stuart emphasized that he would not convey this warning as an official message, "still less as in any sense an ultimatum or threat."[10]

The State Department carefully considered Ambassador Stuart's proposal. In a telegram dated April 6 it authorized him to hold discussions with "the top Communist leaders" and to make the points he had suggested, with one important exception. Stuart was *not* to tell the Communists that the United States might under certain circumstances "assist a nucleus of organized opposition" or "use every available resource to restore real liberation to the Chinese people." In the department's view such statements, even though unofficial, could be interpreted as threats; moreover, there was "little ground for assuming that the U.S. Government would at this juncture embark on a program of all-out military and economic aid for [Nationalist] China."[11]

Three days earlier British Foreign Secretary Ernest Bevin had telegraphed a report to the Foreign Office of a conversation he had had with Acheson in Washington that reflects the U.S. mood at the time Stuart was authorized to hold discussions with the Communists leaders. Acheson told Bevin that Americans considered the Chinese Nationalists about finished and that there was a widespread feeling that the policy of supporting the central government was bankrupt. On the other hand, it would take a long time for the new administration in China to get going. The Moscow-trained Communists would "get diluted" and "the corruption and general inefficiency of the Chinese would gradually get them down." But the State Department had to be careful of being accused of cutting away support for the Nationalists. When fifty-one congressmen had written to the president to express their concern, Acheson had explained the situation frankly, and "they had reluctantly accepted that there was really nothing more the U.S. Government could do."[12]

6

The Stuart-Huang Discussions

It was not long before Ambassador Stuart had the opportunity to hold talks, if not with the "top Communist leaders," at least with a Communist official who had direct access to Chou En-lai. The opportunity was brought about by the PLA's conquest of Nanking the latter part of April. On April 16 the Communist negotiators had given the Nationalist government delegation in Peiping a draft peace agreement, setting a deadline of midnight April 20 for its acceptance. The Nationalists did not accept the draft agreement, describing it as "tantamount to disposal of conquered by conqueror," but they requested a cease-fire so that discussions aimed at achieving an acceptable settlement could continue.[1] The Communists' answer was an order from Chairman Mao and PLA Commander in Chief Chu Teh to the whole army "to advance and strongly, definitively, cleanly to wipe out entirely all that Kmt reactionary clique which dares to resist inside Chinese territory, to liberate whole country, to protect sovereign indepdendence and integrity of Chinese territory."[2]

Ambassador Stuart's diary entries for the next few days highlight the impact of this order on Nanking and on the American embassy.

April 22, Friday. Early morning . . . George Yeh [acting Chinese foreign minister] called advised me officially move to Canton. . . .
11:00—Meeting Diplomatic Body on moving to Canton—unanimous not to move—all watched USA.
April 23, Saturday. CCP took Hsiakuan last night—police disappeared—turn over is in process.
CCP broadcast 300,000 have crossed River—defections everywhere. Long Staff Conference—plans for our own safety . . . stay in compounds.
Widespread looting.
April 24, Sunday. Last night—fires, shooting, explosions all night. . . .
CCP came in early this morning—quietly observed by local people—orderly—business-like.[3]

For about a week after the PLA's capture of Nanking, Ambassador Stuart stayed at home "to avoid unpleasant issues."[4] On May 7, he reported to the State Department: "I have been coming regularly to Chancery once a day without hindrance since May 3, and have been several other places in city. Guards were removed from my compound morning of May 6."[5]

On that same day Stuart's trusted Chinese confidant and personal secretary, Philip Fugh, called on Huang Hua, the newly arrived chief of the Alien Affairs Office, Nanking Military Control Council. This was the first of some dozen meetings during the course of the next three months between these surrogates of Ambassador Stuart and Chou En-lai, and it served as a preliminary to Stuart's initial exchange with Huang which took place a week later.

The role played by Philip Fugh during Dr. Stuart's ambassadorship is probably unique in the annals of American diplomacy. As a Chinese citizen he did not have access to American classified documents, but his conversations with both Nationalist and Communist officials on a variety of subjects touching on Sino-American relations provided the substance of many a classified embassy report to the State Department. Moreover, Fugh lived at Stuart's official residence, and this arrangement, initially at least, was regarded as scandalous by security officers. According to Stuart, even General Marshall "raised his eyebrows."[6] But Stuart regarded Fugh, who had functioned in a somewhat similar capacity when Stuart was president of Yenching University, as all but indispensable to his diplomatic career, almost as an alter ego. Thus he wrote of Fugh's contribution: "He constantly called upon those with whom it was desirable to keep in touch when it would not have been entirely dignified, or for other reasons suitable, for me to do so. Almost invariably when calling on Chinese officials, I took him with me, and he never betrayed a confidence. All of this meant that I had far more intimate and extensive associations with Chinese of all classes than would otherwise have been possible, and that *he* could represent me on most occasions without question."[7]

Huang Hua, the official the Communists had sent to Nanking to deal with the diplomatic mission chiefs and other foreigners who had remained there after the Nationalists had fled, was a protégé of Chou En-lai's, a young man destined to have a brilliant diplomatic career culminating in the post of foreign minister of the People's Republic of China some thirty years later. Huang was also an alumnus of Yenching University, and so had the kind of personal connection with Stuart and Fugh, a fellow Yenching alumnus, that Stuart valued so much. If such relationships counted for anything, they would facilitate Ambassador Stuart's discussions with him.

In fact, however, in his meetings with Fugh and Stuart, Huang Hua would hold to the anti-American CCP policy reiterated by Chairman Mao in his New Year's message and to the line Mao had laid down to the CCP's Central Committee on March 5. "In each city or place where the Kuomintang troops are wiped out and the Kuomintang government is overthrown, imperialist political domination is overthrown with it, and so is imperialist economic and cultural domination. . . . Refuse to recognize the legal status of any foreign diplomatic establishments and personnel from the Kuomintang period, abolish all imperialist propaganda agencies in China, take immediate control of foreign trade and reform the customs system—these are the first steps we must take upon entering the big cities."[8] The line followed by Huang Hua reflected not misconceptions based on suspicion and misapprehension but the CCP's clear intent to carry the revolution through to the end by destroying the Kuomintang government and expelling the forces of U.S. imperialism.

In his initial meeting with Fugh on May 6, Huang delivered "a tirade against U.S. foreign policy" and gave Fugh reasons the CCP considered the USA an enemy. Huang also told Fugh that the Communists' objectives were "to eliminate (1) feudalism and (2) American, British imperialism" in China. Huang agreed to Fugh's suggestion that it might be appropriate for him to call on his "old college President," but he did not recognize Stuart as ambassador, and he was careful to avoid using that title in his several references to Stuart, since Stuart was accredited to "the KMT Government."[9]

When Huang called on him a week later, Stuart took a generally conciliatory line. He spoke of the need to avoid war and relieve "present tension." He said he was glad he could remain in Nanking long enough to demonstrate the American people's interest in the welfare of the Chinese people as a whole. He wished to restore the friendly relations of the past. When Huang Hua expressed interest in recognition by the United States on terms of equality and mutual benefit, Stuart replied that such terms, together with accepted international practice with respect to treaties, would be the only proper basis for recognition. What kind of national government China had was purely an internal matter, Stuart said, but the Communists had not yet established any national government at all. Until the Communists established a government, the United States and other countries could do nothing but await developments in China. Stuart also explained the functions of foreign consulates in maintaining informal relations with the de facto regional authorities.[10]

In his first meeting with Huang Hua,Stuart apparently did not specifically raise the special U.S. concern about Consul General Ward and his staff in Mukden. On April 15 the State Department had instructed Clubb in Peiping to inform the Communist authorities that unless they would "promptly correct unsatisfactory situation Mukden and allow American consular officers there facilities universally recognized necessary proper to discharge their duties, American Gov't will have no alternative withdraw them." Clubb was also to point out that "in China as elsewhere in world, only presence American consular officers free to discharge their duties responsibilities can in view my Gov't provide services and safeguards essential to trade and commerce with the US."[11] But Clubb's representations had elicited neither response nor action from the Communist authorities. By mid-May, Ward and his staff had been held incommunicado in Mukden for nearly six months. Under these circumstances the Department of State instructed Ambassador Stuart to bring to Huang's attention the "intolerable conditions" at the U.S. consulate general in Mukden and the efforts of the U.S. government to have these conditions improved. Stuart was to explain to Huang that the matter was being brought up with him because it had been impossible to ascertain whether previous messages had ever reached high Communist authorities and because of the responsibility that Stuart in his position bore for Consul General Ward and his staff. It was hoped that Huang would bring the matter to the attention of the responsible authorities in Peiping.[12]

On the same day, the State Department decided that enough time had elapsed without a reply since Clubb's last approach to the Communist authorities. It instructed him to inform the Communists that the U.S. government was withdrawing its staff and closing the consulate general in Mukden because of "their imposition arbitrary unreasonable restrictions." Clubb was to request that Ward and his staff be provided with transportation and other facilities to enable them to depart Mukden with their personal effects and appropriate office supplies and equipment. As usual, Clubb's letter went unanswered.[13]

On June 6 Ambassador Stuart had his second meeting with Huang Hua, who had invited him for tea. It was a regular old-school-tie affair, for Philip Fugh accompanied the ambassador, and Huang's assistant, Ling Ke-yi, another Yenching alumnus, also attended. Stuart took the opportunity to raise the Mukden problem, telling Huang that he attached great importance to the solution of this impasse and that he would be very reluctant to leave China in compliance with his orders to go to Washington for consultation until the consular staff had been safely withdrawn from Mukden. Huang said this matter was outside his province, but when Stuart pointed out to him "that through Clubb we had exhausted every process we could think of without even a reply from Peiping," Huang said he would think again about what it would be possible for him to do.[14]

For the most part, Huang had little new to say, although his superiors in Peiping had had three weeks to ponder Stuart's remarks at their previous meeting. Huang again stressed the need for the United States to break with the Nationalist government, and he again raised the question of recognition. In reply, Stuart point out that "after all Communist regime was at present nothing more than People's Liberation Army defeating Kuomintang troops and occupying steadily enlarging parts of country; that there were still very large areas nominally under Nationalist Government and that there was as yet not even pretense on Communists' part of administrative agency on national scale with which it would be possible for foreign countries to deal."[15] On the other hand, the "presence in Nanking of chiefs of diplomatic missions (with exception of Soviet) after arrival of PLA could be regarded as significant." Stuart also told Huang, in reply to a question, that "in all probability" the United States would not follow the government to Taiwan if it moved there.

It is significant that Huang offered no response to the statements Stuart had made at their previous meeting about the desirability of restoring friendly Sino-American relations. Indeed, when Stuart now gave him an opportunity to respond by asking what he could do to further good relations between the United States and China, Huang replied—"almost brusquely," according to Stuart's report—that China needed to be allowed to work out her own destiny without interference, that all the Communists wanted was for the United States to stop aiding the Kuomintang and to sever relations with the Nationalist government.[16]

7

The Chou Demarche

Several days before the second Stuart-Huang meeting took place, U.S. officials in Peiping had received a signal from the Communist leadership quite different from the negative one Huang had conveyed—or so it seemed at least. On May 31 Michael Keon, an Australian correspondent, had relayed to Colonel David Barrett, an American assistant military attaché with long experience in China, a remarkable message purporting to be from Chou En-lai to the American and British governments. The thrust of Chou's message, which Barrett gave to Consul General Clubb for transmission to the Department of State, was that the leadership of the Chinese Communist party was bitterly divided between a strongly pro-Moscow radical faction under the leadership of Liu Shao-ch'i and a liberal faction under Chou En-lai's leadership. The latter advocated early establishment of relations with the Western powers since they alone could help China out of its dire economic straits. Above this factional struggle stood Mao Tse-tung, the unchallenged leader, but the ultimate direction of party policy would be determined by which faction won out. A victory for the Chou faction would mean that the CCP would not always follow Moscow's foreign policy lead but would exercise a moderating influence, thus reducing the danger of war. Meanwhile, Chou deplored the vitriolic anti-American and anti-British outpourings of the party propaganda machine, which had always been beyond his control.

The Chou message dwelt at length on China's serious economic plight, Chou's faith in American economic prowess, and the need for American economic aid. According to Clubb's telegraphic version of the message, Chou argued that "China still not Communist and if Mao's policies are correctly implemented may not be for long time." Chou recalled friendly wartime contacts between Americans and the CCP and hoped "American authorities remembering this would believe there were genuine liberals in party who are concerned with everything connected with welfare Chinese people and 'peace in our time' rather than doctrinaire theories."[1]

Neither Barrett—who had known Chou well ever since he had commanded the U.S. Army Observer Group in Yenan, headquarters of the CCP, in 1944[2]—nor Clubb seems to have questioned the authenticity of the Chou message. For Clubb, the question was whether to take the message at face value or as a plea for economic assistance made with the full knowledge of the party apparatus, perhaps even with the approval of the USSR. Clubb decided on the latter explanation. He saw the Chou demarche as a move "of high Communist policy" based on China's "grave economic debility" and consequent need for American economic aid. He felt that it was probably clear to both the Soviets and the Chinese Communists that the USSR would be unable to supply China's economic needs. Both, he thought, had become reconciled to the necessity of dealing with the United States to avoid a "calamitous economic collapse." At the same time, the Chinese Communists would maintain close political ties with the Soviet Union, desiring to "continue diet of Soviet political bread but eke out diet with American economic cake."[3]

Even though Chou had emphasized that no reply should be given to his message, Clubb recommended a reply, one that would make clear that the United States wanted to maintain relations with the Chinese nation but that these relations "must be based on mutual understanding, respect and cooperation, on reciprocity as well as egalitarianism."[4] Relations of this kind, Clubb apparently felt, would not allow China to be run for the political benefit of the Soviet Union at the economic expense of the United States.

Ambassador Stuart noted in his diary on June 3 that he had received a "top secret message from Barrett through Clubb and Department reporting what Chou meant to reach British and USA authorities—extremely hopeful line of effort."[5] In a telegram of June 7 to the State Department he opined that the Chou message was "a call for help" containing "an extremely important indication as to possible American policy"; obviously, these were not the words of a man skeptical of the bona fides of the message. Stuart recommended replying to Chou that the United States "would be as ready now as we have always been to assist" the people of China in their struggle "to attain independence and national sovereignty and in their need of economic betterment and technological progess," provided that a "basis of mutual self-respect and confidence could be reestablished between China and US." He suggested closing the reply with a statement sincerely welcoming Chou's protestations of pro-Western sentiment but pointing out that "they cannot be expected to bear fruit until they have been translated into deeds capable of convincing people of US that continued American support of Chinese objectives is in mutual interest of both countries."[6]

The State Department accepted Clubb's and Stuart's judgment as to the authenticity of the Chou message and the desirability of replying to it. In a message later approved by President Truman, the department on June 14 instructed Clubb to "prepare a reply on plain paper without signature or designation source" but to transmit it only if he could do so either directly "or thru completely reliable intermediary without danger of disclosure."[7]

In substance, the reply expressed the American hope "to maintain friendly relations with China and continue social, economic and political relations with that country insofar as these relations based on principle mutual respect and understanding and principle equality and are to mutual benefit two nations." The message went on to express American concern over certain occurrences that departed from such principles, as well as from accepted international custom and practice. Three examples were cited: repeated bitter propaganda misrepresenting U.S. actions in China and elsewhere, arbitrary restrictions on the movements and communications of the U.S. consul general in Mukden and failure to reply to the repeated U.S. representations in this matter, and failure to take action to release Smith and Bender (two U.S. servicemen whose plane had strayed over Communist territory the previous October) or to reply to representations about them.[8]

The American reply to the Chou demarche was never delivered, though not for want of effort on the American part. The department instructed Clubb not to give the reply to Keon; but he did use Keon as an intermediary to try to make arrangements for either Colonel Barrett or Clubb himself to give the reply directly to Chou or to his secretary. However, the Communists were unprepared to make such an arrangement and told Keon not to approach them again. According to Clubb's telegram to the department, June 24: "Intermediary expressed to us chagrin, said willing assist in any other way possible, make approach by new channel if desired. I said it appeared to me that Communist side had given firm reply after due deliberation, if they were undesirous receiving reply of whatever character from American side I perceived no point asking him pursue matter further. . . . Barrett agreed."[9] Earlier, Barrett had recommended, in light of Mao's speech to the Preparatory Committee of the People's Political Consultative Conference (PPCC) June 15, that the whole project be discarded.[10] As Barrett saw it, Mao's speech gave little promise of rapprochement between the United States and China.[11]

Mao had made it abundantly clear that he expected the imperialists to continue to behave as enemies of the revolution. Thus Mao thought it "necessary to call people's attention to the fact that imperialists and their running dogs . . . [would] use all possible means to oppose the Chinese people." They would bore into China and cause "disintegration and disruption." They would not only "egg on" the Chinese reactionaries but would even come "with their own forces to blockade the seaports of China," and it was not impossible that they would send part of their armed forces to "encroach on China's frontiers." He warned against relaxing "vigilance towards wild retaliatory plots of imperialistic elements and their running dogs."[12]

Although the American attempt to reply to the Chou message proved fruitless, Clubb believed it had served the purposes of "(1) testing willingness Chou's group continue with matter and (2) exploring field." The most logical explanation for the unwillingness of the Communists to receive the American reply, in Clubb's opinion, was that the Chou demarche "was designed serve political purpose of causing USA view Communist leaders more sympathetically, and perhaps letting sympathy affect US attitude re trade or direct aid, but did not constitute sincere expression of Communist views."[13]

Although Keon had told Barrett that Chou wanted what he said to be conveyed to the British, the State Department did not see fit to share the Chou message with the Foreign Office.[14] The first word the Foreign Office had of the Chou message was in a "very top secret" telegram from Governor Alexander Grantham of Hong Kong received in London August 10, which reported: "Fitzgerald, former British Council Representative in Peking, arrived here three days ago from Peking. He was the bearer of an important message from Chou En Lai for H.M.G. This message was passed to him by Michael Keon. . . . Chou did not wish to use consular channels for transmitting a message to H.M. Government and in giving Keon message he emphasized repeatedly that greatest care should be taken to keep his name out."[15]

The main thrust of the message C.P. Fitzgerald brought to Hong Kong was similar to that Keon gave Barrett in Peiping more than two months earlier, but there were some significant differences, differences that seem to have been deliberately tailored to meet differences in British and American outlooks. As given to the Americans, for example, the message dwelt at length on China's serious economic plight, Chou's faith in American economic prowess, and the need for American economic aid. The Fitzgerald version said nothing at all about American aid, and a more detailed version provided the British by Keon himself when he came to Hong Kong in mid-September even held that China could not expect aid from the United States, which had aided the Kuomintang. The plea for aid contained in the American version argued, "China still not Communist and if Mao's policies are correctly implemented may not be for long time." The British version, according to Fitzgerald, held that the Chinese Communists "are hundred percent convinced communists and they consider communism is the only answer to China's problems."[16]

The first Foreign Office reaction to the Chou message was contained in a minute by Guy Burgess, who noted that the "fairly extensive diffusion of this top secret information by Chou and his choice of journalistic channels makes the thought of a plant very obvious indeed." Burgess went on to point out that saying "I and my friends are moderates, let's collaborate to keep the extremists out" was "a trick . . . much used by the Japanese as well as the Nazis to get concessions even when a hostile policy had in fact been decided on." Burgess concluded, however, that insofar as Chou's possible aim was economic collaboration with the West, British policy appeared not to be much affected whether the Keon story was believed or not.[17]

Patrick Coates—unlike Burgess, who had no China experience—was a China specialist, having served in four posts in China between 1937 and 1946, the latest at the British embassy in Nanking, where he was assistant acting Chinese secretary. He was also on active service with the army for some two years during this period, part of which he spent attached to the Chinese (Nationalist) army. Agreeing that "the possibility that this message is a plant" could not be dismissed, Coates felt "an air of verisimilitude" was lent to the message by Chou's "disarming statements" that the Chinese Communists were 100 percent Communist and that one of his leading supporters [Lin Piao] "nourishes a strong hatred for all foreigners."[18] Had Coates had access to the American version of the Chou message, he might have reacted differently, since neither of the disarming statements he cited was in it.

On August 16 Assistant Undersecretary Esler Dening, a Japan specialist, sent a memorandum to Foreign Secretary Ernest Bevin on the Chou message. Pointing out that it was now clear "the Americans have had the gist of this message for sometime" but had "not disclosed this to us or discussed it with us," Dening asserted the message should be regarded as of some importance and that on the whole it had "a ring of truth." He did not think the British attitude should be unduly affected by the possibility that Chou had employed the "time-honoured technique for a party to say that it is moderate, and that unless one makes concessions to it a more extreme party will gain power," after all Chou had not concealed the fact "that his party are one hundred percent Communist and consider that Communism is the only answer to China's problems." He went on to warn: "The Americans will no doubt argue that the message is a plant and that we should ignore it. . . . If, in the terms of Chou En-lai's message his opponents win, then we will be thrown out neck and crop, and the Americans will say 'I told you so.' "[19]

Dening's rather sad misapprehension of the American reaction to the Chou demarche would have been avoided, of course, if the State Department had been frank with the British about it to begin with. In reality, the American reaction to the Chou message had been more forthcoming than the British. Far from regarding the message as a plant, the Americans took it seriously and tried to reply. As matters turned out, it was His Majesty's principal secretary of state for foreign affairs, Ernest Bevin, who, in a brief note dated August 17, dismissed the message as a plant. "The S/S says that this move of Chou En Lai's reminds him very much of the attitude adopted at one time or another by various less extremist politicians in Soviet satellite states. He points out that whether we responded to approaches from so called moderates or not, the extremists always won. All in all, the S/S tends to the view that this move is in accordance with standard Soviet tactics."[20] It seems apparent that Bevin's reaction to the Chou demarche was based on his own experience with Eastern European Communists, which he trusted in this instance more than he did the judgment of his Foreign Office experts Dening and Coates. Bevin shared essentially the same suspicions of the message as Burgess had expressed, but it is interesting that he cited his own experience with the Soviet satellites whereas Burgess took his examples from Japanese and Nazi behavior.

Coming after the foreign secretary had already pronounced on the subject, the comments of Sir Ralph Stevenson, British ambassador in Nanking, on the Chou message are somewhat anticlimactic; nevertheless they are worth recording, not only because they represent a view from China but also because they provide a contrast to the eager reaction of Stevenson's American colleague, Leighton Stuart. The differing reactions of the two ambassadors may have resulted from their contrasting backgrounds. Stevenson was an experienced diplomat with no China background, and Stuart was an inexperienced diplomat with vast China background.

Noting that the roundabout method of delivery of the message and the lapse of time since it was orginally given to Keon militated against its accuracy, Stevenson found it difficult to disentangle what was original to the message and what was interpretation of the persons through whom the message had passed. He felt that "neither Keon nor Fitzgerald can be regarded as very reliable" (a view the Foreign Office disputed at least insofar as it pertained to Fitzgerald, a reputable scholar). Stevenson thought the "genuineness of Chou's alleged motives at least open to suspicion" and found it difficult to judge the purpose of a communication "to which Chou can scarcely have expected any reply, or even any indication as to how it may have been eventually received."[21]

Although Sir Ralph felt that the message confirmed his views on some points—for example, the opinion, widely held by foreigners in China at the time, that two opposing groups existed in the Communist hierarchy—he had reservations on other points. Thus for him, "repetition by Chou of pretence already voiced by Communist intermediaries in Shanghai that we need not (repeat not) take too seriously the fervent advocacy of pro-Soviet anti-British policies by Chinese Communist party machine is far from being convincing." Stevenson was also skeptical of Communist professions of a desire to trade. In his view, "So long as the ideological and anti-foreign bias continues to predominate . . . they will be in no hurry to take concrete steps to relieve British and other foreign business from disabilities which they are now suffering."[22] His judgment, unhappily for foreign businessmen, proved all too accurate.

There are those who are deeply skeptical of the authenticity of the Chou message because they were well acquainted with the messenger.[23] Philip Fugh did not know Keon, but he strongly doubts that Chou, with whom he was long acquainted, would have sent such a message in such a way.[24] Nevertheless, it is difficult to dismiss the fact that three of the most knowledgeable Americans in China at that time—Barrett, Clubb, and Stuart—all accepted the message as having come from Chou and took it seriously, and when British officials later received the Chou message, they also accepted its authenticity. Moreover, the Chou message provides a plausible explanation for a sudden shift in Huang Hua's line that is otherwise hard to explain. On June 8, Philip Fugh called on Huang Hua at Huang's request. Huang said he could not answer the question Fugh had raised at an earlier meeting about whether the CCP desired communization or industrialization first, but he said the CCP was eager for economic recovery, and American aid would be decisive. Stuart reported to Washington that this was the first time Huang had raised the subject of American economic assistance, "albeit indirectly." Indeed only two days before, in a long conversation with Stuart himself, Huang had said that "all CCP wanted from US was stoppage of aid and severance of relations with 'KMT Government.' "[25]

The abrupt change in Huang's attitude toward American aid between June 6 and June 8 could only have reflected new instructions from CCP headquarters consistent with the Chou message given Colonel Barrett on May 31. It does not necessarily follow that Huang knew of the message itself, but the fact that he was now affirming the importance of American aid, one of the most sensitive aspects of the Chou message, does lend credence to the authenticity of the substance of that message.

Clearly, whatever the authenticity of the demarche, the U.S. attempt to reply to it demonstrated that the United States hoped and expected to continue de facto relations with China after Communist victory and that it wanted to overcome obstacles to such relations through discussions between Communist and American officials.[26] As Clubb pointed out at the time, the U.S. reply was a "clear and firm" statement of American policy. It is unfortunate, therefore, that Clubb's efforts to have it delivered came to naught. On the other hand, much the same signal had already been sent by Ambassador Stuart in his discussions with Huang Hua, and there can be no doubt that Huang had fully reported these discussions to Chou En-lai.[27]

8

The Shanghai Blues

The capture by the Communists on May 26 of Shanghai, China's largest city and largest port, multiplied the opportunities for friction and misunderstanding between the Communists and British and American officials. From the standpoint of the Communists, and probably of most Chinese, Shanghai epitomized what was undesirable in the Western presence in China. In a vivid portrayal of the origins of the city, veteran journalist and observer of China Richard Hughes suggests why.

> Shanghai was born in Chinese mud—the muddy shore of the Whangpoo River, on which the British intruders, their visas granted by Jardine, Matheson and Palmerston and validated by gunpowder, first landed in 1843. . . .
>
> The foreign devils built the International Settlement and Frenchtown. They swallowed up more than a score of neighboring Chinese villages. They imposed their own foreign laws and regulations. . . .
>
> Shanghi persisted and flourished because it could levy tribute on all the wealth, trade and life blood of the Yangtze valley, with half the total population and half the total trade of all China. . . . The new industrial and commercial China was controlled by the Western-bossed twelve square miles of the International Settlement and the French Concession.[1]

Shanghai presented a new kind of challenge to the triumphant Communists. Schooled for so many years in making revolution in the countryside, they were ill prepared to handle the complex technical problems inherent in governing big cities, especially Shanghai, which had the largest foreign population in China. This at least was the judgment of many Western officials and businessmen in China at the time, who felt the Communists' predicament might make them more conciliatory than they had been in the northern cities. On the eve of Shanghai's fall, British Ambassador Stevenson telegraphed the Foreign Office: "Our expectation that the Communists would lack experience and administrative competence in dealing with economic problems of large industrial areas has on the whole been justified by events since Tientsin fell into their hands. Shanghai will present them with an infinitely more complex problem and their need for foreign assistance will shortly become increasingly evident and urgent." Stevenson warned, however, that despite their needs, the Communists would not yield to economic pressures from the West. "There is little doubt," he said, "that the Communists would not hesitate to impose extreme hardships upon the masses of their countrymen for the sake of ideological principles and rather than to appear to yield to economic pressure." He therefore opposed any attempt to use economic sanctions for political ends, which he rightly suspected was the American proclivity.[2]

Stevenson also thought it futile to try to work out a common economic policy with the United States because of differences in British and American means of control over commercial concerns and in their commercial interests in China. U.S. trade was less concerned than

British with local operations such as banking, coastal shipping, spin-
ning, and other productive enterprises. Therefore, the China-based
categories of economic enterprise in which the British were heavily
involved would be most difficult to control under any common economic policy and would be most susceptible to heavy losses or ruin as a
result of economic sanctions and Communist retaliation.[3] British economic interests in China were not only substantially larger but were
different in kind from American, and these differences were the principal but not the only factor accounting for the different responses of the
two communities when the Communists took over Shanghai.

To those in the British and American communities who expected
that the complexities of running Shanghai would oblige the Communists to come to them for help, Communist behavior came as a severe
disappointment. Not only did foreign businessmen experience many
of the same problems of red tape and poor communication with Communist officials as had their compatriots in other cities under Communist control, but they were confronted with a more disquieting pheno-
menon—what American Consul General Cabot called "the 'shut-in'
labor troubles."[4] In labor disputes, which erupted all over the city after
the Communist take-over, workers would lay siege to the premises
where they worked, refusing to let the managers out until their demands were settled.

Both British and American businesses suffered such troubles, but
the American businessmen were less willing to put up with these and
other vicissitudes of doing business under the Communists than were
their British competitors. The British business community, deeply
entrenched in China's internl trade and with bigger total investments
than the American, was firmly committed to a policy of staying put; the
American, much less so. As Cabot observed at the end of a long
telegram to Washington on June 26, a month after Shanghai's fall:
"Incidents of last few weeks involving foreigners have dampened any
initial optimism with which the foreign colony may have regarded
future under Communist rule. . . . Increasing mood among American
businessmen is that of packing up and leaving Shanghai rather than
submit to humiliations and insecurities of present situation."[5] Two
days earlier Cabot had noted in his diary: "To Chamber of Commerce
meeting—dismally pessimistic atmosphere. Gould and Coltman [Stan-
vac] described troubles—practically everyone present would like to
leave."[6]

Like the British and American private firms but unlike the British
consulate general, the American consulate general in Shanghai experi-

enced shut-in labor troubles. Workers once employed by the U.S. navy who had been suddenly discharged when the navy had pulled out of Shanghai early in the year were now out of work and dissatisfied with their severance pay. After rejecting a settlement of their demands offered by consular officials on behalf of the navy, the former employees were ready to use mass action. On June 28 Cabot reported rumors, to which he gave credence, that a "mass visitation" from the former employees, "including occupation ConGen premises entire group plus families relatives on pattern established other recent labor incidents foreign establishments," could be expected.[7] An entry from Cabot's diary the following day reveals the psychological consequences of such harassment: "We discuss using hoses and tear gas if mob invades [consulate] building, but I find other senior officers are opposed—and probably rightly. . . . I feel utterly discouraged, frustrated, sick, nervously exhausted, anxious only to get away."[8]

Besides the shut-in labor troubles, American consular personnel were subjected to other forms of harassment not experienced by their British colleagues. The most notorious example was the detention and beating of American Vice Consul William Olive as the result of a minor traffic charge.[9] The inability of U.S. consular officers to deal with such cases in a conventional, or even rational, manner heightened American frustration. Thus, when officers from the consulate general went to make inquiries at the police station where Olive was being detained, they were abused, threatened, and ridiculed. According to the consulate general's report of this incident, it was clear that the police commissar "was determined do everything possible humiliate Consulate General officers before large crowd of police, military personnel, onlookers. More crowd gathered more loud and aggressive he became. Consulate General officers were addressed as if criminals and kept continuously standing."[10]

When Olive was released after three days' confinement incommunicado on rations of bread and water, the consulate general suggested that the State Department "release story of jailing and beating Vice Consul William Olive, pointing out it seems part of systematic plan to humiliate foreigners."[11] Whether or not there was such a plan, local media quickly exploited the Olive case to reinforce yet again the Communists' image as the liberators of Shanghai from foreign imperialist oppression. The Shanghai *Liberation Daily,* for example, sounded this note:

After violating traffic regulations, Olive still behaved arrogantly and savagely in the manner of an imperialist towards the personnel and police of our Public

Security Bureau. He still wanted to treat them with the attitude of "a master" with which an American vice-consul treated the Kuomintang reactionaries in the past.

But Olive had erred completely. The people have become the masters in liberated Shanghai, and the People's Government will neither tolerate nor allow foreign nationals to insult and ride roughshod over our people!

Under the rule of the People's Government, all provocative acts of the imperialists in violating the law will be duly punished! All imperialist aggressive forces must get out of China![12]

Cabot commented to the State Department, "This grim affair impressively confirms my conviction that no American now safe in China."[13]

9

An Invitation from Mao

On June 28 Ambassador Stuart received through Huang Hua what he called "almost an invitation" from Mao Tse-tung and Chou En-lai to "talk with them while ostensibly visiting Yenching." In reporting "the background of this suggestion" to the State Department, Stuart indicated that early in June Fugh, without instructions from Stuart, had "casually" asked Huang if it would be possible for Stuart to travel to Peiping on his birthday (June 24) to visit his old university as he had been in the habit of doing in previous years. Huang made no comment at the time, but on June 18 he raised the question with Fugh "of whether time permitted" Stuart's making a trip to Peiping. Fugh commented only that "he himself had made this suggestion 2 weeks earlier."[1]

These exchanges between Fugh and Huang, which had not been authorized by the State Department and were not even reported to Washington until after Stuart had received the invitation from Mao and

Chou, seem to have generated an expectation in Peiping that Stuart would go there. Thus he records in his diary:

June 26, Sunday
Chou Yu-kang returned from Peiping. . . . learned H.H. [Huang Hua] sent here because of me—reports of my going Peiping—Mao announced I would be welcome as old friend of many CCP—nothing hide from Americans, etc. Apparently H.H. reported my trip.
June 28, Tuesday
Philip [Fugh] called on H.H. telling of a strongly phrased letter from C.W. Luh [chancellor of Yenching University] assuming that I was to visit Peiping. He said Mao, Chou would heartily welcome me but apparently confirmed this by another telegraphic exchange to this effect which he called in p.m. to report—H.H. came to bring the message and stayed about an hour.[2]

In reporting Huang's message, Stuart made no recommendation to Washington; he merely listed the advantages and disadvantages of his going to Peiping and asked for instructions. The principal advantages, as Stuart saw them, were that he would have a chance to present American views directly to Mao and Chou and to take back to Washington the "most authoritative information regarding CCP intentions," that his going to Peiping might strengthen the more liberal, anti-Soviet wing of the CCP, and that it would be an "imaginative, adventurous indication of U.S. open-minded attitude towards changing political trends in China and probably would have beneficial effect on future Sino-American relations."[3]

One senses that Stuart wanted to make the trip—so at least Consul General Cabot in Shanghai thought. A July 1 entry in his diary records: "I am sure he wants to go. I shoved in my two cents worth to help him by suggesting [to the State Department] that both general situation in Shanghai and the protection of Western interests here would be furthered."[4] The State Department, however, was more impressed with the disadvantages Stuart had cited and gave them as the principal reasons for instructing him "under no circumstances" to visit Peiping.[5] Stuart had noted that the trip would break the "united front" of the diplomatic corps in Nanking, which the United States had sponsored, causing a parade of mission chiefs to Peiping. Moreover, "a trip of US Ambassador to Peiping at this time would enhance greatly prestige, national and international, of Chinese Communists and Mao himself and in a sense would be a second step on our part (first having been my remaining Nanking) toward recognition Communist regime."[6]

Mao, in any case, did not wait for a response to his invitation to Stuart before issuing one of his strongest affirmations of the CCP's alignment with the Soviet Union and hostility toward the United States. In his essay "On People's Democratic Dictatorship," published under a June 30 dateline (the same date on which Washington first learned of the invitation), Mao wrote:

"You are leaning to one side." Exactly. . . . All Chinese without exception must lean either to the side of imperialism or to the side of socialism. Sitting on the fence will not do, nor is there a third road.
"You are too irritating." We are talking about how to deal with domestic and foreign reactionaries, the imperialists and their running dogs. . . . the question of irritating them or not does not arise.
"We need help from the British and U.S. governments." This, too, is a naive idea in these times. . . . Internationally we belong to the side of the anti-imperialist front headed by the Soviet Union, and so we can turn only to this side for genuine and friendly help, not to the side of the imperialist front.[7]

Mao's lean-to-one-side stance was by no means new; it had not resulted from developments of the past few months. As Ambassador Stuart pointed out in a telegram to the State Department analyzing the article, Mao was "merely dotting i's and crossing t's of his previous writings, of political theory formulated in his 'New Democracy' and solidarity with the USSR expressed in many important CCP pronouncements."[8] In "On New Democracy," published in January 1940, Mao had described alliance with Russia as one of the "Three Great Policies" of the "new or genuine Three People's Principles." "Once the conflict between the socialist Soviet Union and the imperialist powers grows sharper," Mao predicted, "China will have to take her stand on one side or the other. This is an inevitable trend. Is it possible to avoid leaning to either side? No, that is an illusion."[9]

By the fall of 1948, the conflict between the "imperialist powers" and the Soviet Union had unmistakably grown sharper, and Mao returned to his theme in his article "Revolutionary Forces of the World Unite; Fight Against Imperialist Aggression," published in the Cominform journal November 1, 1948. "Has not the history of these 31 years," Mao wrote, "proved the utter hypocrisy and complete bankruptcy of all who are satisfied neither with imperialism nor with the Soviet Union, of all those so-called 'middle-road' or 'third force' attempts to stand between the imperialist counter-revolutionary front and the people's revolutionary fighting front against imperialism and its running dogs in various countries?"[10] This article or a precis of it was republished in newspapers in Communist-controlled areas of China in subsequent months.[11]

In the face of Mao's strong reaffirmation of the lean-to-one-side policy while the U.S. reply to his "almost an invitation" was pending, it is hard to take seriously speculation that "an extraordinary opportunity to explore terms of accommodation" was missed.[12] Mao had reiterated his allegiance to the antiimperialist camp headed by the Soviet Union in the full knowledge of the U.S. desire to maintain an ongoing relationship with China. Stuart not only had conveyed the American position in his talks with Huang Hua but had given it on June 10 to a "third force" intermediary, General Chen Ming-shu, who later in the month had talks with both Mao and Chou. Stuart's comments to Chen, as might be expected, followed the same lines as those he had made to Huang. "Americans," he said, "believe states with different ideologies can live together." The Americans "are primarily concerned in Chinese people rather than in form of government they choose themselves, provided only government has support of whole nation and is willing and able to maintain accepted international standards." The attitude of the United States "is one of waiting, observing. However, fact of my remaining Nanking together with other chiefs of mission (excpet Soviet) has significance which must surely be appreciated by CCP."[13]

On June 24 Stuart reported to the State Department that he had heard indirectly that Chen had already had conversations with both Mao and Chou.[14] Apparently, on that same day he told his British colleague Sir Ralph Stevenson about Chen and his conversations in Peking. Thus, Ambassador Stevenson reported to the Foreign Office on June 25:

> My United States colleague has informed me in strictest confidence that he has been in touch with Ch'en Ming-shu, the Secretary General of Li Chi-shen's Kuomintang Revolutionary Committee. He called on Dr. Stuart recently on his way through from Shanghai to Peking and was then briefed on the advantages to China of friendly relations in the future with Western democracies.
>
> His visit to Peking was evidently regarded as being important as . . . he seems to have had conversations with Mao Tse Tung and Chou En-lai.[15]

Whatever hopes Stuart and Stevenson may have had riding on Chen's conversations in Peking, they came to naught. When, on his return from Peking, Chen gave Stuart a written report of these conversations, Stuart found them "discouraging," observing that they contained "no hint of any deviation from present political course set, including relations with the USA."[16]

The uncompromising way in which Mao embraced the Soviet Union in "On People's Democratic Dictatorship" and rejected any thought of asking the West for help must have come as a severe blow to those both within and outside China who had felt that economic necessity would force the Communists into some sort of accommodation with the West, particularly with the United States. Mao's stance flatly contradicted Huang Hua's statement to Fugh of June 8 that China would need U.S. aid. As we have seen, that statement of Huang's was made deliberately and represented a change in his line of two day's earlier. Mao's essay rejected the line of the Chou demarche and was consistent with the refusal of the Communists to receive a U.S. reply to it.

In this light it is not surprising that in Ambassador Stuart's last lengthy interview with Huang Hua, several weeks after the publication of Mao's article, Huang reverted to the same line he had taken before June 8. As Stuart reported this conversation, Huang said "that best American policy would be to keep hands off China, that any merchant, peasant, student would agree to this. He said China could face her industrial and other problems unaided." Stuart reported that he came away from this one-and-a-half-hour conversation "with a feeling of discomfiture" and that Huang's mind was "impermeable to argument and even to facts." Stuart, the man who had once put such hope in changing the Communists' minds through discussion, confessed that he doubted that "either one changed other's opinions."[17]

Ambassador Stuart used his failure to go to Peiping to see Mao as an argument against going to Canton to see Chiang. President Truman had told Secretary Acheson on July 11 that he believed it to be "important and desirable for the Ambassador to visit Canton before returning" to the United States. Truman reasoned that "it would not be understood in the United States for the Ambassador to return after being out of touch for so long with the Government to which he is accredited."[18]

At first Stuart did not demur very strongly when instructed to proceed to Canton.[19] When he learned, however, that Generalissimo Chiang Kai-shek had just gone to Canton, he pleaded that it would be undesirable for him to visit Canton because, if he did so, he could not avoid calling on Chiang. Stuart did not want to jeopardize his usefulness in dealings with the Communist leadership. Thus, he pointed out: "It is certain that visit to Canton and meeting with Generalissimo (which could not be avoided) promptly following my refusal travel to Peiping would appear to Commies studied insult to which they might be expected to react vigorously. . . . My flying to Canton to see their arch enemy would certainly never be forgiven me and any future usefulness I might have had in Commie China entirely vitiated."[20] Stuart argued further that his going to Canton might increase "difficulties which Americans are now facing in Shanghai, Hankow," possibly provoking "retaliatory measures" against the embassy and other official U.S. establishments. He concluded: "While I concur in Dept's decision that I not travel to Peiping with hat in hand to call on Chairman Mao, by same token I feel it unwise to change my course and pay visit to Chairman Chiang."[21]

By refusing to authorize Stuart to go to Peiping, the United States had demonstrated there were limits to how far it would go in pursuit of a modus vivendi. It would not take the "second step" toward recognition of a regime that had not yet formed a national government, nor would the United States contribute to the prestige of leaders who, as Clubb had recently pointed out, had given "clear proof present hostility . . . toward USA."[22] On the other hand, by agreeing with Stuart that he should not go to Canton either, Washington showed it did not wish to antagonize these leaders needlessly or to close off a possible future channel of negotiation.

10
Fewer Stay Put

The month of July, which had opened inauspiciously from the Anglo-American point of view with Mao's public reiteration of the lean-to-one-side policy, brought more frustrations and irritations for British and American officials, especially the latter. The cumulative effect of these troubles was to bring about a modification of American policy. In his autobiography, Ambassador Stuart recalls: "The trends in Communist policy led me to recommend to the Department that plans be made to evacuate Americans from Communist-controlled areas, especially Shanghai. The anti-American propaganda was becoming more vitriolic, the allegiance to the Soviet Union more frank, the discrimination against foreign and indeed all private business more flagrant, the techniques of police-state repression and of state-operated trade more true to form."[1]

On July 15 the Foreign Affairs Bureau in Shanghai called in the acting director of the U.S. Information Service there and "aggressively" ordered him to stop all USIS operations immediately. The activities of the service included "the Consulate General's movies, concerts, library as well as news and publicity."[2] In Peiping on July 19 the consulate general received a similar directive in writing. The order was being issued, the directive said, because "the People's Government has no diplomatic or consular relations with USA."[3]

This reasoning, of course, was all too familiar to American consular officials, and they replied in their usual way that the USIS was a part of the consular establishment and did not "depend on official diplomatic recognition for its existence." In Shanghai, Consul Walter McConaughy also protested that the order violated a principle "recognized in all parts of the world" that informational and educational activities "form a legitimate part" of the work of a consular establishment; furthermore, it discriminated against USIS activities "as compared with certain similar activities of the Soviet Union, which are still carried on unimpeded in this city."[4]

The surprising thing about the Communist move against USIS, perhaps, was that it was not made earlier. In his March report to the CCP Central Committee, Mao had said not only that the Communists should "refuse to recognize the legal status of any foreign diplomatic establishments and personnel of the Kuomintang period" but also that they should "abolish all imperialist propaganda agencies in China." In its story on the order closing USIS, and the British Information Service as well, NCNA asserted that "these two services never ceased their propaganda activities" after the "liberation" of Shanghai.[5]

The Communists' crackdown on the USIS offices in the cities they controlled came at just the time Ambassador Stuart was becoming increasingly frustrated by his inability to depart China for the United States on consultation. His departure had been targeted for July 18 but was delayed some two weeks beyond that date by the Communists' insistence that, like any private citizen, he must have a "shop guarantee" of any unpaid debts or unsettled claims he might leave behind before being granted an exit permit. The State Department took a very dim view of this demand "on grounds of principle, prestige and precedent" and gave instructions that no American in Stuart's party was to accept any guarantor. Eventually a compromise was reached, and the authorities agreed to exempt Stuart from the shop guarantee and from baggage inspection.[6]

Stuart speculated that his departure problems were related to his refusal to go to Peiping to see Mao. Thus he told the State Department on July 14: "When I refused to go I feel that they all lost some face but particularly Huang Hua who first took the initiative here. My suspicions this respect are confirmed by recent remark Huang Hua's number two, Ch'en Ying, who, in connection with some difficulties I and my party are having in obtaining exit permits from China said to Fugh, 'If Stuart had gone to Peiping all these little questions would have been easily settled.' "[7]

In this matter, unlike some other instances of friction between Communist and American officials, the British were sympathetic to the American position. In a message to the Foreign Office July 15 on Stuart's problem, Ambassador Stevenson reported that he and his commonwealth colleagues unanimously regarded the Communist attitude as "indefensible." The "right of unhindered exit" for ambassadors and their staffs had "never been questioned," Stevenson pointed out, "even by states at war." He hoped that the U.S. government would not "give way on this matter of principle even if it means the heads of mission will be held here as hostages." Indeed, on July 14 Stuart had noted in his diary that he had had lunch with the commonwealth mission chiefs and that "they felt even more strongly than I on diplomatic objection to shop or individual guarantee."[8] Commenting on Stevenson's report, Coates in the Foreign Office thought the Communists' "object may be to make foreign diplomatic personnel lose face." Coates had "little doubt" that the Communists had a "set policy of making persons of European descent in China lose as much face as possible."[9]

Though it seems unlikely that the Communists had any such set policy, their policies in general had by now persuaded the three top-ranking U.S. officials in China to revise the U.S. policy of keeping consulates open in cities taken over by the Communists. In their view, not only should no more consulates be "liberated" but those already in Communist territory should have their staffs reduced to a minimum. So recommended Minister-Counselor Lewis Clark after he had had discussions in Okinawa with Ambassador Stuart and Consul General Cabot, who were en route to Washington. Clark in a telegram from Canton on August 5 reported that Stuart and Cabot "having experienced living under Communist regime feel more strongly on subject than I who have not suffered that experience. . . . Their experience indicates complete inability of Consular officials perform their functions. To leave them at mercy unfriendly Communist regime is to incur personal danger needlessly." Clark's message continued: "I gather that there has grown out of experience in Communist China an increasing realization that it will be impossible to 'do business' with Communists on any other than intolerable terms; that the Communists are determined to eliminate American interests and institutions from China when to do so suits their purposes; that no friendly approach on our part will change pattern of events and that as a result our best interests dictate that we treat any forthcoming Communist regime at arm's length."[10] Clark generally agreed with Stuart and Cabot, but he went even further, recommending that all U.S. official personnel be withdrawn if an international repatriation vessel could be arranged.

Stuart's and Cabot's skepticism as to the future utility of consulates in Communist-controlled areas of China had undoubtedly been strengthened by the knowledge that when they departed China on August 2, Acting Consul General Walter McConaughy had been barricaded in his office in the U.S. consulate building in Shanghai for four days, while a substantial number of disgruntled Chinese former employees of the U.S. navy and their families occupied another part of the building. In his report on this incident McConaughy remarked: "Although authorities eventually intervened in covert manner . . . they still have given us no redress, they do not openly admit they intervened, of course have expressed no regrets, have not disavowed action officials who refused intervene and have given us no assurance they would behave differently if we are subjected to similar indignity in future labor crises."[11]

When Ambassador Stuart and Consul General Cabot arrived in Washington they were able to present their views directly to the State Department. On August 12 they participated in a meeting with Deputy Undersecretary of State Dean Rusk, Ambassador-at-Large Philip Jessup, and other State Department officials, at which a decision was reached to close the consulate general in Canton before that city fell to the Communists.[12]

The State Department had already decided to close the consulates at Chungking, Kunming, and Tihwa, where there were no substantial American interests.[13] Before Stuart left Nanking, he had recommended closing the consulates at Tsingtao and Hankow in view of the impossibility of effective representation for the protection of American interests, possible future hardship and danger to the staffs, and the probable impossibility of sending replacements from outside of China "prior to recognition."[14] Thus, on the basis of the experience of those officials who had tred to maintain consular establishments under the Communists in China, the United States by mid-August had decided to close consular offices in six cities, rather than subject them to the same ordeal. The closures also recognized, of course, that in the more remote cities, such as Tihwa, Chungking, and Kunming, remaining American interests in the area would hardly justify keeping consulates functioning under any circumstances.

These decisions significantly modified the policy the United States had followed since the fall of 1948 of keeping its consular establishments open in Communist territory; but they did not reverse that policy, for U.S. consulates were to remain open in Tientsin, Peiping, and Shanghai, along with the embassy at Nanking, Ambassador Stuart's departure notwithstanding. The decision in May to close the consulate at Mukden, as we have seen, was made under special circumstances and did not represent a change in the general policy on consulates.

The American decision to close six consulates had a significant impact on the British. Not only did it deviate from what had been a common Anglo-American policy of retaining consulates in Communist territory, but it brought an added burden to British consular representatives in China and to the Foreign Office when the United States asked the British to protect American interests in the consular districts from which American official personnel had been withdrawn.

Rather surprisingly, the State Department approached British consular officers in the field on this matter before taking it up with the Foreign Office in London. Thus, in a telegram dated August 15, British Consul General Gerald F. Tyrrell in Canton notified the Foreign Office: "My United States colleague has now received instructions from Washington authorising him to place United States movable property and Government owned buildings in my custody provided I am willing to assume this responsibility. The State Department have asked him to let them know whether it would be necessary to negotiate with His Majesty's Government in this regard."[15] Tyrrell informed his U.S. colleague that he would have to await instructions from the Foreign Office before he could assume such a commitment, which he thought would inevitably be extended to the protection of U.S. nationals. He told the Foreign Office that he did not "feel inclined to assume responsibility for any United States interests after they officially evacuate Canton, a step they are presumably taking because they anticipate that they would run into so much trouble were they to stay after the Communist occupation." Tyrrell noted, "If this is so, too close an association with American interests might well result in involving this Consulate General in purely American troubles to the point where it might be impossible for us to carry on at all." He also worried that if the

British agreed, "we shall presumably in due course find ourselves looking after United States interests in the other part(s) of China as well."[16] On this last point, he was exactly right.

Until it received Tyrrell's report from Canton, the Foreign Office had not heard that the United States wanted the British to protect American interests in Canton or even that the United States expected to close its consulate there. Coates shared Tyrrell's misgivings about complying with the American request. He felt that the United Kingdom had an "excellent excuse" for declining the American request in the Communists' refusal to recognize the official status of foreign consulates. The British consulate in Canton would therefore "have no *locus standi* with the Communist authorities to attempt protection of U.S. Government property . . . or the interests of U.S. citizens."

Coates' superior in the Far Eastern Department, F.S. Tomlinson, saw the matter in a somewhat different light, however. Noting that it seemed "anomalous in the extreme of the Americans, who have been enlisting our support for a policy of scuttle, to approach us in this way," Tomlinson thought he saw a British interest in returning "as favorable a reply as possible," since the Americans could scarcely attack the British for their stay-put policy, "while they are benefitting from the services of the men who have stayed put."[17]

Ambassador Stevenson in Nanking agreed with Tyrrell in Canton that there were obvious difficulties, perhaps even dangers, involved in accepting "responsibility for the custody of the United States Consulate General and charge of United States interests in Canton (and presumably progressively elsewhere in China)." Nevertheless, he felt sure that "in the long run" it was in the British interest "to take on this friendly task much as it is liable to add to our immediate embarrassment."[18] Stevenson recommended acceptance of the U.S. request but proposed a number of conditions aimed at reducing the burden, financial and otherwise, on the British consulates involved.

Although the British saw immediately that the United States would seek protection of its nationals as well as its property in China, this possibility seemed to come almost as an afterthought to the State Department. The initial memorandum presented by the U.S. embassy in London to the Foreign Office on August 17 requested only that British consular officers accept custody of U.S. government properties in Canton, Tihwa, Chungking, and Kunming and promised that the United States would "make funds available . . . for salaries of caretakers and for essential upkeep of U.S. properties." The following day the Foreign Office informed the embassy that His Majesty's consular officers would be instructed to accept custody of U.S. government property but warned that the degree of protection they could afford "must inevitably be limited since their consular status is not recognized by the Chinese Communist authorities."[19] Only on August 19 did the American embassy, in a further memorandum to the Foreign Office, request that British consuls in China "afford American citizens protection similar to that afforded British nationals." The Foreign Office promptly informed the embassy that it was also prepared to accede to this further request but again emphasized the limited protection the British would be able to extend.[20]

Though willing to extend British protection to American nationals and property in China, the Foreign Office wanted to make clear that the British government did not intend to imitate American policy. In a memorandum of August 16 Esler Dening reminded Bevin, "The present Cabinet policy is that we should stay in China and keep our foot in the door." He recommended that the Foreign Office News Department say in connection with a State Department announcement about the closure of U.S. consulates in China that "no similar steps are being contemplated by the United Kingdom." Dening felt that such a statement was necessary to reassure British subjects in Shanghai and elsewhere, whose morale was "already shaken by the Nationalist blockade and the consequent failure to resume trade."[21] Dening's recommendation was approved.

11

Blockade

The Nationalist blockade referred to in Dening's memorandum had been inaugurated by the Chinese government toward the end of June, when it had taken action to close ports no longer under its control along with adjacent territorial waters.[1] Both the British and U.S. governments called the Chinese action illegal, but the tenor of their protests foreshadowed a marked difference in their ultimate reactions to the new Nationalist policy. A note to the Nationalist Foreign Ministry delivered by the U.S. embassy office in Canton June 28 stated, "Despite the friendliest feelings," the U.S. government could not "admit the legality of any action" declaring ports and adjacent territorial waters closed unless the Chinese Government declared and maintained an effective blockade of them.[2] In their protest the British deliberately omitted any hint of sympathy for the Chinese action.[3] Moreover, they stressed the presumed ineffectiveness of the "attempted blockade" and declared that the Chinese government, having never admitted a state of war existed in China, had no claim to belligerent rights.[4]

The Chinese Government's retort to all this was summed up succinctly in a message dated July 4 to the Foreign Office from the British embassy office in Canton: "British and American notes about closure of ports were despatched this week and received prompt replies based on the thesis that a state may close any port of its territory when conditions make it necessary."[5]

The Nationalists' port closure decree was no mere paper declaration insofar as Shanghai was concerned. It was enforced by naval vessels stationed near the mouth of the Yangtze and by aerial bombing of the Yangtse estuary and the port of Shanghai. Soon after the announced date of the port closure, June 25, British naval vessels on patrol off the estuary reported that there were sufficient Nationalist warships in the area to blockade the river.[6] Earlier, Nationalist p-51s had bombed the British merchant ship SS *Anchises* in the estuary, bringing a strong protest from Foreign Secretary Bevin to the Chinese ambassador in London.[7] How effective the Nationalists' measures proved to be is indicated by a telegram to the State Department from the American consulate general in Shanghai, reporting that "during July and since the beginning of the so-called blockade June 25" the only two foreign ships to enter the port were a British tug, which towed the disabled *Anchises* to Kobe, and a small Japanese vessel.[8]

The effectiveness of the Nationalist blockade not only created morale problems for the British community but posed a challenge to the British government's "stay put" policy—a policy that counted on the Communists' need, especially in Shanghai, for foreign trade and technical assistance. The British business community in Shanghai became desperate to break the blockade and reestablish trade. But could this be done short of the use of force? If not, where would the force come from? The Communists seemed unable to cope with Nationalist naval and air power, having little or none of their own.

From the beginning, Ambassador Stevenson in Nanking opposed any effort by British ships to force their way through the Nationalist blockade. He doubted that the potential profit from trade under existing conditions in China would be worth the damage to ships and the loss of lives and taxpayers money that would result from such a course. Thus he urged the Foreign Office to adhere as strictly as possible to "our declared sympathetic neutrality in the Chinese civil war." He argued that it was contrary to Britain's ultimate interests to run the risks involved in helping the Communists to obtain supplies "when they are not (repeat not) able to, in return, provide protection to British merchant ships in their zones, though at the same time they so insistently oppose the presence of British naval units in territorial waters." Stevenson contended, "If we discreetly hold back, Communists may by force of circumstances begin to appreciate important role which our trading interests can play in China and modify their attitude towards us accordingly.[9]

Stevenson's cautious approach to the blockade was indirectly supported by the U.K. shipping representative for the Far East, Derek Allen. In a letter of June 27 to Major General R.C. Money at the Ministry of Transport, Allen said the "only shipping service with Chinese Communist ports is Butterfield and Swire." Allen said it was no longer the unanimous view "of the more thoughtful businessmen" in Hong Kong that "we must pursue unconditional trade at all costs with this new largely unknown China."[10]

Butterfield and Swire's different view of the blockade and the Chinese psyche was summed up in a letter addressed to Messrs. John Swire & Son, Ltd., London, on July 22 as follows: "The West is denied the opportunity of demonstrating to the newcomers how much they have to gain by compromising with it. . . . We should prove ourselves indispensable to the process of individual gain which alone fundamentally interests the Chinese. . . . We are sure it is of quite the first political importance that the Communist access to western fleshpots should be restored at once. We hope our policy makers are thinking boldly."[11] What Butterfield and Swire meant by "thinking boldly" was illustrated by a telegram the firm sent several days later to John Swire in London urging that he bring pressure on the government to provide naval escort for British shipping to Shanghai.[12]

Butterfield and Swire, among the first British companies to enter the China trade, may have overestimated the temptations posed by the capitalist fleshpots of Shanghai to the average Chinese, but it should be noted that several months earlier, Mao Tse-tung himself had warned the Central Committee of the CCP thus: "There may be some Communists, who were not conquered by enemies with guns and were worthy of the name of heroes for standing up to these enemies, but who cannot withstand sugar-coated bullets; they will be defeated by sugar-coated bullets."[13] In this light, Mao and the CCP should have welcomed the blockade. And perhaps they did; it provided them with a scapegoat for the economic problems of Shanghai, which they could now blame on the Americans who had provided the Nationalists with the ships and planes used to enforce the blockade.

Be this as it may, on July 20 the Communists approached British Consul General Robert Urquhart and leading British shipping firms in Shanghai ostensibly for help to break the blockade. The intermediary was one Han Ming, a newspaperman known for some years to a member of the British consulate general staff and considered by him to be "upright and honest."[14] At a meeting with the British (minus Urquhart, who did not think he should go), Han said the Communists had a few bombers, but they were ill equipped with radar; thus the only way to get merchant ships into Shanghai would be to escort them by warships as far as Woosung (at the mouth of the Whangpoo). The ships would have to take a chance between Woosung and Shanghai, but the Communists would provide antiaircraft artillery cover. They would turn a blind eye on escorting foreign warships below Woosung, that is, in the Yangtze estuary.[15]

Coincidentally, on the same day Han Ming approached the British in Shanghai, Foreign Secretary Bevin instructed the British embassy in Washington to request the views of the State Department on a proposal to provide some relief to the foreign community in Shanghai "by organising deliveries of essential supplies, notably rice and fuel." Bevin professed to "fully share the views of the United States Government as to the undesirability of relief measures on a scale sufficient to benefit the Communist economy so long as the Communits maintain their present attitude toward our business interests," but he felt the danger to the foreign community from a breakdown of public utilities due to lack of fuel or food riots could not be ignored. As to the Nationalists' blockade, he wondered whether pressure could be brought to bear on them to relax the blockade for the passage of relief ships or whether such ships might "travel in a protected convoy."[16]

But the State Department did not wish to cooperate in a move that might alleviate the problems of the Communists in Shanghai. On July 21 it made an oral reply to the British embassy rejecting the idea of joint Anglo-American arrangements for delivering supplies to Shanghai and advising the British that if they undertook the deliveries of such supplies they should do so as "a temporary measure for relief purposes."[17]

These developments were reviewed in a minute written by Peter Scarlett for Foreign Secretary Bevin July 22 to prepare him for a cabinet meeting that afternoon. According to Scarlett two points had now emerged. First, Sir Ralph Stevenson in Nanking, though he fully agreed with the need for supplies, opposed any attempt to force the Nationalist blockade under naval escort, since both the Communists and the Nationalists would be equally ready to make political capital out of any incident that might ensue. Second, the State Department was not ready to join in any such task, and in the Far Eastern Department's view the United Kingdom could not undertake such a task without U.S. support. This view prevailed with the cabinet. On July 23 the Foreign Office telegraphed the British embassy in Washington that the question of relief supplies for Shanghai had been considered by the ministers, and they had ruled out any possibility of forcing the Nationalist blockade by convoys under naval escort.[18]

A week later Han Ming in Shanghai, "with the authority of Chou En-lai," told representatives of British shipping interests that the Communists would welcome British naval assistance to bring ships in. They would agree to penetration as far as Woosung if necessary; there would be no Communist gunfire on anything as far as Woosung. Reporting these favorable developments, Consul General Urquhart commented that British "restraint and pertinacity" were "beginning to prevail." He said, "It is really not our fault that American volatility has got them into their present mess."[19]

In Urquhart's opinion there had been an abrupt and unwelcome change in American policy. He reported this "Shanghai view" to the Foreign Office on July 29 in a telegram "of particular secrecy":

4. For a month or so after the capture of Shanghai the Americans here followed the same courses as ourselves. . . . We both assumed that the Communists had come to stay, and we sought by suitable speech and gesture to break down their hostility, to initiate commercial relations and to establish a *modus vivendi* pending recognition. . . .
5. . . . We had nothing to offer comparable to cotton stocks which United States Ambassador came here to release, nor have we made attempts comparable with those of United States Ambassador and United States Consul General to make contact with local officials, unsuccessful as they were.
6. . . . my United States colleague . . . said that it was unthinkable to allow a city of this size to drift into chaos, dependent as it was on E.C.A. supplies. He

insisted particularly that utilities must be kept running, and you will recollect that before the capture the Americans agreed to keeping in hand of a month's stock of essential supplies accepting the fact that this would benefit the new regime.

7. This attitude has changed abruptly and entirely and the British here are alarmed. . . . The blockade, which the Americans are now thought to support, is a disaster first for foreigners and next for those moderate Communists who favor overseas trade. . . . It cannot seriously impede the development of political or military programmes now in train.[20]

As already noted, there had been a modification of the U.S. stay-put policy during July in reaction to what American officials perceived as unremitting CCP hostility toward Americans, both in word and deed. However, at this stage, it was too much to say that the United States supported the blockade, even though such a perception on the part of its victims was quite understandable.

The hostility Urquhart expressed toward the blockade was largely shared by the American community in Shanghai, but for somewhat different reasons. Unlike British businessmen there, whom Urquhart had described in his telegram as "patiently enduring discomforts" of the changing times, the majority of the American businessmen were ready to call it quits and get out, blaming the Nationalists and the Communists alike for their problems. The Nationalist blockade, piled on top of their troubles with the Communists, had destroyed their will to carry on in Shanghai. A long memorial to the State Department from the American Chamber of Commerce in that city revealed their feelings in such statements as:

Last vestige Nationalist resistance taken form blockade Chinese ports and aerial bombardment Chinese cities made possible by American warships, planes, fuel, bombs, ammunition. One result these terroristic tactics is American residents China subjected further hazards by mobs inflamed with anti-foreigner propaganda.

. . . .

General opinion many American businessmen who fought losing battle in China throughout postwar era is that continued resistance will be costly, dangerous, and that time liquidate and leave China over due.

. . . .

Entire American community without protection due process law and faced with dangerous possibility food riots, cause for which distorted in terms American inspired, supported blockade by Communist propaganda.[21]

. . . .

Trend recent events indicates consideration safety foreign staffs American companies dictates complete evacuation such persons.[22]

The Chamber of Commerce went on to ask the State Department to arrange safe transportation out of China for the staffs of American companies through negotiations with the Communists and the Nationalists, even if it had to break off relations with the latter or at least to withhold further support until Americans were safe. A few days later, in a statement giving general support to the representations of the Chamber of Commerce, the president of the American Association in Shanghai went even further, urging the State Department to use "every possible means" to bring about the lifting of the blockade permanently, for "otherwse evacuation will be blocked."[23]

Before receiving these representations the State Department had already recognized that the situation in Shanghai was "becoming increasingly intolerable" for some American citizens and that it might be necessary for the government to "assist in arranging for evacuation facilities."[24] This perception apparently led to a slight modification in the American position with respect to the shipment of relief supplies through the blockade. Counselor Charles Meade of the British embassy in Washington spoke with Philip Sprouse, director of the State Department's Office of Chinese Affairs, on August 1. In the event that American orgaizations in Shanghai wanted and were able to arrange for shipment of relief supplies, Sprouse said, the U.S. government would be willing to associate itself with the British government "in approaching the Chinese Government in connection with the passage of evacuation ships carrying such supplies." He warned, however, that the Nationalists might agree to the safe passage of evacuation ships but "might not be willing to allow the entry into Shanghai of such ships if they carried foodstuffs for the foreign community."[25]

In its report of the Sprouse-Meade conversation to the Foreign Office, the British embassy pointed out that the State Department, seriously afraid that the Communists would use foreigners as hostages, had linked the relief ship proposal with evacuation. F.S. Tomlinson, deputy head of the Far Eastern Department, found the "State Department's attitude far from satisfactory," though it did provide "the basis for joint action." He also noted that it was clear that the Americans attached much more importance to getting Americans out of Shanghai than to keeping Shanghai going.[26]

The State Department's emphasis on evacuation of foreigners from Shanghai, as opposed to providing them relief supplies, was explained in part in a conversation Sprouse had with First Secretary J.F. Ford of the British embassy August 20. According to Ford's report: "Sprouse said that he would have liked to see every American citizen out of China. It was regrettable that the Chinese Communists had so many Americans to use as 'hostages' whilst the United States had no power at all over the Communists."[27] Sprouse also expressed American frustrations with the blockade. "The State Department," he said, "had hoped to use the control of trade with Communist China as a means of leverage and it was most exasperating that the blockade had removed even this possibility."[28]

The U.S. attitude toward the blockade was ambivalent. On the one hand, it fitted the American theory that CCP policies could be moderated by economic pressures; on the other, the blockade was the wrong instrument, for it was designed to prevent all trade and could not be manipulated as could trade controls to bring optimum results. Moreover, the blockade provided opportunities for Communist political exploitatin at the expense of the United States; it enhanced the Communists' efforts to divide the Western powers.

The Communist efforts continued to be centered on the British. Thus on August 26 British Consul General Urquhart was called in for an interview with Chang Han-fu, head of the Foreign Affairs Bureau in Shanghai, and asked not to inform his American and French colleagues. Chang told Urquhart that despite their nonrecognition of foreign diplomatic and consular offices, the Communists wished for normal relations with foreign business communities. Blaming the present difficulties in Shanghai on the blockade, which he was convinced was supported by the Americans, Chang said the Communists were prepared to lift the blockade by capturing the Chusan Islands. But there could be no question of British warships convoying merchant ships to Woosung; the Communists would break the blockade by their own efforts. Commenting on his interview with Chang, Urquhart said it was the sort of development "we are entitled to expect in due course," but he acknowledged that it had undoubtedly been accelerated by the blockade.[29]

The Communist authorities continued their campaign of reassurance by granting John Keswick, chairman of the British Chamber of Commerce in Shanghai, interviews with Chang Han-fu on August 28 and with Mayor Chen Yi on August 30. According to Urquhart's report to the Foreign Office, the mayor told Keswick that the impression that the Communist government was trying to squeeze foreigners out was entirely mistaken. Chen asked that foreigners be patient and hope for better times to come.[30]

Urquhart admitted it was possible that the Communist authorities were counting on being able to reassure foreigners by comforting words and were prepared to do nothing further, but he said Keswick and the British Chamber of Commerce were much encouraged.[31] Their relief was natural enough, since up to this time the foreign business community had been cold-shouldered by the authorities. Only a few weeks earlier the Shanghai Chamber of Commerce had complained to the China Association in London that it had not found a way to establish contact with the responsible authorities and so had been unable to make its views known.[32] Such treatment had been the norm, of course, in cities under Communist control. In a report to the Foreign Office in early July, for example, the British consul general in Tientsin had complained that "no written reply or guidance on any problem is obtainable by foreign merchants from ignorant minor officials by whom they are treated with suspicion and contempt and frequently also with open hostility."[33]

What now appeared to be a moderation of Communist policy, toward British business at least, was being manifested not only in Shanghai but in Tientsin and Peiping as well. The British embassy in Nanking noted a common theme in telegrams from these posts: the authorities were denying any intention of injuring British interests and were displaying readiness to establish business relations. The embassy observed, however, that so far these protestations of goodwill lacked "convincing practical proof" and were "belied by Communist performance." In the embassy's view, the governing factor was political; the Communists were playing a waiting game, hoping for a split among the powers, especially in Anglo-American unity in the Far East.[34]

In Shanghai, U.S. Consul General McConaughy sounded a similar note. In a message to the State Department commenting on Keswick's call on Mayor Chen Yi, McConaughy said he assumed the Communist authorities were "up to their old device of playing one group of foreigners against another." This assumption was "borne out by conspicuous absence direct and pointed attacks on British over past 3 or 4 weeks . . . [and] other indications of contacts between British representatives and Chinese Communists" not only in Shanghai but in Tientsin and Peiping as well. Such an attitude was not in evidence toward Americans, however. McConaughy reported: "It seems to be settled Communist practice harass and heckle American citizens especially American government employees at every turn as means provoking minor incidents which can be used in anti-American propaganda campaign and by discriminatory treatment undermining any tendency toward united front among various western communities Shanghai." In the face of these "petty annoyances," McConaughy thought a "large measure of forbearance" was called for and that, in general, it was "being displayed by American community." He noted that the British ambassador was coming to Shanghai on September 12 "with intent discuss united front with British, US consular and business representatives during course of week."[35]

For his part, the British ambassador had already expressed to the Foreign Office the hope that the Americans could be convinced of the mutual benefit of "our policy of holding out" and dissuaded from undermining the British position by "embarrassing opposition and destructive criticism."[36]

12

Anglo-American Policy Differences

The need for closer British-American consultation on China had been recognized for some time in both Washington and London. On July 20 Secretary of State Acheson had instructed U.S. Ambassador Lewis Douglas to see Foreign Secretary Bevin for a frank exchange of views on the Far East, referring to attitudes toward the Chinese Communists as among the "most immediate problems" to be taken up. Acheson specifically mentioned the question of continued recognition of the Nationalist government and the corollary question of nonrecognition of the Communist government, "especially as it may spread its control and, possibly with Soviet backing, assert that it is the govt. of China." Trade with the Communists was another question Acheson felt should be discussed. He was "somewhat disturbed" by reports that British business interests were approaching Communist officials and "suggesting cooperation."[1]

In response to the Acheson initiative, Assistant Undersecretary

Esler Dening urged a somewhat reluctant Bevin to welcome discussions with the Americans. In a memorandum to Bevin, Dening asserted that "for the past three years" the British had been trying to get the Americans to be frank with them over China and Japan, but all their efforts had failed; that the Americans had "gone their way with unhappy results"; and that Anglo-American discussions were the best way "to try to keep American policy on the right lines."[2] Bevin agreed, and the upshot was a series of exchanges of views and meetings at the official and ministerial levels in August and September. The first substantive presentation in these exchanges was contained in a British memorandum handed to First Secretary Arthur Ringwalt of the American embassy by Esler Dening August 16, with the caveat that it "represented interdepartmental views on the China problem but not necessarily ministerial opinion."[3] The Foreign Office warned the British embassy in Washington that it "should not be considered as committing HMG."[4] However, the memorandum was later approved by Bevin and other cabinet ministers and became the basis for discussions with Acheson when Bevin went to Washington in mid-September.[5]

The memorandum expressed the view that relations of the British commonwealth and the North Atlantic Powers with a Communist Chinese government would, at the worst, "follow the pattern of their relations with Soviet satellite states in Eastern Europe." There was a possibility, however, that the pattern would eventually develop along the lines of the relationships with Yugoslavia. Therefore, "the Western Powers should be careful not to prejudice future possibilities by developing an openly hostile attitude towards a Communist regime from the outset." Acknowledging obvious "political objections to precipitate recognition," the memorandum pointed out that withholding recognition from a government in effective control of a large part of China would be "legally objectionable" and would lead "to grave practical difficulties regarding the protection of Western interests in China." It was "most unlikely that the fulfillment of any special conditions can be exacted in return for recognition," for the Communists were "unlikely to be seriously inconvenienced by the withholding of recognition." Therefore, it was probable that after a certain stage "delay in proceeding with recognition might seriously prejudice Western interests in China without any compensating advantages being obtained."[6]

Several days after the delivery of the Foreign Office memorandum, Foreign Secretary Bevin told Ambassador Douglas that the British "attitude to the whole problem of China was much influenced by past history." For example, he thought it had been a serious mistake to have so long continued the recognition of the Manchu regime. The British also believed that "the Chinese Communits were first and foremost Chinese and that they were not capable of becoming Russians over-night." Bevin summed up his "general approach" by saying that his "inclination was to stay where we were in China and try to avoid having to withdraw or being pushed out, and at the same time try to arrange for the minimum supplies to be sent through the blockade."[7] Douglas rejoined that the United States was inclined to take the opposite view on the blockade.

Differing British and American attitudes toward the blockade were largely influenced by their differing attitudes toward trade with the Chinese Communists and toward Formosa. The Anglo-American dis-cussions on applying the so-called R-procedure to trade with China, which had begun in March, continued into the summer. The British did not object in principle to trade controls, but they wanted them to apply to a much narrower list of commodities than did the Americans. Moreover, the British were more concerned about obtaining the cooperation of France and other western European countries than were the Americans, and they were reluctant to impose controls on trade with entrepôts such as Hong Kong and Singapore, which the Americans thought would be necessary to prevent leaks in the control system.[8]

The differences between the American and British positions on trade policy were summed up in aide-mémoire of September 12 from the British embassy in Washington to the Department of State. As was so often the case, the two allies agreed on objectives but disagreed on how these objectives could be obtained. The British aide-mémoire affirmed that there was "no difference between His Majesty's Govern-ment and the United States Government as to the importance" of the aims set forth in the American proposal on trade controls—that is, to influence the orientation of the Chinese Communist regime and to ensure that Western trade does not enhance its military strength. "In-deed," the aide-mémoire declared, "His Majesty's Government be-cause of their position in Hong Kong and South-East Asia, have immediate and compelling reasons to secure the achievement of both objectives." The British had no difficulty with one of the objectives; they were already preventing weapons of war from going to China or to Hong Kong for reexport to China. The differences between the United States and the United Kingdom centered on the means to accomplish the other objective. The British were skeptical of the efficacy of export controls "aimed at the modification of the political alignment of the Chinese Communist regime" and were "not disposed to institute controls for such a purpose."[9]

In a meeting with British representatives on September 9, Walton Butterworth had suggested that the United States, together with the British and other Western governments, should "control selected goods of importance to the Chinese economy, not with the idea necessarily of arbitrarily preventing the flow of such goods, but as a symbol of our ability to take punitive measures against the Chinese Communists if such action should be made necessary in the future."[10] But the British did not want even to appear to threaten the Chinese Communists with punitive action. They did not agree with the Americans that such a threat would influence the Chinese Communists in a desirable way. Moreover, they believed such a policy would undermine the position of British business in China. Despite inauspicious beginnings, the British still thought there would be a period of grace during which the Communists would need the expertise of the foreign business community in trade, shipping, banking, and manufacturing. This view was strongly held both by the British business community in China and by its representative in London, the China Association. British policy was also influenced by a desire to hold on to the island of Hong Kong and the adjacent New Territories, whose viability depended on continued trade with the China mainland.

The differing British and American evaluations of their commercial interests in China, on the one hand, and the political effectiveness of trade controls, or the threat of them, on the other, obviously affected the attitudes of the two governments toward the Nationalist blockade. Having less to lose in trade and believing more in the efficacy of economic pressure as a political tool, the Americans were much less inclined than the British to do something about the blockade.

The different attitudes of the two governments toward Formosa and the Nationalist forces there also affected their views of the blockade. As noted in Chapter 4, the Joint Chiefs of Staff regarded Formosa as strategically important to the United States, though not important enough to commit U.S. forces to its defense. For this reason the National Security Council had adopted a policy of trying to deny Formosa and the Pescadores to the Communists by political and economic means.

On August 4 the Department of State, noting that "since there now appears no certain assurance that the islands can be denied to Communist control by political and economic means alone," recommended that the JCS review its memorandum of February 10 on the strategic importance of Formosa to the United States.[11] The JCS did so and, in a memorandum to the secretary of defense on August 27, reaffirmed their opinion that Formosa was "strategically important to the United States" but that its strategic importance did not justify overt military action, "so long as the present disparity between our military strength and our global obligations exist."[12]

In the Anglo-American official meeting of September 9, Livingston Merchant of the State Department (who had recently spent several months in Formosa on special assignment) explained that since it was "beyond the present capabilities of the U.S. to undertake a military defense of the island," it had been determined that the U.S. would "concentrate on diplomatic support of the present government on Formosa and economic assistance to the island." Despite such support, "the probabilities were that the island would eventually be taken over by the Communists," but as Walton Butterworth noted, it would "require some time and careful preparation before a Communist take-over could be effected."[13]

The British also believed there was a "strong possibility" that Formosa would fall into Communist hands, but their attitude was more fatalistic. Since a take-over could not very well be prevented, all that remained was to hope that occupation of the island by the Communists would "not prove disastrous." Dening raised the possibility of an appeal by the Formosans to the United Nations, "with a view to holding a plebiscite or establishing a mandate under the UN," but he and Butterworth agreed that the possibility of such an appeal remained remote as long as Chiang Kai-shek controlled the government on Formosa.[14]

There was a curious parallel between the State Department attitude toward Formosa and the Foreign Office attitude toward maintenance of the British commercial position in China. The State Department believed Formosa would inevitably fall into Communist hands but wanted to deny it to them as long as possible. The Foreign Office thought the Communists would inevitably drive British businessmen out of China but wanted to postpone the day as long as possible. Commitment to these short-term goals exacerbated Anglo-American differences over the blockade, which undermined the British commercial goal but tended to support the American objectives.

On September 13 Acheson and Bevin capped the series of Anglo-American meetings on China policy with an extensive discussion in Washington. Telling Bevin he would read from a memorandum on the China situation because it "expressed our views so clearly," Acheson read paragraphs from telegram number 1994 of September 3 from Counselor of Embassy John Wesley Jones in Nanking.[15] Jones's telegram asserted that U.S. policy toward China should be based on three premises: that the Chinese Communists would remain in power "for some time," that no resistance movement would succeed unless it was purely Chinese and not dependent on foreign aid, and that no anti-Communist leadership capable of leading a successful revolution against the CCP was on the horizon. Under these circumstances, the United States would have to await the "develpment of Chinese 'Titoism' " to accomplish its goal of splitting China from the Soviet Union. In the meantime, the United States should not adopt a policy of "outright hostility toward the rulers of China," since that would only arouse Chinese chauvinism against America rather than against Russia and thus would not contribute toward the goal of detaching China from the USSR. On the other hand, the United States should avoid "conciliatory gestures" toward China's new rulers, not only because such gestures would be opposed by American public opinion but also because the CCP would see them only as confirmation of the "Communist theory of inner weakness of USA," that is, a "desperate need for markets and raw materials." The CCP should be left to learn "the hard way" that China "will lose much more than it will gain" by its association with the Soviet Union. The United States should do nothing to "contribute to the comfort of new bed which CCP has made for China"; so long as it remained a satellite of USSR, China should get no assistance from the United States.[16]

Significantly, Bevin and Acheson differed on the effect recognition would have on promoting their common objective of splitting China from the Soviet Union. Bevin maintained that "by being too obdurate we will drive the Chinese into Russia's hands, but by playing a careful role we can weaken Russia's grip." Acheson, however, doubted that recognition would be "a strong card in keeping China out of Russian hands"; they would be there anyway. Acheson did agree with Bevin that British and American differences on China were "in tactics not in objectives."[17]

It seems doubtful that the differences between the United States and the United Kingdom were merely tactical, but Washington and London do seem to have agreed on basic objectives. Both wanted to split China from the Soviet Union, and both expected to establish relations with the Communist regime at some time in the future. Events of the past several months had nevertheless revealed major differences in how the two countries would work toward those objectives, and the Acheson-Bevin talks had done little to resolve these differences. Even so, the Foreign Office in a message to Nanking

September 30 optimistically declared that "the danger of a marked divergence between the U.K. and the U.S. policy over China has been averted" and added, "it should not be assumed that we shall necessarily differ from the U.S. on recognition when the time comes."[18]

The Foreign Office had perhaps been encouraged by indications that the United States intended to stay on in China, with the clear implication that it expected eventually to recognize the Communist regime and that it intended to consult with the United Kingdom and other Atlantic allies on the matter. The British, for their part, had assured the United States that they did not expect to rush into recognition and that they too intended to consult with their allies and the commonwealth. But the United States had placed great emphasis on the conditions under which recognition might take place, especially on the importance of the Communists' recognizing China's international obligations. This condition alone should have been seen as an insurmountable barrier to recognition in any foreseeable future. Butterworth had succinctly defined the United States–Chinese Communist clash on this issue during the Acheson-Bevin talks. The Communists, he said, had stated they intended unilaterally to abrogate various treaties regardless of the provisions for termination, and the United States regarded any such abrogation as intolerable.[19] Although Bevin had said at the time that "it would be necessary to insure that [the Communists] accepted their international obligations," the British later receded from this position.[20]

The American and British attitudes toward trade were also likely to lead to a clash on recognition. During his August 26 conversation with Bevin on China policy, Ambassador Douglas had said that the main point of differences between the two governments was that the United States, to quote Bevin's memorandum of that conversation, "considered that every attempt should be made to put pressure on the Chinese Communists by reducing to the minimum the amount of trading intercourse between them and the Western Powers . . . this would bring home to the Communists how essential it was to them to have proper trading relations with the West."[21] Thus, though recognition of a Communist regime would be entirely compatible with the British policy of maximizing trade and avoiding restrictions (except on arms rules), it would be incompatible with the American policy of trying to change the Communists' behavior by bringing economic pressure to bear on them. In the familiar terms of the carrot and the stick, recognition was logically a part of the British carrot, but it would weaken the American stick.

It was clear, too, that the British and American concerns for the futures of Hong Kong and Formosa also pulled in opposite directions as far as recognition was concerned. The British hoped they could keep Hong Kong out of Communist hands by emphasizing its importance to China's trade and by showing willingness to discuss its political future with the Communists; both these objectives would be promoted by recognition of a Communist government. For strategic reasons the United States wanted to keep Formosa out of Communist hands as long as possible, but this objective could not be furthered by recognition. In the circumstances then prevailing, the Communists would not have been willing—as they were in fact, if not in principle, some thirty years later—to forgo military "liberation" of Formosa. In sum, British and American perceptions of their own interests and of how to influence Chinese Communist policy led them to different conclusions insofar as early recognition of the soon-to-be-born People's Republic was concerned.

Part II
Recognition and Withdrawal

13

The People's Republic Proclaimed

On October 1, Chou En-lai sent a public statement by Mao Tse-tung to the foreign consuls in Peiping and asked them to transmit it to their governments. The statement announced, among other things, the establishment of the Central People's Government of the People's Republic of China, the election of Mao as chairman of the CPG, the appointment of Chou En-lai as premier of its Administrative Council and concurrently minister of foreign affairs, and the shifting of the capital of China to Peiping, now to be called Peking once again. Of particular interest to the various consuls in Peking and to their governments was the final paragraph of the announcement: "At the same time it was decided to proclaim to the governments of all countries that this government is the sole legal government representing all of the people of the People's Republic of China. This government alike is willing to establish diplomatic relations with any and all governments of foreign countries which wish to observe principles of equality, mutual benefit, and mutual respect for territorial sovereignty."[1]

In his letter to the consuls, Chou went beyond Mao's public statement that the CPG was "willing" to establish diplomatic relations with foreign governments by saying: "I consider that it is necessary that there be established normal diplomatic relations between the People's Republic of China and all countries of the world."[2] It is also significant that Chou omitted the qualifying clause that had appeared after "foreign countries" in Mao's statement. Even this clause, which was taken from Article 56 of the Common Program, a kind of provisional constitution for the People's Republic passed by the People's Political Consultative Conference just three days earlier, did not reveal the full extent of the qualifications laid down by the Common Program for the establishment of diplomatic relations with the CPG. According to Article 56, foreign governments had also to "sever relations with the Kuomintang reactionaries and adopt a friendly attitude toward the People's Republic of China."[3] This proviso turned out to be the key to the establishment of diplomatic relations with the new Chinese government, and Peking was the sole arbiter of what constituted a "friendly attitude." So that it could make this determination, the CPG would require non-Communist states recognizing the PRC to send representatives to Peking to have their qualifications examined.

No such requirement was made of the Soviet Union or of other Communist countries. Peking and Moscow established diplomatic relations with lightninglike rapidity. On October 2 Soviet Deputy Foreign Minister Andrei Gromyko informed Chou that the Soviet Government, confident that the CPG represented the will of the "overwhelming majority" of the Chinese people,"had adopted the decision to establish diplomatic relations between the Soviet Union and the People's Republic of China, and to exchange ambassadors."[4] To have responded so rapidly (and confidently) Moscow must have been informed of the Mao statement and the Chou letter through other channels well in advance of the receipt of the Chou letter by foreign consuls in Peking—at 9 P.M., October 1 in the case of the U.S. consul general. In reply to Gromyko, Chou expressed "the boundless joy" of the Chinese people that the Soviet Union was the "first friendly state" to recognize the PRC and declared: "I hereby notify you that the Central People's Government of the People's Republic of China warmly welcomes the immediate establishment of diplomatic relations between the People's Republic of China and the USSR and exchange of ambassadors."[5]

The establishment of diplomatic relations between the Soviet Union and the PRC was quickly followed by the inauguration in Peking of a Sino-Soviet Friendship Association, presided over by Liu Shao-ch'i, a member of the CCP Politburo and a vice-chairman of the CPG. There were already a number of such associations elsewhere in Communist China, especially in Manchuria. On August 27, for example, NCNA had reported the formation of "the Northeast Sino-Soviet Friendship Association" in Mukden at a "conference of representatives of branch associations."[6] Some of these branch associations had been in existence since early July.[7] In fact, the Preparatory Committee of the Peking Association itself had been in existence for some two and a half months. On July 16 it had issued a statement by the association's 698 sponsors, including Liu and Chou, announcing that the association planned to introduce Soviet science and technology, to use Soviet experience in national reconstruction, and to strengthen the friendship of the two countries in the struggle for lasting world peace. "The direction taken by the Soviet Union," the statement declared, "is the only direction for mankind."[8]

Not surprisingly, Liu Shao-ch'i's speech at the Peking association's inaugural meeting in October reflected similar sentiments. Among the points Liu made were that the industrialization of China could only take place with Soviet aid and its unique technology, which outstrips capitalist technology, and that Soviet aid technicians, unlike British and American, would be assigned their jobs by China and would return to the Soviet Union when they had finished their jobs.[9]

The close political and economic collaboration between the USSR and the CCP that began in 1947 in Port Arthur and Dairen had been extended to other Manchurian cities as they fell to the PLA in 1948.[10] By autumn 1949, a number of industrial plants in these cities were already operating under Joint Chinese-Russian management.[11] On July 31, the Soviet Union had concluded a bilateral trade agreement with what Moscow referred to as the "Manchurian People's Democratic Authorities"—what the Chinese Communist press called the "Northeast People's Democratic Government." Under this agreement Manchuria was to furnish soybeans, vegetable oil, corn, rice, and other goods, and the Soviet Union would furnish industrial equipment, automobiles, petroleum products, cloth, paper, and medicines. The Chinese delegation that negotiated the agreement in Moscow was led by Kao Kang, chairman of the Northeast Financial and Economic Committee and a member of the CCP Politburo.[12]

Thus, by the time the People's Republic came into being, extensive working relationships had already been established between CCP officials and Soviet advisers in Manchuria, if not in other areas under CCP control, and the fact that Moscow continued to maintain diplomatic relations with the Nationalist government had not prevented the development of these relationships. Yet continued diplomatic relations with the Nationalist government on the part of Washington and London had been constantly thrown up by CCP officials as an impediment to the development of any kind of modus vivendi with American and British officials.

Before he knew of the Chou letter of October 1, Ambassador Stevenson had proposed making "an official communication to the Ministry of Foreign Affairs," even if no direct notification of the formation of the new government had been received, and he had sent the Foreign Office a draft text of such a communication. The Foreign Office made only one change in Stevenson's draft before using it to reply to Chou's letter. Prime Minister Clement Attlee, possibly reflecting his socialist sensitivities, suggested substituting "advantageous" for "profitable" in the Stevenson text. The British reply to Chou's letter thus read, in part: "Friendly and mutually advantageous relations, both commercial and political, have existed between Britain and China for many generations. It is hoped that these will continue in the future. His Majesty's Government in the United Kingdom therefore suggest that, pending completion of their study of the situation, informal relations should be established between His Majesty's Consular Officers and the appropriate authorities in the territory under the control of the Central People's Government for the greater convenience of both Governments and promotion of trade between the two countries."[13] In a circular telegram to British diplomatic representatives in various capitals conveying the text of this letter to Chou, the Foreign Office acknowledged that "from the strictly legal point of view this communication could be interpreted as implying *de facto* recognition" but stressed that its purpose was merely "to induce the Communist authorities to enter into working relations with His Majesty's Consular Officers pending a decision on the recognition question."[14]

Both the American and French governments were concerned about the implication of de facto recognition in the British letter to Chou, which might possibly violate the understandings reached at the tripartite meetings in Washington in September. The Foreign Office agreed that the letter to Chou could be interpreted as British recognition of the CPG as the government of the territories the Chinese Communists controlled but pointed out that in the past the Chinese Communists had shown no interest in de facto recognition. Moreover, Chou's letter had spoken of establishing diplomatic relations; there was no indication of any Chinese interest in anything short of that. Additionally, the Foreign Office stressed that the British desire for the establishment of informal relations between the Communist authorities and British consular officers was quite in line with the policy Britain had adopted early in the year and consistent with the letter sent by the consular body to the mayor of Peiping in April. As to the understandings reached at the Washington tripartite meeting, "the Ministers were concerned with *de jure* recognition" rather than de facto.[15]

The Foreign Office was quite right about the Chinese Communists' attitude toward de facto recognition. They were indifferent to it and ignored the British suggestion of informal relations.[16]

The basic posture of the United States toward the Chinese Communists was much the same on October 1 as it had been in January. Though Washington had decided to reduce the number of consular offices in Communist areas and to close all those in areas the Communists would eventually take over, it was still U.S. policy to maintain an official presence in Communist territory. In fact, when the People's Republic was established, there were about five times as many official U.S. personnel assigned to posts in Communist-controlled areas as in Nationalist-controlled areas; by the end of the year only the post at Taipei remained in Nationalist territory, compared with four still in Communist territory.[17] Thus the United States manifested its intention of staying on in China and of continuing to try to deal with the Communist authorities.

Similarly, although the United States was taking a more restrictive view of trade with Communist areas of China than it had earlier in the year, it was by no means opposed to such trade. The Communist authorities were particularly interested in trade with Japan, and in late April and early May had made inquiries of the American consulate general in Peiping, which were reported to the Department of State by the consulate general and relayed to the supreme commander for the Allied Powers in Japan, General Douglas MacArthur, by the Department of the Army.[18] On May 27 the State Department authorized the consulate general in Peiping to tell the Communist authorities that MacArthur was willing to consider specific trade arrangements and that the consulate general was authorized to transmit concrete proposals to him.[19] Specific proposals for trade with Japan came from private firms in Communist territory, and deals were made involving products supplied by official Communist organs.

In mid-August, for example, the U.S. consulate general in Peiping reported that the San Yang Company offered soybeans, peanuts, coarse salt, sheep and camel wool, magnesite, talc, coking coal, and pig iron, among other commodities, for export to Japan from either Yinkow or Tientsin. San Yang proposed to purchase articles in Japan with the proceeds of whatever deal it might make for its exports. On September 8, the consulate general reported to the State Department that it had received an inquiry from the supreme commander "re offer of coking coal" and had asked San Yang to supply the information. On September 19 the department suggested to the consulate general that it advise San Yang to conduct further negotiations on this matter direct with its Tokyo representative.[20] As a result of negotiations of this kind, there was trade between Communist areas of China and occupied Japan, and it grew in the remaining months of the year.[21]

The United States also traded with Chinese Communist territory, despite the Nationalist blockade, stultifying Communist policies, and U.S. trade controls.[22] Though reduced in size, an American business community, to say nothing of a substantial number of missionaries, remained in China. In sum, at the founding of the People's Republic of China, the United States, like the United Kingdom, still had a foot in the door in China; but unlike the United Kingdom, the United States was not willing to commit itself to a policy of staying put no matter what.

A major influence on the U.S. perspective was the continued detention in Mukden of Consul General Ward and his staff, which had now lasted for more than ten months, despite indications in June that they would soon be released.[23] Indicative of the American preoccupation with the Mukden problem was the U.S. response to the Chou letter of October 1.[24] Clubb addressed this response to General Chou En-lai, Peiping, avoiding any implication of U.S. recognition of the People's Republic by avoiding use of Chou's new official titles—just as the Communist authorities had for so many months scrupulously avoided giving American diplomatic and consular personnel their official titles. After acknowledging receipt of Chou's letter, Clubb continued: "I take this opportunity to bring to your personal attention that the American Consul General at Mukden, Mr. Angus I. Ward, and his staff have been isolated in the consular compounds at that point since November 1948 for reasons unknown. . . . The U.S. Government is deeply concerned with this situation, which is contrary to established principles of international comity and which has been permitted to continue despite representations to the Chinese Communist Military Headquarters, and it is hoped that action will be taken by the concerned authorities promptly to rectify the situation."[25] Clubb's latest representations on the Mukden problem had been made to the PLA commander in chief, Chu Teh, on September 23. They were made after Consul General Ward's three requests of the local Mukden authorities between July 19 and September 3 for departure facilities for the consulate's personnel had gone unheeded.[26] Unfortunately, not only did Clubb's appeal to Chou En-lai to rectify the situation also go unheeded, but matters soon grew worse.

14

The Mukden Ordeal

On October 24 Consul General Ward and four members of the consulate staff in Mukden—two Americans, Ralph C. Rehberg and Shiro Tatsumi, an Italian, Frank Cicogna, and a German, Alfred Kristan—were taken away from the consulate compound by police and jailed on charges of assault brought by Chi Yu-heng, a Chinese laborer employed by the consulate. The first word the State Department had of this incident came in a telegram from Consul General Clubb in Peking reporting a radio news broadcast from Mukden on October 25. The following excerpts from Clubb's telegraphic report give the flavor of the broadcast:

On October 11, Chi Yu-heng went to Ward's office to demand wages due him. . . . When Chi attempted to argue with him reasonably, Ward, acting in his imperialistic and barbarous manner, violently beat and insulted Chi Yu-heng and also incited four ex-Consulate employees. . . . to take Chi into custody and put him in building where he was beaten with fists and feet by group. . . . The 35 Chinese staff members and workers of that place have already lodged stern written protest against violent act of Ward in beating Chinese worker by marshalling mob. . . . public security organizations will immediately take action to investigate case according to law.[1]

Ward not only denied the charges but reversed them, accusing the Chinese employees of assaulting him and his colleagues. Thus he claimed: "On October 11, was assaulted and pummelled by Chinese member of my staff. Due only to quick action by Rehberg, I was saved from being further assaulted by another Chinese armed with cudgel. Cicogna assaulted by group Chinese members my staff and Kristan was assaulted and befouled and badly beaten by Chinese staff member and other Chinese."[2] Although neither Clubb nor the State Department had an opportunity to hear Ward's version of the incident until after he had been released from prison, they were immediately skeptical of the broadcast version, if for no other reason than that Ward and his colleagues had been for many months continuously under the surveillance of Chinese guards posted both outside and inside the consular compound where they had been detained.

While awaiting trial on the assault charges, Ward and the four consulate staff members were kept in solitary confinement on a diet of bread and water and were refused access to other consular personnel or to legal counsel. During their trial they were denied the right to produce witnesses for the defense, the right to question witnesses or plaintiffs, and the right to submit rebutting arguments. All five were found guilty of the charges and sentenced, but their sentences were commuted to deportation. On November 21 they were released.[3]

Four days after the jailing of Ward and the other consulate employees, the State Department, still ignorant of the conditions under which they were being held, instructed Clubb to see Chou En-lai or some other high official dealing with foreign affairs to make "oral representations" on the matter. Clubb was to tell Chou that the United States Government viewed "with greatest concern" the "arbitrary action" by the Chinese Communist authorities against the American consular officials at Mukden and the continued failure to provide facilities for their withdrawal after giving express assurances in that regard.[4] Once again, however, Clubb was unable to see Chou En-lai or any other high official about the detention of the American consular staff at Mukden and had to content himself with sending yet another letter, in which he asked not only that the matter be brought to a "speedy settlement" but "in particular that the British Consular Representative at Mukden be given the opportunity to see Mr. Ward and the other persons charged with assault."[5] When the text of Clubb's letter was released to the press in Washington a few days later, this request was noted with some pique in the Foreign Office, which the State Department had not bothered to consult, taking British assistance "rather for granted."[6]

With the imprisonment of Ward and the others, the usually patient Clubb felt the time had "now come exercise real pressure, if available." He recommended that the Department consider the desirability of temporarily holding up "all commercial negotiations and permits regarding trade between China and Japan. . . . pending release Ward and others from police custody and departure personnel from Mukden."[7] The recommendation found a sympathetic ear in the State Department's Bureau of Far Eastern Affairs. Deputy Assistant Secretary of State Livingston Merchant drafted a memorandum to Secretary Acheson, in which he supported the idea of using Japan's trade with China as leverage to obtain the release not only of Ward and his staff but also of Smith and Bender, who had been detained by the Communists even longer than the Mukden group. Merchant saw a good opportunity at hand. The Chinese wanted to import sixty thousand tons of steel rails and ten thousand tons of spikes, fishplates, and other items from Japan. The supreme commander for the Allied Powers in Japan had indicated strong interest in the transactions and had requested policy guidance. Merchant felt that approaches should be made in Peking and Shanghai to indicate that so long as Ward and his staff and Smith and Bender were held, "it would seem most improbable that these trade talks could come to a satisfactory conclusion."[8]

The Bureau of Economic Affairs, however, opposed going this far, pointing out that Merchant's proposal was contrary to the policy laid down in NSC 41 that it was inappropriate "to use trade controls or transactions to solve incidents or points at issue in noneconomic fields between the United States and the Chinese Communists." The bureau questioned the efficacy of economic pressures that would not be supported either by Western powers or by Japan. He recalled that similar proposals had been made and rejected "with respect to Americans taken into custody by the Czechs and the Russians in Germany," where, he noted, "other measures produced the release of the people."[9]

While the idea of using negotiations with the Chinese Communists on trade with Japan as a lever to secure the release of Ward and his staff was being mooted in the State Department, suggestions involving the use of force were also under consideration there and in the Department of Defense. Both the Joint Chiefs of Staff and the State Department had addressed themselves to this question after President Truman had indicated on November 14 that the possibility of blockading the movement of coal from north China ports down the coast to Shanghai should be explored.[10] Two weeks earlier he had told Acting Secretary of State James E. Webb that if the United States could get a plane in to bring these people out of Mukden, he was prepared "to take the strongest possible measures, including some utilization of force if necessary, and if he was sure it would be effective."[11] On November 17 a contingent from the State Department, led by Acheson and including Stuart, had persuaded Truman against taking radical measures, "military or otherwise."[12] In a memorandum of November 18 signed by General Omar Bradley, the JCS concluded that direct military action might lead to war and would not of itself ensure Ward's timely and safe extrication. It recommended negotiating for Ward's release and offered to supply a negotiator, suggesting, for example, "the Commander of the Seventh Task Fleet."[13]

In a memorandum to the president three days later, Secretary Acheson pointed out that Shanghai was not receiving any significant amounts of coal by sea from north China ports and that even a blockade of all shipping out of China ports would not "create an economic crisis in the Chinese Communist regime. On the contrary, it might well prove useful to the Communists as a propaganda weapon, both at home and abroad, in support of their argument concerning the imperialistic intentions of the United States." Acheson and the State Department strongly opposed blockade or any other policy that would involve the use of force against "other foreign vessels."[14] Such vessels in the case of the China trade would, of course, most likely be British.[15]

Meanwhile, the British were being made aware of the rising American anger, both official and public, over the treatment of Ward and his staff. In a telegram "of particular secrecy" on November 9 Sir Oliver Franks informed the Foreign Office that in a talk with members of the British embassy staff, Ambassador Stuart (who had been in Washington since August) had "referred at length to the anxiety of State Department over detention of Ward by Communists and to the mounting public feeling that little is being done to secure Consul General's release." Stuart himself had even considered the "practicability of landing a strong force of paratroopers at Mukden." What he wanted to suggest to the British was that during unofficial talks on the "idea of recognition" with the Chinese Communists, they might indicate that the detention of Ward made it difficult "to understand Communist intentions towards foreign nationals and, in particular, towards foreign officials." Stuart emphasized that this suggestion was a personal one; the State Department might be reluctant to broach the subject, since the British might consider that "any intervention at this time would strike a jangling note" in their recognition overtures.[16]

Apparently, however, Sir Oliver did not feel Dr. Stuart's proposal would strike a jangling note. He told the Foreign Office he thought "it might be a very useful way of reminding the Communists in advance that there are certain standards of conduct which we regard as basic in the relationship we are hoping to establish." Moreover, it might provide a useful opportunity to help the State Department, which was facing "another heavy onslaught on the alleged incompetency" of its China policy.[17]

A week after forwarding Stuart's proposal to the Foreign Office, Ambassador Franks returned to the subject of Ward's detention, reporting that the American press and radio had considerably increased their interest in the matter. Some newspapers were complaining that just when tension with China was mounting, the British were intending to recognize the Communists. Franks recommended that the United Kingdom should do something promptly to get Ward released "and thereby, to ease State Department's position over their general policy towards China." Although, Franks said, he had not been approached by Acheson, he knew "a friendly act on our part would be most welcome."[18]

Foreign Secretary Bevin agreed; he instructed the British embassy in Nanking to "take an early opportunity of indicating disapproval [of Ward's detention] orally to the highest Communist official to whom you can obtain access." It was Bevin's view that "in the long term we are likely ourselves to feel repercussions if the Chinese get away with such treatment of a foreign official."[19] But the embassy was unimpressed. It replied that "intervention on our part cannot benefit Mr. Ward and might react unfavorably on our own position in China."[20]

Meanwhile, on November 18 Secretary of State Acheson had sent personal messages to the foreign ministers of the countries having representatives in China, asking them, "as a matter of urgency, to express to the highest Chi[nese] auth[oritie]s in Peiping through such channels as may be available to you the concern which your Govt undoubtedly feels over the treatment of the Amer[ican] consular staff in Mukden who have been arbitrarily deprived of their freedom for one year."[21] Acheson's personal message was conveyed to Foreign Secretary Bevin in a "Dear Ernie" letter from U.S. Ambassador Lewis Douglas.[22] In his reply to "Dear Lew," Bevin pointed out that the British government had already been in correspondence with its embassy in Nanking about the possibility of expressing disapproval to the Chinese on the Ward case. On receipt of Acheson's message, the Foreign Office had instructed the British consul general in Peking to express British concern to the authorities, but because Ward's trial had in the meantime come to an end, the British Consul General was deferring action.[23]

On November 26, the day after Bevin's letter to Douglas and five days after Ward's release, the authorities in Mukden suddenly took U.S. Vice-Consul William N. Stokes to court for a hearing on spy charges, though whether as an accused, as a witness, or in some other capacity was unknown to Ward when he reported the incident to Clubb in Peking.[24] Because of the difference in time zones, the State Department received this report on November 25, and it acted with remarkable alacrity. Within twenty-four hours it had sent out another telegram to U.S. embassies in countries having representation in China instructing them to ask governments to which they were accredited to include Stokes in the protest about Ward if such a protest had not yet been made and to make a separate protest on Stokes if a protest on Ward had already been made.[25] It also instructed Clubb to seek an appointment with Chou on the Stokes case and at the same time to send him a letter on the matter.[26] All this the State Department was able to accomplish before it learned that Stokes had been returned to the consulate on the same day that he had been taken to court.

In London the U.S. embassy received the State Department's instruction on Stokes, together with another one indicating that the department did not believe that Ward's release obviated the desirability of appropriate representations to the Chinese Communist authorities about his detention. These sentiments, duly conveyed to the Foreign Office in a letter from First Secretary Ringwalt of the U.S. embassy, immediately encountered opposition. In a memorandum to Sir William Strang dated November 30, Esler Dening said he agreed with British officials in China, who were "most reluctant" to do anything that might "jeopardize their own precarious position." He thought the Americans were "asking too much in suggesting we should take action which would only be appropriate if we were in relations with the Communist authorities, which we are not."[27] This view was incorporated in a reply, dated December 1, to Ringwalt's letter, and its substance, together with that of Bevin's letter of November 25 to Douglas, was sent to the British embassy in Nanking and to the British high commissions in Canada, Australia, and India.[28]

Although it was soon to recognize the People's Republic, India was more sympathetic to the American request than was the United Kingdom. On December 1 the Indian government instructed its ambassador in Nanking to inform the Communist authorities in writing of the concern of the government of India at the treatment meted out to Ward and Stokes.[29] As for Canada, although the Ministry of External Affairs shared the British view that representations relating specifically to Ward and Stokes would serve no useful purpose, the Canadian representative in Nanking was instructed to "take any suitable opportunity of representing to [the] Communist authorities in general terms that consuls should be allowed to perform their functions irrespective of their Governments' attitude on recognition."[30] The British failure to do as much as the Indian and Canadian representatives in Nanking disappointed the State Department.[31]

In view of the strongly adverse affect the harsh treatment of the U.S. consulate general in Mukden had on American public and private attitudes toward the Chinese Communists, it is worth speculating on why that particular consulate was singled out for such treatment.

Inevitably suspicion falls on the presence of strong Soviet influence there; certainly, U.S. officials close to the scene suspected the Soviets. In June, for example, Ambassador Stuart, reporting an NCNA story alleging that the American consulate general in Mukden was operating a spy ring, had asserted that the "whole tenor of charges and attention to detail show Soviet influence." He suggested that "release of charges at this late date was possibly occasioned by Soviet-controlled Chinese Communists in Mukden feeling impelled to justify . . . their arrogant treatment of our consular staff which will redound so to their disadvantage once Ward is free to tell his story."[32] Consul General Clubb, too, frequently expressed to the State Department his conviction that the Soviet Union wielded a powerful influence over Manchurian affairs. For example, in a telegram of November 5 he said it was a "matter of general repute" that "Soviet influence Manchuria is strong," and he speculated, "Perhaps Soviets themselves are responsible for manner handling [Ward] case."[33]

Shortly after the departure of Ward and his staff from China, the U.S. consul general in Shanghai sent the State Department a long telegraphic report on the rising tide of resentment in that city against Soviet "greed" and "encroachments." The consulate's sources differed about the degree of Soviet influence in Peking, but all agreed "on Soviets' powerful position Manchuria," and most asserted their " 'personal conviction' that Soviets primarily responsible for Ward case."[34] The eagerness of the consulate's Chinese sources to blame the Soviets for the Ward case seemed to reflect a Chinese awareness that the case was damaging to Sino-American relations and a desire to exonerate Peking.[35]

The question of Soviet influence in the handling of the U.S. consulate in Mukden was often linked in the minds of Ward and other U.S. officials in China with the presumed existence of a pro-Moscow faction in the CCP. Supposedly dominant in the northeast (Manchurian) branch of the CCP, the pro-Moscow faction was sometimes seen as at odds with the CCP center in Peking on policy matters. Thus, after his release, Ward told the State Department he had "come to believe that pro-Moscow elements of the CCP utilized Consul General arrest to drive wedge between United States and sympathetic elements CCP by aggravating conditions arrest to utmost."[36]

A rare piece of direct evidence of friction between the central Communist authorities and the northeast regional authorities comes from Philip Manhard, the Chinese-speaking vice-consul in Tientsin who made the arrangements with the Tientsin Public Security Bureau for handling Ward and his party when they arrived from Mukden. He clearly recalls that during a meeting at the bureau on this matter two young officials from the Central People's Government in Peking told him emphatically that the way Ward had been treated was unfortunate and did not represent the policy of the CPG. Manhard believes these officials wanted to make sure that the treatment the Mukden consulate staff received in Tientsin would contrast favorably to that which it had received in Mukden, and he was impressed with this scrupulous adherence to arrangements he had made with them.[37]

15

Britain Ponders Recognition

The British were reluctant to risk offending the Chinese over the Ward case partly because the Foreign Office had already decided to lose no time in recognizing the People's Republic of China. On October 22 Assistant Undersecretary Esler Dening had submitted a draft cabinet paper to Foreign Secretary Bevin setting forth the opinion of the Foreign Office's legal adviser that recognition of the Chinese Communist government as the de jure government of China "cannot be said to be contrary to the principles and practices of international law." Bevin approved the paper, noting that he considered that the resistance of the Nationalist government in China "is now ostensibly hopeless and its control over any portion of Chinese territory on the mainland hardly more than nominal."[1]

On October 27 the cabinet considered the cabinet paper on recognition and decided to consult commonwealth and other governments on the subject.[2] The result was a Foreign Office circular telegram to British diplomatic missions asking them to convey British thinking on recognition to governments to which they were accredited.[3] Not surprisingly this thinking was consistent with the views set forth in the Foreign Office memorandum on China policy, which had been presented to the State Department August 16. Now, of course, with the establishment of the People's Republic the time for a decision had come, and the memorandum the British embassy handed the State Department November 1, pursuant to the Foreign Office's circular telegram, reflected developments since August.

In brief the memorandum argued that the Chinese Nationalist government was "no longer representative of anything but its ruling clique," the "communist government of the People's Republic of China" was the "only alternative to the Nationalist Government," and the Communists were "now the rulers of most of China." It would be "a mistake to disregard the fact that they are, on their own statements, orthodox Marxist-Leninists who openly declare their strong partiality for the Soviet Union and its methods," although it had yet to be seen how long this partiality would last. The Soviet Union, for its part, could be expected to "take full advantage of the fact" that it was the first to recognize the People's Republic, and "in the absence of any representation from the West," it would "seek to influence the Chinese communist government in the direction of making matters difficult for the other powers." The Chinese communists need to trade with the West, but "if such trade does not develop they may come to the conclusion that they can tighten their belts and do without Western economic assistance," in which view the Soviet Union would encourage them. The United Kingdom had to consider its own trading interests in China, which were "considerable and of long standing." Finally, "recognition of the communist government as the *de jure* government of China in present conditions" could not be held "to be contrary to the principles and practice of international law." On the basis of these political and legal considerations, the British government had concluded that recognition should be accorded the People's Republic of China.[4]

After perusing the British memorandum, Assistant Secretary of State Butterworth raised three questions with Counselor Hubert Graves of the British embassy, who had handed it to him.[5] Butterworth noted the absence of reference in the memorandum to the "question of obtaining assurances from the Chinese Communist regime, prior to extending recognition, of respect for international obligations" and asked if this indicated that the British government would not expect to obtain any quid pro quo. Graves replied that "it was the British Government's view that the disadvantages of nonrecognition were so great as to outweigh any possible advantages to be obtained from securing Chinese Communist assurance of respect for international obligations."

Butterworth asked "if the British had had any preliminary conversations with Chinese Communist authorities . . . which would provide some common ground and make the British approach to the question less of a 'bolt out of the blue.' " Graves replied that the British embassy in Washington had no knowledge of such exploratory discussions, but he himself suspected that there might have been. (He was later instructed by the Foreign Office to tell the State Department that no soundings had been made.)[6]

The third point Butterworth raised concerned the countries of Southeast Asia, which, according to American reports, would not favor early recognition. Butterworth said he assumed the British representatives in their forthcoming conference in Singapore (known as the Bukit Serene Conference) would look into this question. Graves said he felt certain the conference would consider this question and that he would obtain information in this regard for Butterworth.

When the information came, it was not quite what Butterworth had anticipated. Commissioner-General Malcolm MacDonald reported to the Foreign Office on November 4:

The Bukit Serene Conference agrees with the views of His Majesty's Ambassador to China and the Governor of Hong Kong that British interests in China and in Hong Kong demand earliest possible *de jure* recognition of the Communist Government in China.

This Conference is of the opinion that from the point of view of the situation in South-East Asia and the Far East generally such recognition is desirable as early as possible and in any case by the end of the year.[7]

When Butterworth saw these conclusions, he told Graves he understood the British view of recognition insofar as the British position in Hong Kong and British investments in China were concerned, but he could not follow Britain's reasoning with respect to Southeast Asia. He and Sprouse pointed out that it had been the State Department's opinion that the effect in Southeast Asia of early recognition would be generally unfavorable and that the estimate of the conference in Singapore had "not actually differed materially from the Department's estimate."[8]

The State Department's surprise when the Bukit Serene Conference endorsed early recognition was understandable. Earlier in the year MacDonald himself had suggested to the Foreign Office that the politically influential Chinese communities in the British territories in Borneo, Malaya, and Singapore (where the Chinese constitute the large majority of the population) were "a consideration on the side of postponing as long as possible diplomatic recognition of a Communist Government of China." MacDonald feared that Chinese Communist consular representatives "amidst the local Chinese populations would be dangerous," since many in the Chinese population would be sensitive to pressure from Chinese consular representatives.[9] But at the conference itself fear of adverse reaction in the Chinese communities if the British did not recognize the new government overcame fears of what Chinese consuls might do in these communities after recognition.[10] Curiously, British officialdom in Southeast Asia did not apply the same reasoning to their neighbors.On December 15 Commissioner-General MacDonald reported to the Foreign Office his worries about the possibility of having a Chinese Communist consul in Songhla in southern Thailand near the Malayan border. A Chinese consul there could assist the Communist terrorists on both sides of the border and so "would be a grave menace to the security of Malaya." MacDonald felt, therefore, that it was "of primary importance that Siamese Government should delay recognition of Chinese Communist Government as long as possible."[11]

MacDonald need not have worried about what the Thai government would do about recognition. As the Thai prime minister told the British ambassador in Bangkok, his country had adopted a wait-and-see policy on recognition. Since diplomatic relations had first been established between Thailand and Nationalist China, the Chinese embassy in Bangkok had been telling the Chinese community in Thailand, which is very large, to look toward China. The Thais feared what a Chinese Communist embassy might do.[12] Indeed, the Thai fears were wise. The CCP was at this time trying to replace the Kuomintang in Thailand, and its policy "was in many ways reminiscent of the policy of the KMT," according to Stephen FitzGerald. It was entirely possible that the CCP would try to use the overseas Chinese as a fifth column.[13] In the event, Thailand waited some twenty-eight years before recognizing the People's Republic.

The attitude of independent Thailand toward recognition foreshadowed that of Malaya and Singapore. The recommendation by British officials at the Bukit Serene Conference did not reflect the attitude of local leaders if their subsequent actions are taken as a guide. For example, a year after British recognition of the People's Republic, the Association of Chinese Chambers of Commerce of Malaya, which included chambers of commerce in Singapore, sent a telegram to the

British government asserting that recognition of the "Chinese Communist Government in Peking by His Majesty's Government has done immeasurable harm to Malaya when the Government and the people are fighting against Communist banditry." The telegram went on to "respectfully request that His Majesty's Government will now see fit to withdraw recognition of the Chinese Communist Government in Peking."[14] Significantly, after becoming independent, Malaya waited nearly twenty years to recognize the People's Republic, and Singapore has waited even longer.

The Bukit Serene Conference evidently saw no difficulty in reconciling the recognition of the Communist government in China and the suppression of the Chinese Communist "terrorists" in Malaya.[15] It did apparently fear that popular misconceptions might arise, however. Thus, it recommended that "an extensive propaganda campaign should be launched to explain that the recognition does not involve any inconsistency with our policy of opposition to Communism in South-East Asia."[16]

One of the targets of this propaganda campaign should have been the British War Office, which was worried about the impact of recognition on the security situation in Southeast Asia. On November 18 it told the Foreign Office that recognition might "stimulate the morale of the bandits" (terrorists) and have an "adverse effect on the flow of information re their movements." The greatest misgivings in the War Office centered around the establishment of Chinese Communist consulates in Malaya, which the office felt "should be delayed by all means possible." The War Office was also concerned about the effect of recognition on the French position in Indo-China and warned that the inability of France to prevent the spread of Communism in Indo-China would "constitute a grave military threat to our position in Southeast Asia." Thus, though the War Office believed that recognition was inevitable and clearly desirable from the standpoint of Hong Kong, it urged that from the military point of view the timing should be chosen to minimize its effect on Indo-China.[17]

Only a few days before, the Foreign Office had heard from the French about their concern for Indo-China. In an aide-mémoire dated November 12 the French Foreign Ministry worried about the "worldwide consequences" the arrival of Chinese Communist troops in the immediate vicinity of Vietnam might have. The French hoped the British would consider the special situation of France and the Associated States (Vietnam, Cambodia, and Laos) and avoid recognition of the People's Republic, "which might be deemed premature."[18]

The reactions of other governments to the British soundings on recognition were not all as predictable as those of the French (and American) governments; yet most of them were in favor of postponement. Of the commonwealth countries, India favored early recognition and wanted to make sure that Britain did not recognize the People's Republic first, and Pakistan and Ceylon also generally agreed with the British decision. The rest of the commonwealth favored postponement, however, as did all Britain's European allies.[19] The British decision in mid-December to recognize the People's Republic on January 2 (later deferred to January 6) thus represented a minority viewpoint in NATO and even in the commonwealth.[20]

The news of the British decision, and the reason for it, was conveyed to all commonwealth capitals in similar top secret messages from prime minister to prime minister on December 16. The message to the prime minister of New Zealand, for example, expressed the familiar British view that "the only way to counter Russian influence will be for Communist China to have contacts with the West. The sooner these are established the better." The message assured the prime ministers that this decision did "not in the least lessen" British determination to resist communism in Southeast Asia and elsewhere; the United Kingdom in fact intended "to stimulate resistance to Communism" with all means at its disposal and hoped other countries would do the same. The message acknowledged that Britain did not expect to carry the United States with it on the recognition question, but it had reason to believe the U.S. administration "understand our position and realise that we have far more immediately at stake than the United States." Finally, the message stressed that the views "of our Asian friends" had to be taken into account "in this primarily Asian problem."[21]

On the same day, Bevin sent Acheson virtually the same message as the prime ministers received, along with an additional paragraph in which Bevin said he had hoped to the last that "we might be able to take action together in this matter," but he would "quite understand the position" if the United States felt unable to accord recognition. "As you know," he wrote, "we want to keep a close association with you, but we have to be careful not to lose our grip of the situation in Asia and to take into account the views of our Asian friends."[22]

It is rather hard to believe that Bevin could really have hoped to the last that the United States would be prepared to take joint action with the United Kingdom at this time. There had been frequent communication between the two governments at the official level, and Acheson on at least two occasions since the cabinet-level talks in Washington in mid-September had conveyed his views to Bevin. At the meeting of the Council of Foreign Ministers in Paris on November 11, he had repeated the U.S. view that there was "no need for haste" in approaching the problem of recognition. He had again stressed that the Chinese Communists must first satisfy certain conditions—such as releasing the U.S. consul general in Mukden, agreeing to respect international agreements, and issuing assurances on U.S. property in China.[23]

On December 8 Acheson had called in Ambassador Franks to discuss the question of recognition. The secretary once more went over the familiar American arguments against hasty recognition, making clear that "regardless of the action taken by other powers," the United States "would not act hastily."[24] He came back to Ambassador Stuart's thesis, expressed some seven months earlier, that recognition should be used as a bargaining tool when he told Franks: "Given the fact the Chinese Communists do want recognition by other powers than the USSR and its satellites, it would be regrettable that the powers should give up the opportunity of thus bringing pressure to bear for recognition of existing obligations."[25]

Both Acheson and Bevin miscalculated the importance of recognition as an influence on the policies of the People's Republic of China. Acheson and the State Department assumed Peking wanted recognition from the West badly enough to make concessions to get it. Bevin and the Foreign Office thought that by recognizing Peking the United Kingdom would automatically establish diplomatic relations with the People's Republic and gain influence vis-à-vis the Soviet Union. As events were to demonstrate, both these calculations were wrong.

One who got it right was John Hutchison, a third-generation China hand who became British chargé in Nanking after the departure of Ambassador Stevenson. In a telegram to the Foreign Office on November 21 reviewing the extensive pro-Soviet propaganda that had been appearing in the Chinese press, Hutchison pointed out that there was "very little actual evidence that suggestions that Chinese Communists would welcome recognition by other powers, or active assistance from other foreigners as counterpoise against Russian influence, are more than wishful thinking."[26] Hutchison, whom we shall be hearing a great deal from in subsequent chapters, was nevertheless a strong supporter of British recognition policy.

Coincidentally, the day the British messages went out announcing the decision to recognize the People's Republic, Mao Tse-tung arrived in Moscow in a dramatic enactment of the CCP's lean-to-one-side policy. Of course, this development only made the advocates of the counterpoise policy more eager for recognition. Curiously, Chinese contacts of the American consulate general in Shanghai explained Mao's trip to Moscow as a kind of counter-counterpoise ploy on the part of the Kremlin. It was to be expected that Mao would sooner or later visit the Soviet Union, but according to these sources, the timing of this particular trip "was related to British and other western nation 'moves toward recognition.'"[27] No evidence was forthcoming from these or any other sources to support this speculation, whose logic seemed to be that moves in the West toward recognition of the Central People's government actually worked against the common Anglo-American aim of splitting the People's Republic and the Soviet Union. A feature of such speculation was that Mao's journey was the result of pressure from Moscow rather than the result of the CCP's perception of China's self-interest, but this theme had long been played by various Chinese sources to explain every strongly pro-Soviet move made by the CCP. There is no evidence that Mao's trip to Moscow was forced upon him; it was in fact wholly consistent with the tenor of CCP words and actions in the months before and after the establishment of the People's Republic.

Mao's trip to Moscow was timed to enable him to participate in Joseph Stalin's seventieth birthday celebrations, and the Kremlin gave him special treatment. At the ceremonies congratulating Stalin on his birthday, Mao stood immediately on Stalin's right and was chosen to speak first.[28] He took the occasion to stress that in "their hard struggle against the oppressors" the Chinese people were "deeply aware of the importance of Comrade Stalin's friendship," and he hailed "the great Stalin—leader of the world working class and of the international Communist movement."[29] The Soviet press made sure that the world would understand that Mao acknowledged Stalin's leadership, by revealing that among the collection of presents to Stalin in the Museum of the Revolution was a large, signed photograph of Mao inscribed in Chinese characters "To our leader Comrade Stalin from Mao Tse-Tung."[30]

Mao's presence in the Soviet Union at this time was symbolic of the failure of the United States and Britain to make any appreciable progress toward their common objective of splitting the CCP and the Kremlin.[31] In fact, Mao's journey to Moscow was an indication that this Anglo-American objective was quite beyond their power to achieve.

16

The United States Ponders Formosa Policy

Following the establishment of the People's Republic of China on October 1, 1949, the fortunes of the Nationalist government continued their rapid decline. After the government had moved its temporary capital from Canton to Chungking in mid-October, the division between Generalissimo Chiang Kai-shek, whose headquarters had been formally set up in Taipei on August 1, and President Li Tsung-jen seemed to grow deeper than ever, and the United States, disinclined to throw good money after bad, turned a deaf ear to Nationalist pleas for military assistance.[1] The following extracts from a telegram of November 15 to the Department of State from Chargé Robert Strong, who had followed the government to Chungking, convey the gloomy picture:

Earlier hopes of high officials that substantial progress could be made in southwest toward political unity and military unity and reform have been blasted.

. . . .

Military scene is still one of retreat; defection; uncorrelated commands; long lines of 'defense' with great gaps; inadequate pay, food and clothing for troops; financial and material stringency and mutual distrust.

Political scene is one of continuing deep division between Generalissimo and Li-Pai groups with no prospect of any healing of the breach;

. . . .

US aid and/or third World War are regarded as only means of saving remnants of government and some of its territory.[2]

In these circumstances, it was not long before the government was forced by the military pressure of the Communists to flee its capital for the third time. When it did so, British Consul General M.C. Gillett described government strategy thus: "The Nationalists had no fight left. Still their motto was: 'Don't fight. It isn't really necessary. Keep a Government in being. Then, when the 3rd World War comes (and may it come soon!), the Americans will be forced to fight for us and on our own terms, much as they did in the last war.' "[3] Gillett, who had been "specifically authorized to maintain contact with the National Government" by the Foreign Office,[4] went on to describe how the PLA had arrived on the south shore of the Yangtze on November 28 and the next day had started across the river unopposed, as the last two Nationalist regiments left in the direction of Chengtu, their new capital.

The elements of the Nationalist government that relocated to Chengtu hardly had time to catch their breath, however, before being chased out of their last foothold on the China mainland. On December 6 the government was moved to Taipei. Its removal to Formosa effectively ended the regime of President Li Tsung-jen and his principal military supporter, General Pai Chung-hsi. Although Chiang did not officially resume the presidency until some three months later, the government's move to Formosa restored him to unrivaled power over it, and Li went to the United States for medical treatment.

The Nationalist government's abandonment of the China mainland again confronted the U.S. government with the need to decide whether to maintain diplomatic contacts with the Nationalists or to reduce contacts to the consular level as the British had already done. The Department of State had informed Ambassador Stuart in June that it wanted to maintain continuity of diplomatic contact with the Nationalist government so long as it remained on the mainland and was the sole government of China.[5] Now neither of these conditions existed. Chargé Strong had flagged the problem in his telegram of November 15. "Whereas enough of a government may exist while on continent for Embassy to follow and maintain contact new decision by Department will be required with regard to relations with island government."[6]

Strong had not followed the remnants of the government to Chengtu; some days before this move he had left Chungking for Hong Kong.[7] Foreign Minister Yeh was already there, and it was in Hong Kong that Strong and Yeh concluded arrangements for President Li to go to the United States on an unofficial visit.[8] Li proceeded on this visit at just about the time that the Executive Yuan (the executive branch of the Nationalist government) fled from Chengtu to Taipei.

The "reunification" of the Nationalist government on Formosa made any distinction in U.S. policy between Formosa and that government quite impractical. Formosa could not very well be preserved from the Communists by political, economic, and diplomatic means if contact with those in power there were severed. Therefore, the United States decided in mid-December to maintain contact with the Nationalist government at the diplomatic level. Strong was ordered to proceed to Taipei if the U.S. government received "official notification from the

Chinese Government of the removal of the capital to Taipei" and if Foreign Minister George Yeh no longer remained in Hong Kong "in that capacity."[9] Both of these conditions being fulfilled, Strong proceeded to Taipei, where he found Yeh, during his initial call on him on December 26, "brimming with self-confident good-humor."[10]

Meanwhile, U.S. policy toward Formosa had once again become a cause for British concern. The Foreign Office worried about the continued flow of war material from the United States to Formosa, and Bevin raised the subject with Acheson during the course of their conversations in Paris in early November. The British embassy in Washington followed this up with a memorandum handed to the State Department on December 6, in which mention was made of the quantities of tanks and B-25 bombers being shipped to Formosa from the United States. The British did not think this equipment would prevent the capture of Formosa by the Communists, and they were concerned about what the Communists might do with it when it fell into their hands.[11]

Ambassador Franks discussed the subject with Secretary Acheson on December 8, expressing particular concern that the medium and heavy tanks being sent to Formosa, should they fall into Communist hands, might be used against Hong Kong. Acheson pointed out that there was less than $8 million worth of equipment left to be shipped from the $125 millon in grants made by the China Aid Act of 1948 and that to cut off these shipments arbitrarily would "be of insignificant practical value" in view of the "wealth of materiel" already in Formosa. However, since Ambassador Franks had told him that Hong Kong did not have antitank weapons to deal with medium and heavy tanks, Acheson agreed to look into this question; he thought something might be done if export licenses had not already been issued for them.[12]

Franks also asked Acheson whether the U.S. attitude toward Formosa had changed since the mid-September Bevin-Acheson talks in Washington. Acheson replied that President Truman "had approved the recommendations of the Joint Chiefs that Formosa was not of sufficient strategic importance to make it desirable for the U.S. Government to employ force to prevent the Island from falling under the control of the Chinese Communists though we were seeking by political and economic means to do everything feasible to prevent that." To this end, Acheson pointed out, the United States had recently exhorted Generalissimo Chiang Kai-shek "to consolidate the position since all the ingredients for success were available on the Island."[13]

Despite its message to Chiang, the State Department had little more confidence than the British Foreign Office that Chiang could hold Formosa against a Communist attack. On December 23 it issued a confidential document entitled "Policy Information Paper—Formosa," which addressed the problem of formulating "information policy which will minimize damage to United States prestige and others' morale by the possible fall of Formosa to the Chinese Communist forces." This document claimed that the loss of Formosa was "widely anticipated" and that "the manner in which civil and military conditions there have deteriorated under the Nationalists add weight to the expectation."[14]

On the same day the State Department issued its information policy guidance on Formosa, the JCS sent a memorandum to Secretary of Defense Louis Johnson, which concluded, "A modest, well-directed, and closely-supervised program of military aid to the anticommunist government in Taiwan would be in the security interest of the United States." On the basis of these conclusions, the JCS wanted to "make an immediate survey of the nature and extent of the military assistance required in Formosa in order to hold Formosa against attack."[15]

On December 28 the JCS met with Acheson, Deputy Undersecretary Rusk, Butterworth, and Merchant to discuss this memorandum, which had been submitted to the NSC. Defending their recommendation, members of the JCS argued that from the military viewpoint the Nationalists' position on Formosa was stronger than it had been and that "by comparatively small expenditures Formosa might be placed in a position where it would hold out longer than otherwise, with a consequent significant effect on the ability of the Chinese Communists to consolidate their regime." So long as the Communists had Formosa to contend with or subdue they might be deflected from extending their domination to countries in Southeast Asia.[16]

In rebuttal, Acheson contended that the way to prevent Communist domination of Southeast Asia was to help countries in the area "build up their internal stability, help them produce more food and raise even moderately their standard of living" by programs such as Point IV. "Above all," Acheson said, "we must get ourselves on the side of Nationalist movements, a task which is easier now that the dead hand of European colonialism has been removed." Assuming that the fall of Formosa could be postponed for a year by adopting the JCS recommendation, Acheson rhetorically asked what price would have to be paid for this delay: the price would be the involvement of U.S. prestige in another failure and, more important, the encouragement of the "united Chinese hatred of foreigners." This price might be worth paying if the United States acquired an island essential to its defense, but in Acheson's view there did not "appear to be demonstrated a claim that the loss of Formosa really breaches our defense."[17]

At the conclusion of the meeting, General Bradley "reiterated that the Joint Chiefs were presenting a purely military point of view which reflected the fact that Congress had appropriated money to support these people who were resisting Communism."[18] Bradley was referring to a $75 million fund, appropriated by Congress pursuant to authority contained in Section 303 of the Mutual Defense Act of 1949, for use in the "General Area of China." Section 303 gave the president wide latitude to deal with the rapidly changing situation in China and the area around it, and he was not required to account for expenditures from the fund. Although the State Department opposed using the fund for direct military assistance to the Nationalist government, it was willing to consider support of covert anti-Communist activities on the China mainland and had advocated use of some of the fund to step up anti-Communist propaganda activities directed against China.[19]

Acheson's and the State Department's opposition to military aid for the Nationalist armed forces prevailed in the National Security Council, which on December 30 reaffirmed the policy of attempting to preserve Formosa from Communist conquest by means short of U.S. military assistance.[20] This policy was then reflected in an important public statement by President Truman January 5, 1950, in which Truman announced that the United States government would "not provide military aid or advice to Chinese forces on Formosa," nor did it "have any intention of utilizing its armed forces to interfere in the present situation" there.[21] Although the statement did not represent any change in U.S. policy, by making U.S. intentions so explicit and so public Truman sent a clear signal to the People's Republic that it had nothing to fear from the U.S. militarily even if it invaded Formosa. A week later Acheson repeated the signal by indicating in a speech to the National Press Club that both Taiwan and Korea were outside the U.S. defense perimeter.[22]

Before Truman's announcement of January 5, but after the NSC decision of December 30, Deputy Undersecretary Dean Rusk assured Sir Derick Hoyer Millar of the British embassy that U.S. policy toward Formosa had not changed. Moreover, the United States would now not allow such items as bombers and heavy tanks to be shipped to Formosa, but the Natioanlists would be allowed to purchase other supplies with their remaining funds. Hoyer Millar restated Britain's concern that military equipment on Formosa might fall into Communist hands and then be used for an attack on Hong Kong.[23]

It is worth noting that Truman's and Acheson's public declarations that the United States would not provide military assistance or protection to Formosa were not made in a vacuum, but in a situation where a Communist invasion of Formosa was anticipated as early as March, and in any case by summer. In the expectation of an early Communist invasion, the already small staff of the U.S. consulate general in Taipei was further reduced, and the families of those who remained were evacuated.[24] There were constant references in the Communist media to the forthcoming "liberation of Taiwan." As early as September, *People's Daily*, inveighing against suspected U.S. plans to annex Taiwan, had warned: "The People's Liberation Army which is now victoriously advancing into Kwangtung and Fukien Provinces is mopping up enemy remnants along the Fukien coast. It will not be long before the people's army drives across the sea into Taiwan to liberate its fellow countrymen."[25] Now, there were reports of troop movements to areas opposite Formosa and of the massing of junks and other small craft in adjacent harbors. The British consulate in Canton reported on January 20 that a Major General Chao of the PLA had told a source that his troops would participate in an invasion of Formosa in March, for which both aircraft and landing craft were being prepared. Commenting on this report, Burgess noted the U.S. prediction of an attack on Formosa "by the middle of 1950" and said recent NCNA broadcasts had declared the invasion of Formosa to be first among the tasks of the Chinese armed forces.[26]

17

Britain Recognizes the People's Republic

The British Government announced its recognition of the People's Republic of China the day after Truman announced the hands-off-Formosa policy, and the coincidence, in the opinion of the British embassy in Washington, "drew the fire away from the recognition announcement." Moreover, the embassy found the U.S. press and radio reaction to the British announcement "surprisingly favourable," partly because of "some excellent educational work on the part of the State Department."[1] Before the Truman announcement, Ambassador Franks had been somewhat worried about reaction in the United States to British recognition, though not about that of the Truman administration. In a telegram of particular secrecy on January 3, he had reported to the Foreign Office that the atmosphere in Washington was "less favourable than it was a month ago and we shall probably be in for a sticky patch immediately after our recognition of Communist China." Franks had commented also that the "bipartisan idea has never extended to the Far East and some of the Republican leaders in Congress will hardly be able to resist this opportunity for making capital at the Administration's expense."[2] Sir Oliver believed, however, that Truman and Acheson would firmly maintain "their present attitude," which he summed up as follows:

(a) Although they regret our decision to recognize the Communists, they will not recriminate.
(b) They are against military intervention in Formosa and the despatch of military missions. . . . Nevertheless the President might, for political reasons, have to bow to Congressional pressure over measures designed to throw a defensive screen round Formosa or in some way keep the island out of Communist hands.[3]

The reaction the British received from another American quarter may also have come as a pleasant surprise to them. On January 13, the British diplomatic representative at the SCAP headquarters in Tokyo, Sir Alvary Gascoigne, reported on a conversation with General Douglas MacArthur.

Speaking of our recognition of the Peking Government, General MacArthur confirmed to me today that he did not think that it would have an important reaction in Japan. He understood perfectly well, he said, why we had to recognise the Chinese Reds. It was purely because of our economic interests. . . . Our move had done nothing, he said, but accelerate events that would have taken place over a longer period of time. . . . The United States would obviously have to recognize Peking but the people of America must be made to understand that recognition of a Government did not necessarily carry with it approval of the said Government. While he hoped that we should get some concrete advantage by our recognition, he felt that we should not be able to save much from the wreck.[4]

The Foreign Office deliberately gave the CPG twenty-four hours to prepare for the formal announcement of British recognition by sending the British chargé in Nanking his instructions en clair. Thus it was no surprise to the Chinese when Consul General Graham met with Foreign Ministry officials Wang Ping-nan, head of the General Affairs Department, and Huan Hsiang, director of the Western European and African Department, on the afternoon of January 6 to present the formal British notification of recognition.[5] On the previous day the Chinese Nationalist ambassador in London had been called into the Foreign Office and informed that the British were withdrawing recognition of his government as the government of China.

In the United States and elsewhere in the West, debate raged on the question of recognition as though it were tantamount to establishing diplomatic relations, but Mao's proclamation of October 1, 1949, and Chou's letter transmitting it to foreign governments referred only to the establishment of diplomatic relations. As the first country to respond to Mao's declaration, the Soviet Union also omitted any reference to recognition, stating simply its desire to enter into diplomatic relations. The eastern European Communist governments followed suit.

All of this might have encouraged the belief that recognition and the establishment of diplomatic relations amounted to the same thing or at least that diplomatic relations would follow recognition more or less automatically. When the Burmese government informed the CPG on December 16 that it wished to establish diplomatic relations, however, the CPG asked the Burmese to send a representative to Peking "to begin negotiation of this matter." Clearly, the procedure for establishing diplomatic relations would be different for the non-Communist states from that for the Communist countries.[6]

The implications for the British of Peking's response to the Burmese government were seen in the Foreign Office well before the

United Kingdom's recognition announcement. In a minute dated December 30, A.A.E. Franklin of the Far Eastern Department asserted that Peking's response had a "very unpleasant ring" and that it might prove to be "the beginning of an attempt by the Communists to make recognition 'conditional.' " Franklin conjectured, all too accurately as it turned out, that if this were so, the Communists might "before agreeing to establish diplomatic relations want all sorts of points cleared up with us." He felt such a situation might prove "extremely embarrassing" for the United Kingdom and foresaw that "such negotiations could be expected to drag on for a considerable time." Franklin disagreed with Hutchison, the British chargé in Nanking, who was "inclined to think that negotiations might only cover an extremely limited field such as rank and identity of envoys, dates of appointment, location of embassies, etc." He noted that the Chinese response to Burma's recognition had caused resentment and uneasiness in Burma.[7] Such a reaction was reflected, for example, in an editorial in the newspaper the *Burman*, which called Peking's reply "an unmerited piece of studied coldshouldering" of Burma's sincere offer of friendship.[8]

The pattern established by the CPG in its dealings with Burma and India, which had recognized the People's Republic on December 30, was repeated in the case of the United Kingdom.[9] When the British government, in a note from Bevin to Chou dated January 6, formally recognized the CPG as the de jure government of China, it also asked the CPG to receive Hutchison as British chargé d'affaires ad interim. On January 9 Chou replied that the CPG accepted "Mr. J. C. Hutchison, who was nominated by Mr. Bevin as Chargé d'Affaires *ad interim,* to come to Peking to conduct discussions on the establishment of diplomatic relations."[10] Hutchison noted that the Chinese government had not explicitly accepted him as chargé d'affairs and recommended that the Chinese be asked whether they would receive him in such a capacity, for to do so would imply that diplomatic relations had been established."[11]

On January 13 the Foreign Office instructed Consul General Graham in Peking to inform the Foreign Ministry of the British view that the interchange of notes that had just taken place between the British government and the CPG constituted the establishment of diplomatic relations and to seek acceptance of this view.[12] If acceptance were not forthcoming, Graham should state that it would only be possible for Hutchison to go to Peking in his capacity as chargé d'affaires.[13] When Graham called at the Foreign Ministry and put forward the British view that diplomatic relations had already been established, however, he received a noncommital response.[14] Subsequently the Ministry of Foreign Affairs informed Graham that Hutchison could come to Peking in his capacity as chargé d'affaires to discuss preliminary and procedural questions regarding mutual establishment of diplomatic relations.[15] Although the Chinese had conceded nothing on the main point at issue—whether diplomatic relations had already been established—the Foreign Office decided to send Hutchison to Peking.[16]

Chinese reaction to British recognition was disappointing, and not merely as manifested by Peking's insistence that diplomatic relations be negotiated. British Consul General Scott L. Burdett in Tientsin wrote the Foreign Office on January 14 that recognition had "not made any difference whatever"; no contacts were allowed at any level, and letters were either returned in original without explanation or ignored.[17] From Canton, the consul general reported on January 30 that though there had been "inevitable expectations that recognition would result in a complete change in our situation," there had been no change.[18] Several weeks later there had still been "no relaxation of restrictions to which we are subjected," and the Post Office continued to hold up mail addressed to the consulate general.[19]

The British consul general in Shanghai telegraphed on February 4 that movements of British subjects out of Shanghai continued to be restricted, and he regarded the restriction as normal and obvious in time of war. Yet a police official had told a British businessman who wished to go to Hong Kong via Canton that facilities would be allowed as soon as "recognition was effective." In a Foreign Office minute on this telegram Franklin commented, "Movements are restricted because of non-recognition or non-establishment of diplomatic relations and not because of the war."[20]

The Foreign Office could get little comfort from the Chinese press either. Instead of giving the British government any credit for recognizing the People's Republic, the press emphasized that Britain did so in its own economic interest. Thus the *Ta Kung Pao* in Shanghai, pointing out (correctly) that British industrial and commercial circles had long advocated recognition, declared that Britain's desire to establish diplomatic relations with China was "for the sake of commercial interests." Somewhat ironically, in light of the British Foreign Office view that recognition would give the CPG an alternative to its pro-Soviet policy, *Ta Kung Pao* boasted that the People's Republic had "scored a complete diplomatic victory within only three months since the establishment of the Central People's Government," a victory that was the result of "carrying out Chairman Mao's policy of leaning to one side." *Ta Kung Pao* also claimed that British recognition had widened the divergence between Britain and the United States, and it drew a careful distinction between the friendship of the British people and "the diplomacy of capitalist countries."[21]

An article published in the Nanking *Hsin Min Pao* of February 3, under the heading "Acquaint Yourself with British Imperialism," reviewed Britain's nineteenth-century wars with China and the twentieth-century anti-British riots in such places as Shanghai and Hankow. The article then warned that Britain had only recognized China because it had to; the Chinese should not expect any change in British ways. Imperialists were persistently hostile to the peace-loving peoples of the world.[22]

While Hutchison was preparing to enter into "preliminary and procedural" talks for the establishment of diplomatic relations between the United Kingdom and the People's Republic, British Consul E.T. Biggs in Formosa was seeking to maintain British relations with the Nationalists at the provincial level. Thus the British, with clear consistency, were following the same policy they had followed on the China mainland; they were keeping their consulate open in Chinese territory controlled by a regime they did not recognize. Unlike the Communists, however, the Nationalists, in accordance with international practice, accepted the British position.

When Consul Biggs called on Formosa Governor K.C. Wu to inform him that the Britain had recognized the Communist government, the governor expressed a desire to maintain trade relations and communications with Britain and promised that all measures would be taken to protect Biggs and his staff and the British community.[23] Despite Wu's assurances of protection, a group of soldiers, apparently acting on their own, invaded the British consular premises and hauled down the consular flag.[24] When on January 12 Biggs called on Governor Wu to protest this behavior, Wu was conciliatory. He promised that the offending troops would be withdrawn from the area and that there would be no recurrence of the incident. He agreed that Biggs could rehoist the consular flag. More important, Wu informed Biggs that the Nationalist government had approved continuance of full British consular functions, including the use of cipher, diplomatic bag, and customs facilities. British consular officials could, of course, conduct relations only with the provincial officials and not with those of the Ministry of Foreign Affairs or other central government ministries.[25]

The problem of how best to conduct relations with the derecognized Nationalist regime on Formosa without affecting relatons with the CPG posed a continuing dilemma for the British government. Thus when a Chinese Nationalist air force plane bombed the Hong Kong border town of Shumchun on February 5, the Foreign Office decided to protest to no one but to have the Governor of Hong Kong make a public statement to the effect that any unauthorized aircraft flying over Hong Kong was liable to be fired on. Consul Biggs in Tamsui was then instructed to give the text of the announcement to the governor of Formosa with the request that he convey it to the appropriate authorities and to the commander in chief of the Nationalist air force. The announcement was duly made in Hong Kong on March 10, and its text handed to the governor of Formosa the same day.[26]

A few days earlier, however, Foreign Secretary Bevin had sent a seemingly contradictory telegram to the British consul general in Shanghai, who was greatly concerned by the Nationalist bombing of that city. Bevin said he did not believe "any useful purpose" would be served by protesting to the Nationalist government through the Formosa provincial government. Bevin reasoned: "Our protests had no result even before we withdrew recognition from the Nationalist Government, and if, as we may suppose, some publicity is given to our representations and their inevitable rejection, this might embarrass Mr. Hutchison in his forthcoming discussions with the People's Government, who would be likely to claim that it furnished evidence of our continued relations with the Nationalist Government."[27]

18

American Consular Properties Seized

The day the British government announced its recognition of the CPG, January 6, the Peking Municipal Military Control Commission made a move that squelched any hope of early U.S. recognition. It proclaimed that within seven days land acquired by "certain foreign countries" under "unequal treaties," on which military barracks had been built, would be requisitioned.[1] During the night, copies of the proclamation were posted on the walls of the American, British, French, and Dutch consular compounds. By the next morning posters on the walls of the British compound had been removed, but the property of the other three countries was duly requisitioned. In the case of the United States, this action led directly to the withdrawal of all official American personnel from the People's Republic of China.[2]

The immediate issue was the requisitioning of the property in Peking, owned by the U.S. government, that housed the American consulate general, but there was a larger and more important issue involved, as well: the question of respect for treaties entered into by previous Chinese governments and for customary international practices that had been developed in the West, which the Communists generally ignored. In the latter category, of course, was the tradition that foreign consulates could continue to function at the local level regardless of the absence of diplomatic relations at the national level. As we have seen, the Chinese Communist authorities' refusal to honor this tradition and their insistence on treating foreign consular and diplomatic officials like ordinary aliens not only had created friction with Western powers but had so restricted communication with their representatives in China as to make impossible the orderly negotiation of problems as they arose.

Concomitant with the policy of refusing to deal with foreign consular officers as officials was the Communist authorities' refusal to treat consular property as official property of a foreign government. The consequences of this policy were first apparent when, even before the establishment of the People's Republic, local Communist authorities sought to levy taxes against foreign-government-owned consular properties in Tientsin and Peking as though they were privately owned.

The U.S. position was that taxes were not payable on properties owned and used for government purposes, since, under international law, one sovereign government may not be taxed by another, whether recognized or unrecognized. Acknowledging that the case was stronger for diplomatic property than for consular property, the department admitted that "as a practical matter," it might be necessary to pay the taxes demanded; but they should be paid only under protest and not unless "other Western Powers definitely agreed pay such taxes."[3]

On September 14, the U.S. consulate general in Tientsin paid taxes on U.S.-government-owned consular houses, after the local authorities had turned down its request for exemption and after French and British consuls had paid such taxes. In reporting this action, the consulate general reminded the State Department, as it had "on many occasions during past 8 months," that "Communist authorities have consistently taken line that Consulates not recognized and that consular personnel and property foreign governments will be treated as non-official as long as diplomatic relations not established."[4]

The issue of the treatment of government-owned property also arose in connection with regulations promulgated by the local authorities for the registration of alien property. In Tientsin a rather ludicrous situation developed when the local Land Bureau demanded certain amendments to the applications for registration sent in by the American, British, French, and Italian consulates, as the following excerpts from a Foreign Office minute indicate:

6. Applications for registration of Govt. properties were submitted . . . on the 14 November by the four Consuls-General. H.M.C.G. was informed by the Land Bureau that the forms required the following additions before they [could] be accepted:
(a) the insertion of the word "former" before "British Govt." and "British Foreign Service Officer."
(b) the insertion of the word "bogus" before "deed of ownership."
(c) the application of a personal Chinese seal after H.M.C.G.'s signature
(d) the production of a letter or certificate indicating that H.M.C.G. was authorised to act in this matter.
7. A similar intimation was made to the U.S. and Italian Consuls-General. The French applications were, after minor amendments, accepted, possibly because the word "bogus" had without the knowledge of the French C.G. been inserted, presumably by his Chinese staff, in two of the three French

applications and was not required in the third application [an Imperial title-deed].

. . . .
9. . . . By the 29th. November the British, U.S. and Italian C.G.'s had ascertained that of the four points indicated in para. 6 above (a) and (d) would not be insisted on, and they were prepared to accede to (c). The Land Bureau however refused to admit that the former Nationalist Land Bureau should be described as the "former" Land Bureau and insisted on the word "bogus".
10. H.M. Embassy at Nanking instructed to inform H.M.C.G. that the insertion of the word "bogus" could not be agreed to, since this might be interpreted as invalidating all deeds issued by the former Nationalist Land Bureau, including those held by all British property owners in Tientsin.[5]

The British consul general in Tientsin, in his frustration, saw the Land Bureau's insistence on "bogus" as "merely another typical instance of petty tyranny with which local underlings are allowed to treat foreigners in general and Consuls in particular."[6] Be that as it may, the proclamation of January 6 requisitioning certain foreign consular properties in Peking was certainly not the work of local underlings. The next day U.S. consul general Clubb received a communication from General Nieh Jung-chen, director of the Peking Municipal Military Control Commission, referring to the proclamation and requesting that Clubb dispatch a special messenger with authority to turn over the "former American military barracks" at 22 Legation Street.

Clubb acknowledged this communication and telegraphed the State Department for instructions. On January 9, in accordance with the department's instructions, Clubb wrote to Chou En-lai to inform him that the property at 22 Legation Street was acquired by the United States under the protocol signed at Peking on September 7, 1901, by China and eleven other powers and that this right had been reaffirmed in the Sino-American treaty of 1943, under which the U.S. government had relinquished its extraterritorial rights.[7] Clubb also informed Chou that the so-called military barracks had "long since been converted into an office building and used as the office of the American Consulate General." Clubb concluded his letter to Chou with the statement that the U.S. government expected that no action would be taken "constituting any violation of the rights of the United States Government."[8]

Clubb followed up his letter to Chou with another the next day and with one to General Nieh Jung-chen on January 13. In the latter message he reiterated that the premises the Control Commission sought to requisition were used for the U.S. government's official

purposes, "namely for the housing of the American consular establishment in Peking." He also stated that he was without authority or
instructions to deliver over the property, and any requisition would be
on the "full responsibilit of the Central People's Government and
against the formal protest of the United States Government."[9]

In the meantime, the U.S. government had asked the British
government—which, having just recognized the CPG, presumably
had better access to its officials than did the United States—to deliver a
message to Chou En-lai or to the highest available Chinese official. The
message was to state that the U.S. government would have no objection to turning over to the authorities the Glacis property to the west of
the U.S. consular compounds and the U.S.-government-owned building on this property, but should the Chinese Communist military
authorities requisition any part of the consular compounds, the U.S.
government would consider such action a violation of its rights and
would conclude that it had no alternative but to close all its official
establishments in Communist China and to withdraw its official personnel.[10]

Despite some misgivings in the Foreign office, Bevin telegraphed
the British embassy in Nanking on January 12 to instruct Consul
General Walter Graham, who had been transferred to Peking from
Mukden, "to make every effort" to convey the American message to
General Chou "before the 13th January or as soon as possible
thereafter." Bevin considered that the British government should not
dissociate itself from the problem confronting the American, French,
and Dutch governments, "particularly as this is the first open attempt
by the Communists to disregard China's Treaty obligations." (Neither
the British nor the Americans were yet aware that the Tihwa municipality had requisitioned the U.S. consulate in that city on December
29.) He reasoned that "in view of their general attitude towards the
Western Powers," it seemed "very likely they will be encouraged to try
to take over the rest of the Embassy compounds."[11]

However, Bevin did not want to become too closely associated with
the U.S. message and its "strong language." He emphasized, therefore, that Consul General Graham "should make it clear that in this
matter he is acting merely as a mouthpiece and make it as clear as he
thinks appropriate that, while we have comparable concern, we were of
course not consulted in the drafting of the United States message.
Having delivered the United States message he should however add
that I am disturbed at these developments and that I trust that there is
no intention on the part of the local authorities to disregard the Treaty

rights enjoyed by the various countries concerned in respect of their Embassy compounds."[12] By the time Graham was able to do anything about Bevin's instructions, which had to be relayed to him through the British embassy in Nanking, requisitioning of the U.S. consular premises had already begun. Graham reported on January 14 that requisitioning had begun at ten that morning and that he had seen Huan Hsiang in the Foreign Ministry at three that afternoon. However, Clubb had already had the message delivered to the Foreign Ministry January 12. Thus the Chinese authorities knew of the American offer to turn over other property to them and of the threat of withdrawal before the requisitioning started.[13]

Although Clubb had beaten him to it, Graham delivered the message also. In doing so he elicited a comment from Huan that the existence of the barracks was disgraceful, a relic of unequal treatment that should be recovered by the Chinese. Graham came away from the interview with Huan feeling sure that the Chinese intention was "to take our property too."[14]

The unequal treaties had long been abrogated, of course, and the military barracks had long since been converted to offices, but they continued to have propaganda value for the Communists. An NCNA article of January 19 asserted, for example: "In 1943, the United States, Britain, France and other countries declared the abrogation of their prerogatives in China. But under the rule of the traitorous Kuomintang reactionaries, the barracks of the imperialists which were an infringement on China's sovereignty remained intact. Only the People's Republic of China could really accomplish the task of abolishing the imperialist prerogatives in China."[15]

In a dispatch to the Foreign Office commenting on the background and timing of the Chinese action against the American, French, and Dutch consular properties in Peking, Consul General Graham noted that one speculation rife in Peking at the time was that the requisitioning was "a plan devised exclusively by the military authorities, in which the Wai Chiao Pu [Foreign Ministry] had no part, and to which it possibly was even hostile; that, in fact, Chu Teh [commander in chief of the PLA], taking advantage of Mao Tse-tung's absence from Peking, had forced the hand of Chou En-lai . . . and succeeded in his aim of making friendly relations with America practically impossible." Graham's dispatch continued: "A strong argument against this view is the subsequent recognition, by the Foreign Minister [Chou En-lai] himself, of the Ho Chi-minh regime in Indo-China, which must make it almost as difficult for France to recognize the People's Government as the seizure of their property has made it for the United States. Such parallel action by the Wai Chiao Pu and the Military Control Commission appears to rule out the likelihood of a serious split between the military command and the civil government."[16] Graham believed that the timing of the requisitioning order could "hardly have been chance." It had been obvious for nearly a week that the British government would recognize the People's Republic at just about the time it did. He concluded that the action of the Chinese authorities of posting the requisition notices on the British consulate's walls on the evening of January 6 and then taking them down a few hours later was probably designed to "emphasize the distinction between the sheep and the goats"—between those countries that had recognized and those that had not.[17]

Graham also speculated on whether the Chinese authorities foresaw the consequences of their seizure of U.S. consular property in Peking. He thought that it was by no means certain that they did but that, in any case, opinions within the CPG would differ as to the desirability of injuring Sino-American relations and of getting rid of U.S. consular posts in China. He concluded that many would be glad to see such a development, but there were others, "whose opinions are not at present carrying much weight, who view with misgivings this decisive breach with America and general worsening of relations with the Western World."[18]

In making this comment, Graham was probably not yet aware of the telegram sent to the Foreign Office by the British embassy in Washington three days earlier reporting that "Chinese seizure of U.S. consular premises at Peking has caused marked resentment here, and decision to withdraw all U.S. official representatives from China is generally approved by press." The embassy also pointed out that the "sudden turn of events had checked the growth of the movement in favour of recognition which was noticeable immediately after Mr. Acheson's speech at the Press Club on 12th January."[19]

The American decision to withdraw all its official personnel from the People's Republic if the Communist authorities requisitioned U.S. consular property in Peking was made by President Truman on the recommendation of Secretary of State Acheson. However, as Acheson told an executive session of the Senate Foreign Relations Committee, January 24, he had presented an alternative course to the president, which was to protest the requisitioning, withdraw to what was left of the consular compound, "and see what happened next." He advised against adopting this course because it might simply be "the first in a series of humiliations." There would be more and more U.S. property requisitioned, U.S. officials would be more and more restricted in their movements, "and little-by-little we would be humiliated and imprisoned in China."[20] Acheson's testimony makes clear, however, that the State Department was not merely using the requisitioning of U.S. consular property in Peking as a pretext to pull out of China; it hoped the Communist authorities would change their minds. Thus Acheson told the committee:

We thought that there was a possibility that they might stop, look, and listen, and the President decided that . . . we should notify them that if they took the property, we moved out, everywhere in China, and that information was given to them and they did not stop but went ahead.

During the days from January 6 on until the time that it finally went into effect, we kept this proposed action very secret, because we did not want to diminish any chance that the Communists might turn around and withdraw from this action, and we thought that all possibility of that would be over if this became a public matter."[21]

The State Department lost no time in following through on its threat to recall all American officials from Communist China once the requisitioning of U.S. property began. On January 14 telegraphic instructions went out to the four remaining consular posts in the People's Republic ordering them "to close as soon as transportation from Communist-occupied China could be arranged for all official personnel and arrangements completed for the assumption of American interests by the British representatives at those posts."[22] Nearly four months were to pass before all this could be accomplished and the last official American personnel could leave China.

As we have seen, the British had long since agreed to protect American interests in China and had taken charge of them in all of the consular districts where the U.S. had already closed its establishments. On January 19 the Foreign Office formally agreed to the State Department's request that the British government also assume responsibility for U.S. interests at Peking, Nanking, Shanghai, and Tientsin when U.S. establishments in those cities closed. But the British requested that "U.S. representatives at the four places already named could be instructed to dismantle their own radio equipment before handing their keys to their British colleagues."[23]

British representatives in China were less than enthusiastic about this extension of their responsibilities. Thus British Chargé Hutchison in Nanking, uncertain of how he was going to be received in Peking, wondered in a telegram to the Foreign Office on January 17 if it would be possible to discourage the State Department from asking that representations be made on behalf of the United States, "except in such cases which brook of no delay and cannot be handled in any other way," until diplomatic relations between the British and Central People's governments had been established "and the status and functions of His Majesty's Consular Officers have been recognised."[24]

In Shanghai, Consul General Urquhart reported on January 31 that the British Chamber of Commerce had "expressed misgivings lest our protection of American interests may prove harmful to British interests." Urquhart also criticized the U.S. decision to withdraw from China, reporting the "general feeling" that the "American gesture of complete withdrawal is disproportionate to the provocation" and that it would have been better if the "showdown" with the People's Republic had taken place "on grounds more favourable to Western nations." Urquhart estimated that of the "530 Americans, officials, civilians and dependents" in the Shanghai Consular district, 100 to 125, including 39 officials, would leave.[25]

In an earlier message, Hutchison had commented on the "effects on British interests in China of American withdrawal from China." He noted first that there was no indication that the American reaction "to the high-handed and discourteous manner in which they were deprived of the use of their former military compound may have come as a disagreeable surprise to the Chinese . . . . Government spokesman have not shown any signs of dismay or even surprise." Hutchison was afraid, however, that the American withdrawal would serve to strengthen the extremists in the Communist party while weakening those "who have perhaps hitherto been able to exercise a moderating influence." He went on to say, "If I am right action taken by State Department diminishes the possibility on which we have counted of weaning China from dependency on Moscow."[26]

For its part, the Foreign Office was more worried about the impact of the requisitioning on American policy toward China than about the effect of U.S. withdrawal on Chinese policy toward the West. In a top secret analysis of the "international situation in regard to China," the Foreign Office informed Hutchison that the U.S. administration had "not been unsympathetic towards our act of recognition, and in normal circumstances might have been expected to follow suit when the dust died down." It continued: "But the seizure of the American barracks property in Peking has caused a setback, and it would now in our view be extremely difficult for the United States Administration to make any overtly friendly gesture towards the People's Government. Similarly they will find difficulty in taking any action to deter the Nationalists in Formosa from taking hostile action against the mainland." The message also expressed Foreign Office concern about what the requisitioning of consular property in Peking portended for the imminent negotiations in Peking. It would be "extremely interesting" to learn from Hutchison, when he had held his preliminary discussions in Peking, "whether there is any real disposition to establish relations with us on a friendly basis," for "the action of the Peking Government in seizing the barracks properties and in recognizing Ho Chi-minh certainly suggests there is a pull in the direction of making the establishment of diplomatic relations with the West as difficult as possible. The French would probably have recognized the Chinese Government as soon as they had ratified their agreement with Bao Dai; now, they are in a quandry."[27]

19
Sino-Soviet Accord

Just when Chinese actions affecting British, French, and American interests were causing the Foreign Office to ask whether the People's Republic had "any real disposition" to establish diplomatic relations with the West, Chinese leaders were negotiating a defense treaty and other agreements with the Soviet Union. These negotiations culminated on February 14 when Premier Chou En-lai and Soviet Foreign Minister A.Y. Vyshinsky signed, in the presence of Mao and Stalin in the Kremlin, a thirty-year Treaty of Friendship, Alliance, and Mutual Assistance, together with an agreement dealing with the eventual restoration to full Chinese control of the Chinese Changchun Railway, Port Arthur, and Dairen and another covering the extension of a $300 million Soviet loan to China.[1]

At the direction of Foreign Secretary Bevin, the Research Department of the Foreign Office prepared an analysis of the Sino-Soviet

Treaty, comparing it with similar Soviet treaties with the eastern European satellites and showing striking similarities. For example, Article 1 of the Sino-Soviet Treaty, aimed at preventing an attack by Japan or states allied with it, was almost identical to the corresponding article in the Soviet-Romanian Treaty if "Japan" were substituted for "Germany." Article 3 of the Sino-Soviet Treaty, stipulating that the parties to it should not join any alliances against the other, was very similar to Article 5 of the Soviet-Czech Treaty. Article 4, the clause concerning mutual consultations, appeared in the Soviet treaties with Romania, Hungary, and Bulgaria, and Article 5, concerning economic and cultural ties, was "virtually identical with Article 4 of the Soviet-Czech Treaty."[2]

In the Far Eastern Department of the Foreign Office, Guy Burgess noted that the signing of the Sino-Soviet agreements rounded off a discernible pattern in the "chronological carpet" of Sino-Soviet relations since October 1, 1949. In Burgess's view this pattern revealed "careful, successful and detailed Sino-Soviet planning and co-ordination of several recent moves." Among these planned and coordinated moves were the date of the establishment of the People's Republic and the rapid acts of recognition first by Moscow and then by its satellites; the stress in both Soviet and Chinese propaganda that there had been an important shift in the balance of forces between the Soviets and the West; and the "forward move in South-East Asia," illustrated by Georgi Malenkov's October Revolution anniversary speech of November 6, 1949, and Liu Shao-chi's speech at the World Federation of Trade Unions conference in Peking on November 16, which "took up Malenkov's theme violently and called for the urgent and aggressive stepping-up of specified armed risings by Asiatic peoples." Burgess thought the Sino-Soviet agreements "seemed calculated to strengthen (a) Sino-Soviet relations against the West and (b) the position of the Chinese Communists, both in China and as the supporters of Far Eastern 'liberation.'"[3]

It seemed to the British embassy in Moscow that the Soviet government had "let Mao get all the tangible benefits" from the Sino-Soviet Treaty and agreements, while the Soviets contented themselves "with the propaganda advantages of a notable display of disinterested good will and generosity."[4] The British government hoped to counteract the Soviet propaganda advantages but, poised as it was on the threshold of negotiations with the Central People's Government in Peking on the question of diplomatic relations, did not wish to offend the Chinese. Thus it furnished British high commissioners in commonwealth capitals with ammunition to use against the treaty and agreements but cautioned that it was "essential to avoid any criticism of Chinese Government at this particular juncture." With this caveat the high commissioners were instructed that, if they were "consulted by Commonwealth authorities, friendly colleagues, or journalists," they could point out that while there was no ostensible Chinese quid pro quo for the Soviet concessions to China, the treaty illustrated the "well-known comparison of Soviet policy to iceberg of which only small part is visible." They could also suggest that the economic agreements should be considered in the light of Soviet depredations in Manchuria in 1945 and the Soviet economic penetration of Manchuria since the conclusion of the trade agreement there in July 1949. Furthermore, the Soviet credit of $300 million spread over five years was very small compared to the $2.1 billion spent by the United Kingdom in South and Southeast Asia since the war.[5]

Uninhibited by impending negotiations with the People's Republic, the United States was less subtle than the United Kingdom in its attack on the Sino-Soviet negotiations. Well before the negotiations had concluded, Acheson had publicly accused the Soviet Union of trying to take Manchuria away from China. In his National Press Club speech of January 12 he had offered somewhat dubious evidence, which the State Department tried to substantiate by later releasing to the press "background material based on the large accumulation of reports and data available to this Government."[6]

The State Department also launched a covert attack on the negotiations. Thus, in a top secret "eyes only" message of January 25, it informed Ambassador David Bruce in Paris: "Department has received from several sources interim reports regarding Stalin-Mao negotiations which, while viewed with reserve, may serve very useful propaganda purpose if skillfully released for publication in such a manner that appearance of material could not be traced to this government."[7] The material supplied to Bruce for covert planting included reports that the Soviet Union was pressing the People's Republic to provide 1,000,000 Chinese laborers to work in the USSR and that 300,000 had already arrived. The plants sought to discount the impact of any Sino-Soviet treaty in advance by warning that it would "probably breathe friendship and cooperation with unpalatable Chinese concessions well hidden in secret protocols and agreements."[8]

Following the conclusion of the Sino-Soviet Treaty, the State Department again delivered a one-two propaganda punch. Acheson attacked it in a speech on American policy toward Asia before the

After presenting his credentials as U.S. ambassador to China, Dr. J. Leighton Stuart was photographed with President Chiang Kai-shek and General George C. Marshall at Kuling, July 1946. Embassy Minister-Counselor W. Walton Butterworth is in the second row. Courtesy of Philip Fugh. *Below,* Consul General Angus Ward and Mrs. Ward at the entrance to the American Consulate General in Mukden. The Wards and the consulate staff were placed under incommunicado house arrest after the PLA's capture of Mukden, November 1, 1948. Courtesy of William N. Stokes.

Chou En-lai, General Chu Teh, and CCP Chairman Mao Tse-Tung in Yenan. With other CCP leaders they entered Peiping March 25, 1949. National Archives. *Below,* Ambassador Stuart at the gate of the U.S. Embassy residence. Stuart voluntarily remained at the embassy for a week after the PLA's capture of Nanking, April 24, 1949. Courtesy of Philip Fugh.

Above, British Foreign Secretary Ernest Bevin, 1949. Library of Congress. *Left,* Consul General O. Edmund Clubb and Mrs. Clubb host an Independence Day reception at the American Consulate General, Peiping, in 1949. Colonel David Barrett, assistant military attaché, is on Mr. Clubb's left. Courtesy of O. Edmund Clubb.

Walter P. McConaughy, *above*,
took charge of the U.S. Consulate General in Shanghai upon
John Cabot's departure from
China August 2, 1949; he later
served as consul general in Hong
Kong, 1950-52. Courtesy of
Walter P. McConaughy. *Right*,
Robert C. Strong, who, as U.S.
chargé d'affaires ad interim,
followed the Nationalist government to Chungking from Canton
in October 1949 and to Taipei in
December. Courtesy of
Robert C. Strong.

George K.C. Yeh was for nine years the urbane and accomplished foreign minister of the Republic of China, and subsequently ambassador to the United States.

Secretary of State Dean Acheson, center, conferring with Assistant Secretary for Far Eastern Affairs Walton Butterworth and Ambassador-at-Large Philip Jessup at the State Department, March 1950. National Archives.

Chang Han-fu, vice minister for foreign affairs, People's Republic of China, held inconclusive discussions with British chargé John Hutchison on the establishment of dipomatic relations, March-June 1950. *Below,* Assistant Secretary of State for Far Eastern Affairs Dean Rusk played an important role in consultations between the State Department and the Foreign Office in 1950-1951. National Archives.

Chargé d' affaires Karl L. Rankin in his office in Taipei, February 1953, shortly before his appointment to succeed Leighton Stuart as U.S. ambassador to China. National Archives. *Below,* Missionaries Hugh and Mabel Hubbard at their home in Tung-Hsien during their fifteen-month house arrest in the People's Republic of China.

Opening session of the Korean "preliminary talks" of October 26-December 10, 1953. The U.N. delegation, seated from right to left: Colonel Stanton Babcock, Special Ambassador Arthur H. Dean, Kenneth Young (Dean's deputy), and Edwin W. Martin. *Below*, PRC representative Huang Hua and North Korean delegate Ki Sok Bok at the opening session.

Commonwealth Club of California on March 15, and the department
sent more plants out the next day to Hong Kong and Taipei. Acheson
told his audience that "Soviet Russia has promised to return certain
Manchurian property but not the industrial equipment robbed by the
Red Army in 1945" and that while China "faces a prospect of 40 million
people suffering from hunger between now and the next crops . . .
food moves from China to the Soviet Union." He also belittled the $300
million five-year Soviet loan, comparing it to the $400 million *grant* the
U.S. Congress had voted for China in the single year 1948.[9] The
material sent to Hong Kong and Taipei for "discreet distribution to key
Chinese officials, press and information leaders," for inclusion in
speeches, editorials, and cartoons, pointed out, among other things,
the "similarities between the Sino-Soviet Treaty and other treaties
concluded by the Soviet Government," and gave examples of Soviet
treaty violations and of Soviet imperialism.[10]

Chou En-lai set the tone the People's Republic would take in the
propaganda war over the Sino-Soviet Treaty and agreements at the
February 14 signing ceremony in Moscow, when he declared: "The
conclusion of the treaty and agreements is a special expression of
fervent assistance to the revolutionary cause of the Chinese people on
the part of the Soviet Union directed by the policy of Generalissimo
Stalin . . . . The imperialist bloc headed by American imperialism has
resorted to all kinds of provocative methods attempting to frustrate the
friendship between our nations but these ignominious attempts have
utterly failed . . . . I believe that our treaty and agreements . . . will be
regarded with enmity only by the imperialists and warmongers."[11]

Judging by appearances, Mao himself was well pleased with his
reception in the Soviet Union and with the negotiations. According to
two staff members of the U.S. embassy in Moscow, Mao and his party
attended an all-star ballet performance at the Bolshoi Theater in
Moscow on the eve of the treaty-signing ceremonies, and the audience
gave them a "standing, prolonged, shouting ovation . . . . Mao and
party appeared exhilarated by thunderous enthusiasm."[12] On the
evening after the signing of the treaty and agreements, the Chinese
ambassador in Moscow "gave a grand cocktail party" attended by five
hundred guests including Stalin, Nikolai Shvernik, Malenkov, Lavren-
ti Beriya, and Kliment Voroshilov, as well as Mao and Chou.[13]

Somewhat more tangible evidence of Mao's state of mind came in
his farewell speech at the Moscow station. There, he proclaimed the
fundamental and indestructible solidarity "between our two great
peoples," which would have a great influence on the future of all

mankind in the struggle for peace. This was a conviction the Chinese Communist party had always held, Mao said, and he had now received confirmation of it in the Soviet Union. If he was dissatisfied with the economic agreements, Mao gave no hint of it. "The experience of the Soviet Union in economic construction and construction in other important spheres," he declared, "will be the example for construction of the New China." Mao's speech closed with a ringing tribute to the Soviet leader: "Hail to the teacher of the world revolution, best friend of the Chinese people, comrade Stalin."[14] Not content to leave his praises in Moscow, as he approached the Chinese frontier after visiting six Soviet cities, Mao sent a farewell message to Stalin ending with, "Best wishes for unbounded strength and prosperity to the Soviet Union led by you."[15]

Chinese media took specific note of the American efforts to denigrate the Sino-Soviet Treaty and agreements and counterattacked. For example, an editorial in *People's China* of March 1 alleged:

Ever since the Chinese people drove Chiang Kai-shek's regime from China's mainland, the American imperialists have been forced to rely increasingly on their schemes for driving a wedge between China and the Soviet Union. To date, at least, this apparently remains one of the main strategies they could think of in regard to China.

The signing of the Sino-Soviet treaty and the various agreements reached in Moscow . . . has demonstrated the futility of the State Department's latest policy of trying to stir up ill-will between the two neighbors.[16]

On April 16, an editorial in the same magazine claimed: "The newly-signed Sino-Soviet economic agreements will speed up the process of rehabilitating China's war-torn economy, and thus bring about fundamental improvements in the lives of the Chinese working people . . . . It is not surprising, under these circumstances, that the spokesmen for American imperialism have fumed with such rage against these agreements."[17]

20

British Frustrations

By an odd coincidence, the representative the United Kingdom had sent to Peking to negotiate the establishment of diplomatic relations made his initial call at the Foreign Ministry on February 14, the day the Sino-Soviet Friendship Treaty and other agreements were signed in Moscow in the presence of Stalin and Mao. During the course of this call, John Hutchison restated the British position that the exchange of notes between Bevin and Chou "constituted establishment of diplomatic relations." He also said it had become clear that the Chinese government believed that "preliminary and procedural questions must first be discussed." He wanted to know what these questions might be; but the Foreign Ministry was not yet ready to divulge them.[1] Some two weeks later a courtesy call on Vice-Minister Chang Han-fu, whom Hutchison described as having "no small talk," failed to elucidate the mystery.[2]

Meanwhile, A.K. Sen, the representative the Indian government had sent to Peking for "preliminary and procedural" discussions, had also had his first discussions at the Foreign Ministry. Reportedly, Jawaharlal Nehru had been "deeply irritated" by the demand that the establishment of diplomatic relations be negotiated. Nevertheless, India had acceded to Peking's request that it send a representative to discuss "procedures and preliminaries for establishment of diplomatic relations."[3] In his meeting at the Foreign Ministry, Sen was asked why India had abstained from voting on a Chinese representation question in the UN on February 7 and what the government of India was doing about Kuomintang properties in India. Hutchison reported to the Foreign Office that his Indian colleague was "naturally depressed by this development."[4]

Hutchison's turn for cross-examination at the Foreign Ministry came on March 2. Reading from a document, Vice-Minister Chang informed him that the Chinese government considered that since the British government had announced its desire to establish diplomatic relations with China, "it should not continue to maintain any diplomatic intercourse with the Kuomintang." Chang then cited Britain's abstention in the UN Security Council on a Soviet resolution to unseat the Chinese Nationalist representative and similar action taken in other organizations of the United Nations as evidence that Britain refused to accept the delegate of the legal government of China and continued to recognize the delegate of the Kuomintang "reactionary clique." He also asked for clarification of the British government's attitude toward organizations of the "Kuomintang reactionary clique" in Hong Kong and to Chinese national property there.[5]

The UN Security Council resolution referred to by Chang had been introduced on January 10 by Soviet Ambassador Yakov Malik. The resolution would have had the Security Council declare the representative of the Chinese Nationalist government illegal, revoke its recognition of his credentials, and exclude him from the council. The Chinese Nationalist representative, Ambassador Tsiang Ting-fu was at the time presiding over the council. On January 8 Chou En-lai had sent a note to the United Nations "demanding the United Nations and the Security Council to expel the illegitimate delegates of the Chinese Kuomintang reactionary remnant clique." On January 10 Chou sent a further note informing the UN that the People's Republic had "appointed Chang Wen Tien Chairman of the Delegation of the People's Republic of China to attend the meetings and to participate in the work of the United Nations, including the meetings and work of the Security Council."[6]

On January 12 various delegations made statements on the Soviet resolution. Among these was a statement by U.S. Ambassador Ernest Gross to the effect that the United States would vote against the Soviet resolution, but since the United States considered the matter a procedural one, it would not consider its negative vote a veto and would accept any council decision made by a seven-vote majority.[7] The next day the council voted to reject the Soviet resolution, and Malik walked out.[8]

British recognition of the People's Republic and the U.S. failure to do so had divided their positions in the Security Council on the Chinese representation issue but had by no means polarized them. The British abstained to indicate they did not wish to vote against the majority on the issue, and the Americans were also willing to abide by a majority decision, even if it meant ousting the Nationalists.

The Foreign Office instructed Hutchison to explain the British vote in the Security Council to Vice-Minister Chang and, at the same time, to refute the implication that Britain continued to have "diplomatic intercourse with the Kuomintang." Hutchison was to say:

As already indicated to the People's Government, His Majesty's Government in the United Kingdom withdrew recognition from the former Nationalist

Government since that date. . . . When His Majesty's Government in the United Kingdom abstained from voting in the Security Council on the issue of the expulsion of the former Nationalist representatives, this did not constitute an expression of view in favour of the former Nationalist representative or against the People's Government representative. The decision to abstain was taken because there was at that time no likelihood of a majority decision and it was consequently premature for the question to be raised. The considerations which applied in the Security Council apply equally in other organs of the United Nations. In general His Majesty's Government would of course welcome the appearance of representatives of the People's Government in all organs of the United Nations as soon as the majority of members of those organs are disposed to vote in favour of that Government's admission.[9]

In a follow-up telegram for Hutchison's personal information, the Foreign Office elaborated. There were now only five members of the Security Council in favor of admitting the People's Republic—Soviet Russia, India, Yugoslavia, Norway, and the United Kingdom. Britain would continue to abstain on the issue of Chinese representation until a majority of the members (seven) were in favor of admission. The Foreign Office also strongly felt that "a decision on this important question must be taken first in the Security Council"; it would be "entirely wrong to test this issue out in one of the subsidiary organs of the UN." In the event that the Chinese were to "cast doubts" on this explanation of Britain's abstention in the Security Council, Hutchison was authorized to counter with the observation that the Russian action (of walking out of the Security Council after its motion to expel the Chinese Nationalist representative had failed) was making things "infinitely more difficult" for the People's Republic. He could also point out that the "failure of the People's Government to establish normal diplomatic relations with those governments who have accorded *de jure* recognition has caused natural hesitance on the part of other governments who might be disposed to do likewise."[10] (One such government was the Canadian. The Canadian Department of External Affairs, in fact, had suggested to the Foreign Office that it make this argument in Peking. As it happened the Foreign Office had already thought of the argument itself.)[11] Hutchison was to defend the British position on Formosa as follows: "The existence of a British Consul at Tamsui does not signify the existence of any diplomatic relations. In accordance with the practice of His Majesty's Government in the United Kingdom, he is there to protect British interests and in so doing he had *de facto* relations with the local, but only with the local, authorities. There are many precedents for our action, notably in China both inside the Wall and in Manchuria."[12] Hutchison gave the British reply to the Chinese Foreign Ministry on March 17, but he had to wait until May to get the Chinese reaction.

Meanwhile, the Indian government, though its answers to the Chinese questions were not very forthcoming, was given a passing grade on its examination for entry into diplomatic relations with the CPG. To the Chinese request for an explanation of its abstention on the issue of Chinese representation in the Economic and Social Council, New Delhi instructed its representative in Peking to say that India had no intention of giving any other government an explanation about its votes in the UN.[13] As to the question about Kuomintang organizations in India, the Indian government said it knew of none, but its policy was to grant the right of asylum to individuals.[14] On March 15 Vice-Minister Chang informed the Indian representative in Peking that the CPG was content with India's replies, and negotiations for the establishment of diplomatic relations could proceed. The CPG now recognized the Indian representative as chargé d'affairs ad interim and hoped that an exchange of ambassadors would take place soon.[15] Within a week the CPG gave its agreement to the appointment of Sardar K.M. Panikkar, who had been India's ambassador to Nationalist China, as ambassador.[16]

In the Foreign Office, Franklin, though pleased with the Indian success, doubted that in the British case "the Central People's Government will in fact be content with our replies."[17] In Peking, however, Hutchison was more sanguine. He believed (wrongly as it turned out) on the basis of his "Indian colleague's last interview" that the Chinese government might be satisfied with the British replies.[18]

Though the British were not as vigorous in their support of admitting the People's Republic to the UN as the CPG would have liked, the Foreign Office was in fact working behind the scenes to build a majority in the Security Council in favor of such a move. Thus in a letter to the British ambassador in Paris, dated March 28, Esler Dening pointed out that "the waverers in the Security Council might be more disposed to vote for the People's Government representative if France were to change her attitude." He suggested that in view of the Indian and British experience in the negotiations in Peking, the French would have an easier time when their turn came if they had already voted in favor of the inclusion of the CPG representative in the Security Council.[19]

The thwarting of the British government's expectations that recognition of Communist China would lead directly to the establishment of diplomatic relations was paralleled by the disappointment of British business hopes that recognition would ameliorate business prospects in China. In its *Bulletin* of March 20, for example, the China Association complained that two and a half months after British recognition of the new Chinese government there had been no improvement in the situation of British firms or individuals in China; indeed, their situation was "probably worse." According to the *Bulletin*, trade and industry were almost at a standstill, but regulations of the CPG prevented firms from reducing staffs in response to the decline in their business activities. The bloated payroll was a heavy drain on their liquid financial resources, and the situation had continued for nine months.[20]

In Shanghai the British Chamber of Commerce pointed out that it was not so much the laws and regulations themselves that caused the businessmen's problems as the fact that they were not being implemented.[21] In a report dated March 29 the chairman of the British Chamber of Commerce in Tientsin lamented: "Even now after a year of Liberation, we are still in the melting pot so to speak and are fearfully ignorant of what tomorrow may bring. . . . it is regretted that it cannot be reported that the value of British trade in Tientsin has in any way justified the optimism and hopes with which the year under review opened. . . . The future is obscure and unpredictable. . . . foreigners—other than those of the anti-West bloc—are unwelcome in this great land of our adoption."[22] In a report transmitted to the China Association on April 1 the British Chamber of Commerce in Shanghai pronounced itself "gravely concerned with the trend of events which has affected everyone in business in China today" and pleaded that something be done to "remedy a situation which is rapidly becoming untenable."[23] In a shift away from its previous emphasis on the disastrous consequences of the Nationalist blockade of Shanghai, the chamber now recognised that the plight of foreign business in Shanghai was "mainly due to the upheaval of the economic conditions which have followed the advent of the new régime." Even the lifting of the blockade, said the chamber, "would not of its own be the cure for our troubles." The "plain facts" were that most firms were able neither to continue operating successfully nor "to extricate themselves from their difficulties by their own efforts." The chamber added: "Where attempts at liquidation have been made they have been met with exorbitant demands by labour which are tantamount to blackmail. . . . Foreign managers are being held personally responsible for their firms' obligations towards payment of salaries and taxes, refusal of which, for however good a reason we fear might result in imprisonment with all that implies."[24]

An indication of how little had changed in British relations with the People's Republic despite recognition was provided by the Chinese handling of the former British military barracks. When the requisition posters were removed from the British consular compound in Peking, British officials in China had surmised that the former British barracks would not be given any more than a temporary reprieve. Hutchison told the Foreign Office he would not be surprisd if the military barracks question turned out to be "the one matter" the Chinese would "propose to negotiate before the establishment of diplomatic relations."[25] With the publication on February 15 of a Sino-Soviet communiqué on the signing of the Sino-Soviet mutual defense treaty and other agreements, the British became even more convinced that the days of the military barracks property were numbered. Chou En-lai and Soviet Foreign Minister Vyshinsky, according to the communiqué, had exchanged notes "on the decision of the Soviet Government to hand over gratis to the Government of the People's Republic of China all buildings of the former military cantonment in Peking." After this announcement, Britain became the only one of the eleven powers that had signed the Protocol of 1901 still in possession of its military compound in Peking.[26]

In his speech at the signing ceremony for the Sino-Soviet Treaty and agreements, Chou En-lai singled out the Soviet gesture for special praise. "Transferring gratis buildings in the so-called military cantonment in Peking," Chou declared, was "a demonstration of the great friendship on the part of the Soviet Government and Generalissimo Stalin."[27] Actually, according to a report from the American consulate general in Hong Kong, the Russian military barracks in Peking had been returned to the Chinese in 1920. It had been used as a godown by Bryner and Company for many years until the company was ordered to vacate by the Chinese Communist authorities.[28]

Although Britain believed it had "a good title to the military compound," it was prepared in the interests of good relations with China to renounce it. Explaining its decision to the British ambassador in Washington, the Foreign Office reasoned that to negotiate an agreement with the CPG, even though it meant giving up the military compound, would be preferable to yielding to force with a mere protest, as France and the Netherlands had done. Moreover, to refuse to negotiate would lead to Chinese accusations of imperialism and of being "less appreciative than the Soviet Union of changed conditions in China." Such a propaganda line would be effective in China, the Foreign Office believed, and the possible reaction on the British position in Hong Kong had to be considered. Moreover, in as much as one of Britain's "main purposes in establishing relations with the People's Government" was to exploit any frictions that might develop in Sino-Soviet relations, it would be unwise to begin such relations with a dispute over the military compound.[29]

But the Chinese did not give the British a chance to discuss the subject. British Consul General Graham was handed an order from the Peking Military Control Commission, couched in terms similar to those received in January by the American, French, and Dutch consuls general, requiring the surrender of the British military barracks. Hutchison then sent a letter to the Vice-Minister Chang asking for an opportunity to discuss the matter and saying that he anticipated that there would be "no difficulty in reaching, in a courteous manner, an agreement satisfactory to both our Governments." Hutchison's letter also pointed out the implications of the unilateral seizure of the property. As he reported to the Foreign Office: "I added that I felt sure that the requisition in the manner envisaged, would provoke strong adverse criticism in the United Kingdom which would I felt be particularly undesirable at a time when our discussions for formal establishment of friendly relations were actually in progress and that with a view to obviating any such disagreeable and I felt sure unnecessary appearance of unfriendliness, I was anxious to enlist the Vice-Minister's help in preventing any precipitate implementation of the order."[30] The Chinese authorities gave no indication that they were interested in obviating any appearance of unfriendliness or disagreeableness, however. In response to Hutchison's letter, the Foreign Ministry called him in and requested that he comply with the terms of the Military Control Commission's orders; the vice-minister would not discuss the subject.[31]

Hutchison told the Foreign Office he could do no more than "guess at the reasons which have decided the Chinese Government to take this step at this moment and in this manner," but as he was wont to do, he speculated that "this unfriendly and discourteous action" represented "a victory for the more extreme pro-Soviet and anti-Western Elements in the Government."[32]

Before the military compound was taken over by the Chinese on April 11, Hutchison informed the Chinese Foreign Ministry that the British government considered that "the right to utilize for official purposes the former military compound attached to this Embassy is secured to them by Article 3 (iii) of the Sino-British Treaty of 1943. While they have been and still are prepared unconditionally to relinquish that right by agreement, they do not consider that the Chinese Government would be entitled to requisition the property by unilateral administrative action."[33] The fact that the Chinese authorities requisitioned the military compound, even though the Foreign Ministry had been previously informed by Hutchison that the British were willing to yield it unconditionally by agreement, strongly suggests that they wanted to do it unilaterally for internal propaganda purposes. It enabled the Chinese press to say that the "Military Control Council issued an order to the former consul of Great Britain."[34] Thus, British recognition of the People's Republic had delayed the requisitioning of the former British military compound in Peking for about three months, but in the end, recognition had neither prevented the takeover nor altered the unilateral manner in which it was carried out.

21

The Hazards of Departure

While the British government was seeking through negotiations with the CPG to maintain a diplomatic and commercial foothold in China, the U.S. government was trying to arrange for the departure from China of all its officials and of those American and British private citizens who wished to leave. The problem centered on Shanghai, where foreigners were trapped by the continuing Nationalist-Communist conflict.

When in mid-January the United States announced its decision to withdraw all official personnel from Communist China, the situation in Shanghai was already serious. The Nationalist blockade was preventing all but a few ships, among them vessels of the American-owned Isbrandtsen Line, from reaching that port.[1] Travel on these vessels was hazardous, but the Communist authorities refused to allow Shanghai residents to proceed to other port cities from which they could leave China in relative safety. In these circumstances, the Shanghai consular corps collectively expressed the hope that governments that had recognized the CPG would appeal to it on humanitarian grounds to allow foreigners, especially those needing to return to their homeland for medical or other emergencies, to go to Tientsin and

Canton. But the corps opposed a suggestion from the U.S. consul general that the Voice of America start a publicity campaign on the subject in the name of humanitarianism.[2]

In Nanking, where he was still waiting to proceed to Peking for negotiations on the establishment of diplomatic relations, British Chargé Hutchison felt there was little chance of success for an appeal to the Chinese authorities on humanitarian grounds, and he was "very reluctant to make the attempt especially at the outset." He thought he might eventually be able to take up individual hardship cases, but all this would "have to await full establishment of diplomatic relations between HMG in U.K. and People's Government." Meanwhile, Hutchison hoped that the Voice of America publicity campaign, which he regarded as "a most ill-considered and wrong-headed idea," could be discouraged.[3] Hutchison did not even think it desirable "at this time" to ask the Chinese authorities for an explanation of why they would not permit foreigners who had already been granted exit permits to travel to Tientsin or Canton.[4]

The American decision to pull all U.S. official personnel out of the People's Republic intensified the pressure for finding a way to evacuate those foreigners from Shanghai who wished to leave. The State Department investigated the use of planes, trains, and even small coastal steamers as a means of exit from Shanghai. But the local authorities continued to refuse the use of air or rail transport out of Shanghai for other Chinese ports, and the owners of the coastal steamers did not want to risk them in the narrow North Channel of the Yangtze estuary, which was the only channel not mined by the Nationalists. Finally, the department obtained approval in principle from the Shanghai authorities to use shallow-draft vessels to ferry passengers to larger ships lying in the estuary. The American President Lines then chartered two LSTs for this purpose, which were to rendezvous with the President Lines' passenger ship *General Gordon* on March 20.[5]

The British embassy in Washington suggested on March 6 that the British representative in Peking try to secure agreement from the CPG on behalf of the United States and the United Kingdom for the proposed ferrying operation to and from the *General Gordon,* which would include British subjects as well as American citizens.[6] Hutchison, however, objected. He thought joint action with the Americans in making representations to the Chinese authorities "inappropriate and from point of view of our interests here inadvisable." Hutchison saw "very little basis for a common approach," since the British had recognized the Chinese government and hoped to maintain their consular posts in China, but the United States had withheld recognition from that government and was closing its consulates. Moreover, Britain wanted to bring in British subjects, and the United States wanted to take Americans out. Hutchison concluded that joint action would only reduce Britain's chances of getting favorable treatment for its citizens.[7]

Consul General Urquhart in Shanghai countered Hutchison's views with an assertion that "for our immediate purposes we have a large measure of common interest with Americans." He thought there were "practical reasons" for sharing American arrangements for getting as many British subjects away as possible.[8] In fact, the State Department had indicated a willingness to give British subjects priority among foreigners using American evacuation facilities. Thus the British embassy in Washington reported March 13: "State Department have instructed U.S. Consul General at Shanghai that in ferry arrangements he should 'so far as possible' give British evacuees preference next after Americans."[9] At the China desk in the Foreign Office, Franklin commented, "State Department have shown an extremely cooperative attitude as far as helping British subjects both in and out, in making their plans for the *General Gordon.*"[10] He cautioned, "We must avoid giving the Americans the impression we are not prepared to show solidarity because this might be harmful in our relations with the Chinese."[11] He thought that taking joint action on this matter with the Americans would neither improve nor spoil British chances of getting favorable treatment of British citizens. In any case, the Foreign Office instructed Hutchison to "make a very early approach to the Central People's Government" to request favorable consideration for the entry of the LSTs to Shanghai.[12]

On March 20 Hutchison reported to the Foreign Office that he had made oral representations to the Foreign Ministry about the LSTs and had been advised that the American President Lines should tell its troubles to the Foreign Nationals Department in Shanghai; however, the ministry had also promised to consider the question. Hutchison recommended that the APL make a further approach to the Foreign Nationals Department in Shanghai.[13]

On the day Hutchison made his report, the Shanghai authorities rejected the request APL had made several weeks earlier to use LSTs, whereupon the Department of State issued a press release denouncing this decision, which it attributed to the "unwarranted apprehension of local authorities that these vessels are not commercial ships."[14] The department also instructed American officials in Shanghai to seek reconsideration of the matter.

Consul General Urquhart objected to the State Department's line. He told the Foreign Office March 23 that "American broadcasts to the effect that the *Gordon* is being kept waiting to see if the Chinese authorities will 'reconsider' or 'change their minds' must make matters worse." He recommended that the Chinese decision not to allow the LSTs be accepted and a substitute be found for them.[15] Urquhart had just seen Huang Hua, who had told him that LSTs were irrevocably banned and that "responsibility lay with the Americans for the mess into which they had got themselves." Urquhart suggested to the Foreign Office that if an announcement had to be made, it should simply state that the Chinese authorities had maintained their refusal of naval-type LSTs but that permission was being sought for the use of commercial craft in their place.[16]

It was becoming increasingly clear that the Communist authorities now wanted to be rid of the onus of preventing foreigners from leaving Shanghai. Huang had told Urquhart during his March 23 interview that the Shanghai authorities were negotiating with Tientsin to permit a number of passengers to travel via that port.[17] Three days later the Shanghai press announced that "any person who has urgent reason for leaving the country may apply to the Foreign Affairs Bureau to have exit permit changed so as to leave via Tientsin."[18] On March 29 Urquhart reported a reversal in the attitude of the local authorities; they now seemed eager to furnish Chinese flagships to be used as ferries. Urquhart believed that Hutchison's representations in Peking "must have contributed powerfully to bringing about this favourable turn of events."[19] He later told the Foreign Office that the "Chinese now feel they allowed their resentment [against American handling of evacuation arrangements] to run too far"; this explained their present "relatively helpful attitude."[20]

Whatever the explanation for the change of attitude, new arrangements for evacuation progressed rapidly. On April 7 the Ministry of Foreign Affairs in Peking agreed in principle that a British ship, the *Anking*, and a Dutch vessel, the *Boissevain*, could pick up passengers in Shanghai, but details had to be arranged in Shanghai between shipping agents and the Foreign Nationals Department.[21] Accordingly, arrangements were made for a Chinese-owned river steamer to ferry evacuees, who numbered 300 Americans and more than 450 British subjects, to the *Anking*.[22]

But now a new complication arose. The Nationalists decided to mine the North Channel of the Yangtze estuary, on which the ferrying operation depended, asserting this mining was necessary to forestall a Communist attack on the Nationalist-held Chusan Islands southeast of Shanghai. The deployment of Communist air power in the vicinity of Shanghai had increased Nationalist fears of such an attack. Communist fighter planes were now commonly seen in the skies over Shanghai. On March 25 Urquhart had reported that "fighters patrol every fair day," as many as eight at a time.[23] On April 8 there was an air raid alert in Shanghai, which, according to Urquhart, "evoked prompt and impressive demonstration of jet fighter strength." Moreover, Urquhart told the Foreign Office, since March 16, the Communist military authorities had been in a position to tackle from the air local manifestations of Nationalist sea power.[24]

Despite Nationalist threats to mine the North Channel, the British commander in chief, Far East Station, based in Singapore, was not ready to adandon plans for a sea evacuation of Shanghai. On April 10 he radioed British naval vessels standing off the Yangtze estuary that an order might be given them to delay Nationalist mining of the North Channel long enough to ensure the withdrawal of British and other nationals from Shanghai.[25] Although he alerted his ships to the possible need to delay Nationalist minelayers through persuasion at sea, the commander in chief hoped mining could be delayed through American and British diplomatic persuasion. The Americans, however proved uncooperative. American Chargé Robert Strong was prepared to ask only for a twenty-four-hour delay in the mining of the North Channel. He was concerned the Communists might benefit from further delay and subsequently capture the Chusan Islands, opening the State Department to accusations by the political opposition that assistance had been given to the Communists.

For his part, the British naval liaison officer in Tamsui doubted that his personal approach to Admiral Kuei Yung-ching of the Nationalist navy "would produce any results since the Chinese Navy is convinced it is essential for the defense of the Chusans to block the north channel."[26] Indeed, nothing did come of his approach to Admiral Kuei; nor was the British Yangtze Patrol ever ordered to dissuade the Nationalist minelayers from carrying out their operations.

Instead, the evacuation scheme was abandoned, but not without a furor over who was responsible. A State Department press release of April 12 announced that because the Chinese Communists had not yet granted clearance to the ships to be used in the proposed evacuation of Shanghai and the Nationalists could no longer delay mining the North Channel, "all plans for an evacuation by sea from Shanghai at this time have been abandoned."[27] In Shanghai, Consul General Urquhart and the British assistant naval attaché castigated the U.S. announcement as dishonest, claiming that clearance for the *Anking* and the ferry operations had been approved by the Communists before the press release was issued. Urquhart went so far as to say the "Communists seem honest by contrast."[28]

The Shanghai authorities, too, wanted to set the record straight and did so in a manner that A.A.E. Franklin described as "an interesting example of Communist technique in matters of this sort." They called in British shipping agents in Shanghai. An official read and required them to sign a statement that expressed thanks on their behalf and on behalf of the prosepective passengers for the assistance received from the authorities, explained that the cancellation was apparently due to refusal by the Nationalists to extend the safe conduct, recorded the dates of approval of the operation and the grant of clearance for the ship, and thanked the authorities for their help and regretted that the project had fallen through.[29]

Even though the State Deartment's press release apparently came out after the final clearance of the *Anking* had been given in Shanghai, it is unlikely that the department was aware of this. In any event, Americans who wished to leave China were now permitted by the Shanghai authorities to depart via Tientsin. In the Foreign Office, Franklin's comment summed up the situation well: "The Communists have in this whole withdrawal business tended to adopt cat and mouse tactics, while safeguarding their position against charges they were deliberately bottling up foreigners in Shanghai."[30]

The Communists, of course, shared with the Nationalists responsibility for preventing foreigners from leaving Shanghai, and their reasons are not difficult to guess. By refusing to let foreigners leave Shanghai except by the only means the Nationalists could prevent, the Communists could direct the foreigners' wrath against the Nationalists and so pressure them to reduce their bombing and to lift the blockade. Foreign resentment against the Nationalists had become very strong in Shanghai, particularly after the February 6 bombing of public utilities in that city. The American-owned Shanghai Power Company, which supplied 100 percent of the power for Shanghai's water supply and sewage system, suffered direct hits causing twenty-seven deaths. According to company officials, the bombing destroyed 25 percent of the installed capacity of the power plant and totally shut it down.[31]

The February 6 bombing brought strong appeals for U.S. intervention with the Nationalists. On February 10, for example, the China Association asked Foreign Secretary Bevin to make urgent representations to the U.S. government to use its influence with the "Kuomintang regime in Formosa" to cease the bombing in Shanghai—bombing that had caused an "extremely critical" situation.[32] The American

Chamber of Commerce in Shanghai had already telegraphed appeals to the State Department and the American Chamber of Commerce in Washington for intervention with the Chinese Nationalists to stop the bombing. Additionally, "all foreign civilian, religious and national organizations had addressed an appeal to the United Nations with a view to bringing pressure to bear on the Kuomintang regime in Formosa to stop indiscriminate bombing of Shanghai."[33]

The February 6 bombing did bring an official American protest to the Nationalist government against the "deliberate aerial attacks on American-owned property in Shanghai which have caused extensive damage and endangered American lives."[34] This protest was drafted by Philip Sprouse, who sent it for clearance to Merchant on February 7 with a strongly worded memorandum setting forth its rationale.

> The pace and pattern of recent Chinese Air Force raids on Shanghai, culminating in the raid of February 6 on Shanghai with heavy damage to the American-owned Shanghai Power Company and considerable damage to property of the American-owned Standard-Vacuum Oil Company, together with heavy casualties among the Chinese population, are doing definite harm to American interests, both tangible and intangible. . . . there is the important problem of the inevitable increase in anti-American feeling among the Chinese population of cities which are being bombed by American planes and killed and injured by American bombs carried by planes using American gasoline. The Chinese Communists will need little propaganda effort for their part to stir up feeling.[35]

Sprouse also made the point that the Nationalists' bombing would not really affect the outcome of the Nationalist-Communist conflict. He seemed to be particularly incensed that the Nationalists, who were now carrying out air raids on public utilities, had during their long retreat before the Communist armies, consistently failed to destroy military equipment they left behind. They had failed to demolish even the largest arsenal in China at Mukden. Moreover, "the Chinese Government did not destroy public utilities in any of the cities which they evacuated and for them now to do so from the air, as they are doing at Shanghai with American-owned property cannot be excused or justified in any way."[36]

Chargé Robert Strong duly delivered the U.S. protest in Taipei, but the State Department found the Nationalists' reply unsatisfactory. Acheson described it as "telling us to go to hell with our protest on the Shanghai bombings."[37] In another memorandum to Merchant, the exasperated Sprouse found it "incredible . . . that we permit the Chinese Government brazenly to do the damage to our position in China that it is doing."[38]

While Acheson and the State Department were privately and publicly deploring the Nationalist bombing raids, Communist Chinese officials were accusing the United States of direct responsibility for them, even to the point of manning the bombers. Thus Commander in chief Chu Teh, the highest ranking military officer in the People's Republic, declared in a speech delivered in Peking on February 28: "The Kuomintang gangsters are using war vessels supplied by America to blockade the China coast; using U.S. aeroplanes to bomb Chinese cities and using American and Japanese military personnel sent by American occupationists to take part in bombing and other military actions."[39]

Foreigners, as well as Chinese, were susceptible to allegations that the bombing represented U.S. policy. For example, in a telegram to the Foriegn Office, Hutchison suggested that "however hopeless such an approach may be," the Foreign Office should ask the U.S. government "whether their protestations of friendship with the Chinese people" were consistent "with support of a policy of bombarding utilities virtually defenceless from the air."[40]

Although the United States had protested to the Nationalists against their bombing of Shanghai, it was unwilling to intervene with them to ease their blockade. As we have seen, the United States had differed with the United Kingdom since the previous summer in its attitude toward the blockade, and it was not now prepared to change its hands-off policy. This position was spelled out in a memorandum to Acheson from Assistant Secretary Butterworth dated March 27 regarding an anticipated British overture for U.S. cooperation in a British attempt to break the blockade. The memorandum recalled that on October 1 President Truman had informed Acting Secretary James Webb that he wished "the blockade to be effective."[41] Butterworth recommended that "the British Ambassador be informed of the President's decision . . . and of the Department's belief that under present conditions no attempt should be made to obtain a reversal or modification of this decision."[42]

Although keeping foreigners who wished to leave China bottled up in Shanghai contributed to the objectives of the Communists, they also paid a price for it in foreign ill will. As Urquhart indicated to the Foreign Office, they may have changed their policy because, by the end of March, the price was getting too high. However, there was undoubtedly another reason for the change—the buildup of their own air power in the Shanghai area. The Communists had accumulated sufficient air and naval strength in the area to overcome the military weakness that had made them look powerless in the face of the Nationalists' blockade and bombings. In short, the military reasons for bringing foreign pressure to bear against the Nationalists' bombing and blockade had largely disappeared.[43]

Whatever the reasons for the change in policy, the Communist authorities' decision to allow foreigners in Shanghai to proceed to Tientsin for departure from China permitted the United States to complete the implementation of its policy of official disengagement from the People's Republic of China. On the morning of April 20 a special train left Shanghai for Tientsin with passengers booked to depart on the *General Gordon* from Taku Bar (the port for Tientsin). Joined by other foreigners who had made their way to Tientsin by regularly scheduled passenger trains, the embarking passengers numbered almost one thousand, including "all official American personnel."[44]

Disengagement from the China mainland was now complete, and official American personnel were not likely to return until the CPG mended its ways. This, at any rate, had been the clear implication of Acheson's speech to the Commonwealth Club of California on March 15. Aiming his remarks at the Chinese people, Acheson had said that the representatives of the United States were leaving them "not by any wish of ours" but because "the normal and accepted standards of international conduct have not been observed by the Chinese Communist authorities in their treatment of our representatives and because they have, in effect, even been summarily ejected from their own offices in Peiping. Under such conditions, our representatives could not fulfill their normal functions. We regret this leaving by our people but our Chinese friends will understand where the responsibility lies."[45]

Official disengagement from the People's Republic did not mean complete disengagement, however. An American presence remained, and this was in accord with U.S. government policy. The State Department was still prepared to issue passports on a selective basis to American citizens "desiring to go to Communist areas in China." According to a letter of May 9, 1950, signed by Philip Sprouse and cleared by the redoubtable Ruth Shipley, chief of the Passport Division, each passport application would be examined closely, and decisions would be based on "the merits of each case and the situation existing in the area to which the applicant desired to proceed." Though the

Department of State considered it "inadvisable for dependents and nonessential American citizens to go to China," it did "not wish to interpose objections to the return to China of essential replacement personnel of established American mission and business organizations."[46]

22

An American Probe

In an effort to ensure that the CPG understood the reasons the United States was pulling its officials out of China, and to probe Peking's attitude toward the United States, the State Department instructed Consul General Clubb on March 22 to endeavor to arrange an "informal interview with Chou En-lai" or with the highest available official, making sure that the Chinese did not construe his request as a preliminary move toward recognition or a sign of U.S. weakness under pressure. Clubb was to point out that the U.S. public could not understand such measures as the Communists' refusal to permit the departure of American officials and businessmen from Shanghai, the continued detention of Smith and Bender, the previous detention and ill-treatment of the U.S. consular staff in Mukden, and the seizure of U.S. consular properties in Peiping." He was to emphasize the importance of such measures in determining the attitude of the U.S. public and government toward the CPG. Clubb was instructed to find out what the views of the Communist authorities were and what their attitude toward the West, particularly the United States, was.[1]

Some two months earlier, shortly after the seizure of the U.S. consulate building in Peking, Clubb had recommended to the State Department that he be authorized to seek an interview with the Foreign Ministry some time after Mao's return from Moscow. Clubb wanted authorization to say that the U.S. government assumed and expected that the requisitioned U.S. consular property would be returned at an early date and that "upon such restitution American

Government will be prepared turn its attention again to question recognition." At that time Clubb thought several factors—including the strong U.S. reaction to the property seizure, which, in Clubb's view, exceeded Chinese expectations; disillusionment with negotiations in Moscow, which Clubb thought probable; and the increasingly desperate economic situation of China—might persuade the Communists to consider restitution. Underlying Clubb's request was his conviction that "Communists desire American recognition for both political and economic reasons."[2] The State Department informed Clubb that it was considering his suggestion that the Communist authorities be approached on the question of restitution of the American consular property but cautioned him against giving any indication that restitution "would in any way affect question recognition."[3]

Clubb's belief that Mao and Chou might well return from Moscow disillusioned was not dampened by the conclusion of the Sino-Soviet Treaty on February 14. Clubb reported on February 20: "Scattered Chinese reaction thus far unfavorable. They view alliance as constituting crystallization situation to their disadvantage. . . . Quite apart from fact loan is pitifully short of China's needs, is basic fact that poverty-stricken China must repay loan together with interest."[4] Clubb had expected the CCP leaders to be disillusioned with their negotiations in Moscow, and now he was reporting corroboration of a sort for this opinion. Thus it is perhaps not surprising that on February 23 he informed the State Department that he thought the return of the two Communist leaders from Moscow might occasion a feeler from the Chinese side with a view to improvement of Sino-American relations.[5] No such feeler was ever forthcoming, however; nor was there any tangible evidence that Mao and Chou were disillusioned with the outcome of their prolonged negotiations in Moscow or that they desired an improvement in Sino-American relations. In fact, as already noted, both their own public statements and the PRC media indicated the opposite.

In assessing the desire of the CCP leadership for U.S. recognition, Clubb, like Ambassador Stuart, tended to overestimate the importance of the economic factor.[6] Thus Clubb did not take very seriously a statement recently made to him by Chang Tung-sun, a leader of the Democratic League in Peking and a member of the People's Political Consultative Conference formed under CCP leadership. Chang had warned, according to Clubb's report, that "relaxation of Sino-American relations can come only from either amelioration of American-Soviet relations or American victory in war, for economic competence will not be permitted to overweigh the political for Communists." Another informant, Wang Shu-chih, had opined that "the desire to get rid of foreign influence and even foreigners despite the conflict of this desire with China's economic aspirations" was one of the "factors dominating political scene."[7]

Pursuant to the State Department's instructions, Clubb on April 12 had an interview with "one Lin believed to be head of Australian American Affairs Section" of the Foreign Ministry. After providing Lin with "a sketch of political field," Clubb gave "a few examples of outstanding questions at issue," for example, the Smith-Bender case.[8] Lin characterized Clubb's representations as "worthless talk" and declared that, as long as the United States continued to support Chiang Kai-shek, talk of working toward an improvement in the general situation was ridiculous.

Commenting on this disappointing interview, Clubb put his finger on a significant difference between Peking and Washington in their approach to negotiation of the issues that separated them. Thus, he told the State Department: "The Chinese Communist policy . . . seemingly confirmed by the present instance is patently that if general problem of 'support to Chiang Kai-shek' is cleared up by recognition of Peking regime there might be approach to solution of particular problems otherwise not. My own approach was based upon concept that solution of particular problems might be antecedent to an amelioration of the general situation."[9] The Communists had consistently held that U.S. problems could not be negotiated, or even discussed, in the absence of diplomatic relations—even during the period when no central Communist government existed. On the other hand, as long as the Communist authorities refused to discuss such problems, let alone ameliorate them, it was difficult for the United States to recognize a Communist government. In a conversation with Huang Hua nearly a year earlier, Philip Fugh had made this point. When Huang said that problems such as the Ward case could easily be cleared up as soon as normal diplomatic relations had been established, Fugh had pointed out that such occurrences only made the establishment of friendly relations the more difficult.[10]

It was, of course, clearly in the Communists' interest to bring an end to any relationship between the United States and the Nationalist government, and it is thus not surprising, perhaps, that they should make a U.S. break with the Nationalists a condition for conciliating U.S. grievances. What is surprising, however, if the Communists had any serious interest in promoting such a break, is that they did so much to antagonize U.S. official and public opinion and to raise doubts that a shift in U.S. poicy would reap any benefits for the United States or, indeed, lessen Peking's hostility.

Although the United States had not broken with Chiang and the Nationalists, it had sent clear signals at the highest levels that it had written off the Nationalists and would not assist them against a PLA attack on Formosa, an attack that both the United States and the People's Republic assumed would be successfully carried out during the year. Despite this signal, Peking had seized U.S. consular property in the full knowledge that the seizure would drive U.S. officials from China and had concluded a defense pact with the Soviet Union aimed indirectly, but obviously, at the United States. Moreover, its treatment of the British since the United Kingdom's recognition of the People's Republic had provided no encouragement whatsoever to those in the United States who might favor agreeing to the Communists' terms of recognition first and negotiations second. British recognition had brought neither diplomatic relations nor an amelioration of conditions for British business; nor had it made any perceptible impact on Sino-Soviet relations, which now appeared to be closer than ever.

Peking's treatment of the United Kingdom had served only to warn off other countries. Thus Secretary Acheson told two businessmen with interests in China on March 24 that no action was being taken on recognition of the People's Republic partly because "the nations that have recognized to date appear to be in little if any better position than those who have not."[11] Earlier in the month the American ambassador to Canada, Laurence Steinhardt, had reported: "The delay in recognition has not been caused as much by the attitude of the United States as by the embarrassment accorded to the United Kingdom and the new Asiatic members of the Commonwealth after their efforts to exchange representatives with the Chinese Government. Canadian officials have appeared relieved that Canada was not placed in a similar awkward position."[12]

Despite their disagreement with many aspects of U.S. China policy, it is significant that officials in the Far Eastern Department of the Foreign Office working on Chinese affairs placed major responsibility for the impasse between the United States and the People's Republic on Peking. Thus, in a minute summarizing a lengthy discussion between these officials and British Consul General Urquhart upon his return to London in the summer of 1950, Franklin asserted that

the Chinese Communists have not and never had had any serious intention of establishing normal relations with the United States. Their attitude over the last year or so has made this quite clear. To prevent any risk of relations becoming more normal, they locked up the American Consul General in Mukden, subsequently commandeered the military compound of the Embassy in Peking and when the State Department tried to establish some kind of informal contact through their Consul General in Peking prior to his departure, the Chinese, for reasons best known to themselves, refused to enter into any kind of discussion. I think it is quite clear that over the last year and a half the Chinese Communists were fully aware that had they really wanted to establish some kind of relations with the Americans, it would have been possible for them to do so.[13]

23

Mutual Sino-British Dissatisfaction

Just before the opening of "ministerial conversations" between Acheson and Bevin in London on May 9, the British received the Chinese reply to the statements of British policy Hutchison had conveyed to Chang Han-fu on March 17. It was an unhappy one and may have influenced the gloomy assessment of Sino-British relations Bevin gave Acheson. According to an American report, Bevin expressed "strong doubts about value of present U.K. position, both from general political standpoint, commercial standpoint, and effect on Southeast Asia"; but he emphasized that British policy was "not reversible," and he thought the future might prove it to have been wise.[1]

In their reply the Chinese had expressed dissatisfaction with Britain's continued abstention from voting in organs of the United Nations on the "question of China's right of representation." The British government, Chang told Hutchison, "should show with factual deeds" that it had "definitely severed diplomatic relations with the remnant clique of the Kuomintang reactionaries."[2]

The CPG also found unsatisfactory the British attitude toward Chinese national property in Hong Kong. This question had primarily to do with the disposition of some seventy commercial aircraft located in Hong Kong, which belonged to two Chinese airlines—China National Aviation Corporation (CNAC) and Central Air Transport Corporation (CATC). On November 9, 1949, the general managers and staff members of the two airlines had flown to Peking from Hong Kong and issued a statement breaking off relations with the Nationalist government and offering their services to the CPG. NCNA played the story as an "uprising of the 4000 personnel" of the two companies.[3] Three days later, Premier Chou En-lai declared that the two airlines were "properties of the People's Republic of China."[4] However, following the defection of the airlines' staff, the Nationalist government, supported by the United States, had asked the Hong Kong authorities to impound the aircraft and equipment still in Hong Kong to prevent their transfer to the Communists. On December 10, it was announced in Taipei that both CNAC and CATC had been sold to Civil Air Transport, an airline headed by General Claire Chennault of World War II Flying Tigers fame, and heavily subsidized by the U.S. Central Intelligence Agency.[5] The question of ownership of the CNAC and CATC assets in Hong Kong then came before the courts.[6]

According to General Chennault's widow, Anna, this "brilliant capture-by-purchase" of the entire fleet of seventy-one C-46, C-47, C-54, and Convair transport planes, had in the general's view saved Formosa, since it had prevented their being used in a Communist attack on that island. But the only evidence Mrs. Chennault adduces for this judgment is that the "General was sure that if he were the Communists and had got the planes, this is exactly what he would have done."[7]

Regardless of what use the CPG might or might not have made of these planes, it was incensed that the British government, even after recognizing the CPG, would not release them. The British had refused because the question of ownership was before the courts. Chang claimed that by impeding the aircraft from "taking off and returning to China" and by not "fully protecting the aircraft" (seven had been sabotaged on the airfield in Hong Kong), the British had not yet acknowledged full responsibility for Chinese property and the CPG's right to administer this property.[8]

Chang's presentation of the CPG's views reminded Dening in the Foreign Office "of innumerable communications we used to receive from the Japanese before the war," and the memory made him think the Chinese would be tough. In a memorandum to Sir William Strang, he recommended that the British government be in no hurry to reply and that, when it did, "all the contentions in the Chinese communication" be rejected. To avoid the appearance of "acting at American instance or dictation," Dening did not want to reply to the Chinese "while the Americans are in London." On the other hand, he wanted to avoid any suggestion "that we are too eager or that we are ready to appease them." Ernest Bevin saw and agreed with Dening's memorandum to Strang.[9]

With the Americans safely out of London after the ministerial meetings, the Foreign Office was prepared to reply to the CPG's criticism. Dening's tough line was reflected in the instructions sent to Hutchison, who was to pass it out that His Majesty's government had

clearly stated that they would welcome the appearance of representatives of the Central People's Government in all organs of the United Nations as soon as a majority of the members of those organs are disposed in favor of that Government's admission. . . . In this connexion His Majesty's Government were greatly surprised that the Central People's Government in commenting on this question should have made no reference to the steps which His Majesty's Government have taken to persuade other members of the [Security] Council to cast their votes in favour of the admission of the Central People's Government and thus secure an early decision in that body.

As already indicated . . . the recognition by His Majesty's Government produces the effect in British Law that the right to exercise control of Chinese State property now falls to the Central People's Government. His Majesty's Government consider it necessary to restate their view that where the ownership of property in British territory is in dispute, title can only be established by recourse to the Courts. This principle clearly applies in the case of the C.N.A.C.-C.A.T.C. Aircraft since the ownership of these aircraft is in dispute. . . . His Majesty's Government are quite unable to accept the Central People's Government's contention that the Government of Hong Kong afforded inadequate protection to these aircraft.[10]

Hutchison was to reiterate the British government's desire to establish diplomatic relations with the CPG so questions of substance could be satisfactorily and expeditiously resolved. Clearly, the Foreign Office had strayed from the position it had adopted when Hutchison first went to Peking, that is, that he should avoid discussing substantive matters.[11] Now, Franklin worried that such discussions might be contributing to a delay in the establishment of diplomatic relations. In a minute dated May 22, he commented: "The Chinese may well use it [the existing unofficial channel] as a means to air their various grievances while at the same time continuing to refuse to establish, or delay the establishment, of diplomatic relations. On balance I am rather inclined to feel that the advantages of any such arrangement will be on the Chinese side and that until we establish diplomatic relations we will not get much satisfaction from the Chinese by means of these informal communications."[12]

The British had recognized the People's Republic in the expectation that diplomatic relations would follow automatically, but four months later the Chinese were still denying them such relations. Now the price for diplomatic relations seemed to be resolution of the issues between them to the Communists' satisfaction. Hutchison had already conveyed to the Foreign Office his "impression . . . that the Chinese will make no progress towards the establishment of formal diplomatic relations until we vote in U.N. in favour of their delegates and until it is clear that they will be able to take possession of their aircraft."[13]

Since Hutchison saw the Chinese and British positions on these two issues as "inevitably widely different," he advocated an effort to "bridge the gulf" and the avoidance of "any action or statement which might accentuate the present difference in our points of view." Such a course might ensure the continuation of the "present tacit and undefined working arrangement" between himself and the Foreign Ministry.[14] In this light he asked the Foreign Office whether his instructions took sufficient account of the Chinese point of view, that is, of the "great practical importance [the Chinese] attach both to control of Chinese aircraft in Hong Kong and to active participation in the U.N."[15] In a subsequent message, Hutchison painted a picture of British policy as he thought the Chinese probably saw it. The Chinese government, he said, "expect our policy to be actively pro-American (and consequently thoroughly pro-KMT) and basically opposed to the People's Government, and they tend to interpret our actions in the light of that expectation."[16]

Despite Hutchison's belief that Chinese perceptions made it necessary for the British to try to bridge the gulf and avoid actions that would further antagonize the Chinese, Franklin in the Foreign Office was skeptical. He took the view that the "Chinese know exactly where they stand, i.e., on the Soviet side, and where we stand—on the other side." To talk of friendly attitudes was absurd; the question was whether, in spite of conflicting views and interests diplomatic relations could be established.[17]

Foreign Secretary Bevin, like Franklin, was unconvinced by Hutchison's arguments and in a telegram of June 6 told Hutchison:

"There can be no doubt that it is precisely the failure of the Chinese Government to establish normal relations which restrains other Member States from extending recognition to them or taking any steps to facilitate their admission to the United Nations. I have no doubt that the number of nations according *de jure* recognition to the Chinese Government would have been substantially greater by now had that Government shown more readiness to establish relations with those countries which have already accorded recognition. . . . I should like you to make this point at the time you deliver the reply."[18] Bevin further instructed Hutchison "to make the point that it is the United Kingdom alone which has made serious efforts to secure the necessary number of votes to enable the Central People's Government representative to take his place in the Security Council."[19]

Bevin had still more to say in defense of British actions—in this case his own. The Chinese press had published on May 28 an NCNA item attacking a statement Bevin had made on the Sino-British negotiations during a House of Commons debate May 24. It accused Bevin of adopting "an extremely evasive attitude towards the important questions" of Chinese representation in the United Nations and Chinese state property in Hong Kong. Calling Bevin's statement "extremely unfriendly towards China," NCNA claimed that he "went so far as to say that to establish diplomatic relations with China was an 'unpleasant decision.'"[20] Bevin now instructed Hutchison to say, but only if Chang raised the subject, that reports of Bevin's speech as published in China were inaccurate. Hutchison was then to "point out that the Secretary of State's position was made much more difficult by the unilateral decision of the Chinese Government to publish, the day before the Debate, their version of the exchanges which had been going on between our Governments, and . . . to press home the point that incidents such as this, the unilateral requisitioning of our barrack property in Peking and the failure after many months to establish normal relations have all aroused criticism in the country which was reflected in the Debate in question."[21] As to Bevin's reference to an "awkward decision" (not "unpleasant decision" as stated in the Chinese press), Hutchison was to say that it had clearly been made in the context of the United Kingdom's having made "a decision different from that of Commonwealth and other friendly Governments," for which the British had "received no credit from the Chinese."[22] Bevin's point was well taken. Far from giving the British credit, Peking was accusing them of taking orders from Wall Street.[23]

To be accused of following the American lead, when in fact their policy had diverged widely from that of the Americans, did not sit well with the British and hardly made them more amenable to Chinese arguments. An interesting example of British reaction is provided in a conversation former Minister of State Hector McNeil had with Soviet Ambassador George N. Zaroubin in London May 19. Zaroubin raised the subject of the current Anglo-Chinese negotiations, saying that the British attitude was at first logically based but that now the British were simply reflecting American opinion. In response, McNeil told Zaroubin the United Kingdom had already strained its relationship with the United States over policy toward China. Instead of receiving China's gratitude for this "courageous and morally correct step," Britain had been subjected to snubs and propaganda without parallel in the relationship of two major powers. Britain could do nothing further for China until China had taken "the logical step of exchanging diplomatic representatives with us." McNeil went on to complain that Britain "had taken a step towards China," but China "had taken no step towards us."[24]

In this mood, even when the Foreign Office decided to change its policy on Chinese representation in the United Naions in a way that would be favorable to the People's Republic, it did not wish to appear to be yielding to Chinese arguments and propaganda. Thus Hutchison was instructed to seek an interview with Chang Han-fu and reply to the Chinese arguments on Chinese representation without revealing that the British government intended to vote for seating of the PRC representative at the June 19 meeting of UNICEF. Hutchison was "not to be apologetic to the Chinese and not to disclose in advance an intention to vote for the Chinese on June 19th."[25]

Hutchison objected to withholding information on the change in British policy. He argued that not to give the Chinese advance notice would be to "miss an opportunity to make a friendly and useful gesture that would cost nothing." Moreover, quite understandably, Hutchison did not want to rehash with Chang the arguments for the old policy just before it was to be reversed.[26]

But Hutchison's recommendation was rejected, and he proceeded as instructed to communicate the British positions to Chang at their meeting on June 18. Predictably, Chang was unmoved. Although he said he would report the British views to his government, it was clear he felt nothing had changed. When Hutchison expressed hope that the way was now clear for further steps forward in the negotiations, Chang replied that the issue was really quite simple: it was a matter of demonstrating Britain had really severed relations with the Kuomintang remnants. The responsibility for the delay in establishing relations was the United Kingdom's. Nor was Chang willing to give the British credit for trying. According to Hutchison, he "passed over in silence" Hutchison's reference to British lobbying efforts in the U.N.[27]

Taken together, Clubb's last interview in the Foreign Ministry in April and Hutchison's latest session with Chang clearly defined the CPG's attitude: refuse to negotiate the issues in the absence of recognition; after recognition, refuse to establish diplomatic relations without a satisfactory resolution of the issues. It is difficult to see what advantage recognition had brought the United Kingdom, other than the opportunity to discuss the issues. As we have seen, however, some in the Foreign Office regarded such discussions in the absence of diplomatic relations as simply an opportunity for the Chinese to eat their cake and have it too. On the other hand, recognition probably did give British diplomatic and consular officials in China at least marginally more access to, and effectiveness with, Chinese officials in making representations on behalf of British business and other interests in China than they would have had in the absence of recognition.

24
Foreign Business in a Squeeze

Pursuant to a cabinet decision, the Foreign Office instructed Hutchison on May 18 to take up the plight of British business in China with the Ministry of Foreign Affairs and to do so before an upcoming foreign affairs debate in the House of Commons.[1] The Foreign Office wanted not only to call attention to the hardships of the British community but also to point out the mutual advantage to China and Britain of British firms' remaining in China. Accordingly, Hutchison was instructed to warn that many firms had reached the end of their resources "both inside and outside of China" and saw "no alternative to closing down." He was then to ask the CPG to consider how it could "mitigate the effects of present circumstances on United Kingdom enterprises in China." Hutchison was to offer some suggestions for Chinese consideration; the CPG might, for example, make loans available at reasonable rates of interest to firms whose liquid assets were exhausted; it might strictly enforce labor laws permitting discharge of redundant employees; and it might allow some plants to close down until conditions justified resumption of their operations.

Hutchison was also to seek an amelioration of the "personal position of United Kingdom subjects." He was to ask that they be allowed freedom of movement within China, that they be allowed to leave the country without delay, and that those wishing to enter China to relieve staff of British companies be allowed to do so. The Chinese were to be asked to assure full protection of the persons and property of British subjects managing U.K. enterprises.[2]

There had been some nasty incidents of physical assault and detention of managers by disgruntled workers, with little or no intervention by the local authorities, to which Hutchison had already called attention in a letter sent May 2 to Vice-Minister Chang. He had complained that such incidents "render impossible proper relations between British employers and their Chinese employees" and had suggested that the authorities might wish to "have these incidents thoroughly investigated."[3] In the Foreign Office, Nigel Trench thought Hutchison's letter could hardly be called a protest; he noted that Hutchison had not followed the Foreign Office's suggestion that he point out to the Chinese authorities that they had previously promised to protect the persons and properties of foreigners. In Trench's opinion, normal practice (certainly normal practice for Communist governments) would be to demand punishment of the perpetrators of the violence.[4]

Protest or not, Hutchison appears to have obtained action in the case of at least one victim of labor violence, a Mr. Langford, the manager of the Shanghai Ice and Cold Storage Company. Hutchison had called his case to the attention of the Foreign Ministry on May 8, after Langford had been forcibly detained in his office overnight.[5] A Ministry of Commerce representative had then come down to Shanghai to investigate, and the result had been private assurances to Langford from the police. Attributing this development to Hutchison's "intervention in Peking," Urquhart commented: "We all feel there is little to be done through the Foreign Affairs Bureau here which under Huang Hua seems obstinately hostile."[6] Two days later Urquhart reported that Langford was transferring his office as quickly as possible to Tientsin, ostensibly to supervise his company's business there but actually as a first step toward working his way out of China.[7]

In another case, a British victim of labor violence reported that the Labor Bureau had called him in and expressed regret for the treatment he had received at the hands of the workers. The bureau gave assurances it would not recur. He subsequently learned from his staff that the culprits had been punished after a thorough investigation. This procedure was gratifying to the victim, but it in no way improved the financial prospects of his company, which was consuming capital and had little prospect of recovery.[8]

Those British companies in China that were seeking a way to liquidate and get out had to be discreet about it. Urquhart addressed this problem in a message to the Foreign Office May 27, in which he claimed to have "consistently opposed any proposal which might stimulate our people to pull out." He went on to say: "Whereas Americans have pressed for exit permits regardless of prospects of success with result that a number can be described as being held for one reason or another against their wish, the British generally have refrained from trying to force the issue prematurely."[9] Urquhart cited the British Chamber of Commerce as the source of an estimate that "over twenty firms would close down forthwith if they considered it possible to do so."[10]

Though British firms may have been more discreet about their desire to leave China than American firms, it was plain (as Urquhart's statement implied) that many were staying against their will just as were American companies. For example, one of the largest, the British-American Tobacco Company wanted to cut its losses, get its European staff out of China, and hand over the business to the Chinese, but the People's Tax Bureau in Shanghai told the company representatives there that it was "their duty to continue." In the Foreign Office, Trench commented that when the Chinese authorities say that private enterprise has a part to play in the economy they mean that private enterprise has an obligation to play such a part, like it or not.[11]

Despite the many problems British businessmen faced in China, the chairman of the British Chamber of Commerce in Shanghai, John Keswick, was able to see some favorable omens. In a speech delivered June 7 he noted that since the protests sent by various Shanghai organizations to the United Nations in February, there had been no serious bombings. In a joking reference to the U.S. protest in Taipei, he said: "It was perhaps fortunate that the power company is an American corporation." More recently (within the week in fact), there had been "the first signs, however small, of a start of a period of inflation as opposed to deflation." He hoped that "this slight indication of change" would not be swamped, "as we all may be, by the economics of the New Deomocracy." Noting the exodus of a great many of our American friends and a large reduction in the scope of their business activity in this city," Keswick optimistically hoped that they would "come back."[12]

If there had been a proportionately larger exodus of American businessmen than British, as was probably the case, it had not been because they had received worse treatment at the hands of the Communist authorities. Their experiences appeared to have been roughly the same as those of their British colleagues, but they tended to be less sanguine than the British about the prospects of doing business in China.[13] Moreover, the departure of all U.S. official personnel had caused them some anxiety. When the announcement of the U.S. official withdrawal was made in January, a number of American firms decided to pull out. Thus on January 25 Consul General McConaughy reported from Shanghai that most representatives of American firms with a number of local employees "have been reluctant up till now force issue by any move toward closure with its certain prospects of threats, intimidation, tedious fruitless negotiations, lock-ins, vain appeals police protection, etc. Imminent closure CONGEN brings issue to head, since representatives received modicum comfort knowledge they could pour their troubles out to CONGEN and aprise their head offices actual state affairs through safe channel communications."[14]

Like their British opposite numbers, American businessmen found liquidating their businesses and getting out of the People's Republic no easy matter. For example, when the local manager of the Everett Steamship Corporation attempted to close the company's Shanghai office, eighteen local employees agreed to the plan, but four strongly opposed it. These four were union leaders, who demanded that the office remain open with full salaries for all, even though the company was doing no business because of the blockade. The union leaders were apparently afraid that Everett's closing would set a precedent that would be followed by other steamship companies.[15]

Although authorities of the Shanghai Public Utility Bureau asserted that private ownership of public utilities was against Communist tenets and that transfer of the American-owned Shanghai telephone company was just a matter of time, they were in no hurry to take over the company and allow its American employees to depart. A telegram from the U.S. consulate general on February 5 reporting this situation listed three reasons for this attitude: "(1) Better possibility of extracting

US funds for support of telephone company if nominal ownership remains American; (2) Foreign technical supervision for maintenance and replacement operations still required; (3) American ownership may afford some measure protection against Nationalist bombing."[16] The conditions under which the company was forced to operate make clear, however, why its New York directors wanted to pull out. The Shanghai authorities had persistently refused essential rate hikes, while imposing a 50 percent telephone use tax. At the same time, they had virtually robbed the company's officials of any management power by making it compulsory to transfer all its bank accounts to the People's Bank and insisting that all disbursements be approved by Chinese officials.[17]

Some weeks later when a representative of the Shanghai Power Company and the president of International General Electric Company called on Secretary Acheson to discuss the Shanghai situation, a State Department officer asked them which of the three reasons listed above they believed to be most responsible for the Communist detention of key American businessmen. They replied that probably all three motives were represented, but differed in particular circumstances. In the case of the Shanghai Power Company the motive was probably security against bombings; in the case of the International General Electric Company, the reason may have been the need for continuation of remittances as a measure to solve the social labor problem.[18]

Another company experiencing difficulties getting its American executives out was Standard-Vacuum Oil Company. In a letter to Secretary Acheson dated May 5, its board chairman stated that the company had instructed its five remaining executives in China to apply for exit permits at the time the company learned that the all U.S. diplomatic and consular representatives were being withdrawn from China, but only one of them was able to leave on the SS *General Gordon* on April 30, when the last of the official U.S. personnel left. The letter continued: "From previous action taken by the union of our Chinese personnel, as well as the labor unions of other American companies in China, in holding or detaining business executives unlawfully at their own offices or other places, it became evident to us that the personal safety of our American and non-Chinese personnel in China depended upon our meeting exorbitant and unlawful financial demands made upon the Company."[19]

By May the overriding reason for preventing the departure of American and British businessmen whose companies (or banks) wished to close down their China operations appears to have been financial. The CPG wanted to obtain the maximum amount of money possible from the companies concerned. Upon his return to the United States, Consul General Walter McConaughy reported to the State Department that the "last word" from U.S. businessmen in Shanghai was a request that the "U.S. Government prevent funds from being remitted to China from the United States," "to prevent their being held for ransom as hostages."[20]

Part III
IMPACT OF
THE KOREAN WAR

25

The Neutralization of Formosa

On April 27, 1950, the Nationalists abandoned the large island of Hainan off the south coast of China, after battling local and invading Communist forces for about ten days. On May 16 they completed the evacuation of the Chusan Islands, which had been an important base for their sea and air blockade of the coast around Shanghai.[1] These events plunged Nationalist morale to a new low, and made the fall of Formosa itself seem imminent. From Taipei, U.S. Chargé Robert Strong reported May 17: "In opinion of attachés and myself fate of Taiwan sealed, Communist attack can occur between June 15 and end July. . . . we feel reduction of American staffs to be matter of greater urgency than would have been case had effort been made defend Chusans. We cannot determine how soon Communist air activity over Taiwan will begin, but it is possible from now on."[2]

Strong went on to make a number of recommendations, including reduction of official personnel, issuance of "formal warning to all Americans leave Taiwan soonest," and removal of cryptographic machines. He told the State Department that he would "have all documentation necessary for transfer to British Consul prepared prior to June 15" and would "establish internal and external evacuation units."[3] The department replied on May 26 that it concurred with Strong's view that "early and gradual" measures should be the basis of the evacuation plan and authorized him to "make all necessary arrangements" with the British on a confidential basis for turnover in case of need.[4]

Several days later Strong took the matter up with British Consul Biggs, who reported to the Foreign Office that American officials would not be withdrawn until Communist capture of Formosa seemed certain or imminent, and that they would probably be taken off by warships. Meanwhile, U.S. official staff would be gradually reduced, and a warning would be issued to American citizens if an invasion appeared imminent.[5]

Convinced as he was that Taiwan's doom was sealed, Strong lost no time in paring down the small U.S. official establishment there and otherwise preparing for complete departure. The results were described thus by Karl Rankin, Strong's successor:

When I arrived in Formosa on August 10, 1950, I found our Foreign Service establishment here in the last stage of decay. It had never been designated as an embassy, but was simply a consular office in which the principal officer was also chargé d'affaires, a.i. The staff had been reduced even below what is usually considered a "skeleton," much of the best office and household equipment had been shipped out to save it from the expected communist invasion, while the buildings and remaining equipment were in a sad state of repair. Files had been largely destroyed and operations were virtually limited to keeping evacuation plans up-to-date and exchanging current information with the Department to the limited extent permitted by the tiny staff and other sketchy facilities.[6]

While preparations for a U.S. departure from Formosa were being speeded up, a small group of high-level officials in the State Department was considering a radical change in policy. Such a change had been proposed in a memorandum dated May 18 from John Foster Dulles, who had become a consultant to the secretary of state only a few weeks earlier, to Assistant Scretary of State for Far Eastern Affairs Dean Rusk, and to Paul Nitze, director of the Policy Planning Staff at the State Department. Dulles later sent a copy of his memorandum to Undersecretary of State Webb.

In Dulles's view, the loss of China to the Communists had shifted the balance of power in the world in favor of the Soviet Union and "to the disfavor of the United States." If U.S. conduct continued to show the world a disposition to allow "doubtful areas" (that is, those outside of the Americas and the North Atlantic Treaty area) to fall under Soviet control, a "series of disasters" to the U.S. position could be expected in such places as Japan, the Philippines, and Indonesia, "with its vast natural resources." Even the oil of the Middle East would be "in jeopardy." To prevent such disasters, according to Dulles, it was necessary that the United States "quickly take a dramatic and strong stand that shows our confidence and resolution." The most advantageous of the doubtful areas in which to take such a stand was Formosa. Among the arguments Dulles advanced to urge a stand in Formosa was one that foreshadowed a policy President Truman was to adopt after the North Korean invasion of South Korea: "If the United States were to announce that it would neutralize Formosa, not permitting it either to be taken by Communists or to be used as a base of military operations against the mainland, that is a decision which we could certainly maintain, short of open war by the Soviet Union."[7]

After receiving Dulles's memorandum, Rusk apparently decided to send it to Acheson under his own name, since the State Department's files contain a memorandum from Rusk to Acheson dated May 30 that is identical to the Dulles memorandum of May 18.[8] There is no indication in State Department files that the Rusk/Dulles memorandum was seen by, or even forwarded to, Acheson.[9] According to British documents, however, Acheson was taking part in highly secret State Department discussions on possible changes in Formosa policy at this time. In a letter to Dening, British Ambassador Franks reported that in an "after-dinner chat" on June 5 Acheson had mentioned that he and his staff were giving some thought to the future of Formosa. The State Department was "wracking its brains to see whether conditions conducive to preservation of the present status could not be encouraged or possibly created." Franks's letter continued: "Acheson had nothing to offer. . . . But it was clear that there is pressure in the Administration for another look at the Formosa position and that the attitude of January last . . . is not now quite so firm."[10] Franks did not think for a moment that Acheson would agree to military intervention, but he did think it obvious that the U.S. administration would try "to delay the elimination of the token anti- Communist group." The British therefore could not hope for early easing of the U.S. position on Chinese representation in the United Nations.

Referring to Franks's letter, Counselor of Embassy Graves wrote to John S.H. Shattock in the Foreign Office on June 22: "Curiously enough no one in the State Department, junior to Dean Rusk, knows of this reconsideration, nor have they learned that Acheson has spoken to the Ambassador about Formosa."[11] As a matter of fact, on the basis of State Department documentation, we know that at least two officials below the Rusk level, Sprouse and Merchant, were in on the Formosa discussions.[12] These officials were apparently deliberately keeping their British embassy contacts in the dark; in any case, they maintained they had no knowledge of any impending change in U.S. policy toward Formosa.[13]

Moreover, according to Graves's letter, Sprouse and Merchant were less concerned than was the British embassy about General Mac-Arthur's attempts to persuade the National Security Council to revise U.S. policy towards Formosa. The embassy was worried about reports that the White House was considering a declaration "after the manner of the Monroe doctrine" and that the "army Department" was marshaling arguments in favor of placing Formosa under MacArthur.[14]

Graves may have been aware at the time he wrote that MacArthur had sent a memorandum dated June 14 to the JCS in which he pronounced himself satisfied "that the domination of Formosa by an unfriendly power would be a disaster of utmost importance to the US, and . . . that time is of the essence." MacArthur proposed that he "be authorized and directed to initiate without delay a survey of the military, economic and political requirements to prevent the domination of Formosa by a Communist power and that the results of such a survey be analyzed and acted upon as a basis for US national policy with respect to Formosa." Discussing his memorandum with Dulles in Tokyo, MacArthur made it clear that he wished to make the survey personally, for otherwise, "it would be impracticable to make detailed recommendations regarding methods of accomplishing the desired end."[15]

On June 25 North Korea invaded South Korea. Two days later President Truman declared that in the circumstances of the attack on the Republic of Korea, "the occupation of Formosa by Communist forces would be a direct threat to the security of the Pacific area and to United States forces performing their lawful and necessary functions in that area." He continued: "Accordingly, I have ordered the Seventh Fleet to prevent any attack on Formosa. As a corollary to this action, I am calling upon the Chinese Government on Formosa to cease all air and sea operations against the mainland. The Seventh Fleet will see that this is done."[16]

Truman's decision to reverse the U.S. policy of nonintervention in case of a Communist attack on Formosa followed Acheson's suggestion at a top-level dinner meeting at Blair House the evening of June 25, which clearly reflected the Dulles neutralization formula of May 18. As reported in a memorandum prepared by Ambassador-at-Large Philip Jessup, Acheson suggested that "the President should order the Seventh Fleet to proceed to Formosa and prevent an attack on Formosa from the mainland. At the same time operations from Formosa against the mainland should be prevented. He said that he did not recommend that General MacArthur should go to Formosa until further steps had been decided upon. He said that the United States should not tie up with the Generalissimo. He thought that the future status of Formosa might be determined by the UN."[17]

Consistent with Acheson's advice not to tie up with Generalissimo Chiang Kai-shek was the State Department's explanation, in a secret circular telegram to American diplomatic and consular officers, that the president's action had been "taken as immediate security measure to preserve peace in Pacific and without prejudice to pol[itical] questions affecting Chi Govt."[18] Nevertheless, the Nationalist government's fate was inevitably affected by Truman's commitment to defend its refuge. The Nationalists were beneficiaries almost in spite of themselves, for neither Truman nor Dulles had faith in their fighting capabilities. Dulles bluntly voiced his opinion on this score in a conversation with Hollington Tong, a member of the Kuomintang Advisory Council and head of the Nationalists' broadcasting services, a few days after he had drafted his May 18 memorandum to Rusk and Nitze. "I had in all frankness to say to him," Dulles reported, "that there had been in official quarters and in American public opinion a very complete loss of confidence in the will of the Nationalist forces to fight. The impression prevailed that they had ample material strength to defend Formosa, if they would, but that there was grave doubt that they would. Rumors were current that many of the leaders, including the Generalissimo, were already making plans to get away from Formosa to safety and past performance gave credibility to these rumors."[19]

For his part, Truman blamed the Nationalists for the Communists' victory in China, a particularly sore point with him since his domestic political enemies accused his administration of having lost China to the Communists. Truman let loose his feelings about the Nationalists on a number of occasions. For example, in an unmailed letter to Arthur Krock, Washington correspondent of the *New York Times*, he declared: "Chiang Kai-shek's downfall was his own doing. His field Generals surrendered the equipment we gave him to the Commies and [sic] used his own arms and ammunition to overthrow him. Only an American Army of 2,000,000 could have saved him, and that would have been World War III."[20]

Despite Truman's low opinion of the Nationalists' capabilities, he seems to have considered accepting a Nationalist offer of "one army of 33,000 men, suitable for operations in plains or hilly terrain" to fight in Korea.[21] However, Secretary Acheson, backed by the JCS, opposed the offer on the grounds that the Nationalist troops would be more useful defending Formosa than Korea. Acheson also felt that deployment of the Nationalist troops in Korea might bring Chinese Communist intervention, "either in Korea or Formosa or both." The JCS pointed out that available transport could be better utilized by U.S. troops and supplies.[22] Years later Truman denied he had ever given serious consideration to Taipei's offer of Nationalist troops. Merle Miller quotes him as saying, "They weren't any damn good, never had been."[23]

MacArthur also opposed the Nationalists' troop offer. Among his reasons was his fear that their use in Korea would cause problems for the British in Hong Kong.[24] The upshot was that the offer was politely declined with the suggestion that "it would be desirable for representatives of General MacArthur's Headquarters to hold discussions with the Chinese military authorities on Taiwan concerning the plans for the defense of the island against invasion prior to any final decision on the wisdom of reducing the defense forces on Taiwan by transfer of troops to Korea."[25]

26

Reactions to Neutralization

Peking reacted strongly to Truman's announcement that he had ordered the Seventh Fleet to prevent an attack on Formosa. In an official statement, Chou En-lai described this move as a "violent, predatory action by the United States Government" but claimed that it came "as no surprise to the Chinese people."[1] Indeed it should not have come as a surprise to the Chinese people, since the CPG through its controlled press had been telling them for months that the United States was plotting to seize Formosa. President Truman's January 5 announcement that the United States would not intervene in case of an attack on Formosa had been dismissed by the Chinese media as "a smokescreen," which, by some strange twist of reasoning, was said actually to "confirm the American imperialists' intention to annex Taiwan."[2] Yet even though Premier Chou's claim that the U.S. move came as no surprise was consistent with the Chinese propaganda line, there is reason to believe that it actually did surprise the CCP leadership. Up to this time the United States had refrained from intervening in China's civil war with its own forces. This fact was presumably what prompted Mao Tse-tung to tell Josef Stalin, if Nikita Khrushchev can be believed, that the United States would not intervene in Korea if the North Koreans attacked South Korea because it would be an internal Korean matter.[3]

For those who would prefer not to rely on Krushchev's word, there is other evidence that Peking put more faith in Truman's January 5 statement on Formosa than it admitted. For example, as reported by *People's China*, General Su Yu, vice-commander of Marshal Chen Yi's Third Field Army, which had the responsibility for "liberating Taiwan," publicly acknowledged in February the difficulties of carrying out successful military operations against Formosa but did not even hint that his forces would have to do battle with U.S. armed forces.[4] After Truman's June 27 statement, an article in *World Culture* acknowledged: "Before June 27, the problem of liberating Taiwan pitted the strength of the PLA against the Chiang Kai-shek remnants, with the help of the American imperialists occupying a background position. Since June 27, the problem of liberating Taiwan pits the strength of the PLA against the American imperialists, with the Kuomintang bandit remnants moving into the background."[5]

The strongest evidence, perhaps, that before Truman's June 27 statement the People's Republic did not anticipate that invasion of Formosa would bring about an armed conflict with the United States is that after that statement was made indications of an imminent invasion, previously so strong, soon diminished.[6] Thus, in a memorandum to Secretary Acheson on August 8, George Kennan speculated, "Had we not reacted as we did on June 27, the communist forces would probably already have seized the island." Now he thought the chances were "somewhat less than 50-50 that they will make the attempt in the next six weeks," and "if the attempt is not made within this period, it will probably not be made at all at the present juncture."[7] At about the same time, Averell Harriman reported General MacArthur's views: "He is satisfied that the Chinese Communists will not attempt an invasion of Formosa at the present time. His intelligence and photographs show no undue concentration of forces, although they are building airstrips. He is convinced that the 7th Fleet plus the air jets from the Philippines and Okinawa, B-29s and other aircraft at his disposal, can destroy any attempt which may be made."[8] Some two months later, in a memorandum headed "Threat of Chinese Communist Invasion of Formosa," the CIA concluded that the Chinese Communists would not attempt an invasion during the remainder of 1950 (the period of the estimate). It pointed out that such an attack would involve the risk of war with the United States and that "success would be improbable."[9]

Of course, the risk of war with the United States did not deter the People's Republic from sending hundreds of thousands of troops into Korea, but the military circumstances there were entirely different. When the Communists intervened in Korea, Mao was employing China's greatest military asset—masses of manpower—against relatively thin U.S. gound forces; but an invasion of Formosa after June 27 had to depend on penetration of U.S. naval and air forces by vastly inferior Chinese counterparts. Mao did not win a long succession of military victories on the mainland by pitting his weakness against the enemy's strength.

Initially, at least, the United Kingdom reacted negatively to President Truman's order to the Seventh Fleet. In a letter to Acheson, which pleased neither him nor the president,[10] Bevin asserted: "The United States have the whole-hearted backing of world opinion in the courageous initiative they took to deal with the aggression in Korea. I do not believe they could rely on the same support for their declared policy in connexion with Formosa." Bevin's letter went on to raise the question of "what the attitude of the United States would be if the Russians agreed to help in restoring the status quo in Korea in return for United States readiness to reconsider their present declared attitude in regard to Formosa."[11]

Acheson replied in a letter that the U.S. ambassador to India, veteran career diplomat Loy Henderson, described as "one of the greatest and most inspiring documents which I have seen during my years of service."[12] Acheson left Bevin in no doubt that the United States would have no part of such a deal. Repeating the U.S. position that the "ultimate fate of Formosa should be settled by peaceful means either in connection with a Jap[anese] peace settlement or by the UN," Acheson warned, "but we are not willing to see it go involuntarily to Peiping in the present state of affairs in Asia." In a separate message Acheson asked Ambassador Lewis Douglas to "emphasize to Bevin that this reply which has been approved here at the highest levels represents both my own strong personal views and has fullest concurrence of all official quarters here."[13]

Several days after this Bevin-Acheson exchange, Permanent Undersecretary Strang again emphasized to Ambassador Douglas the importance the British attached to "avoiding any step that would tend to line up Asian countries against the West."[14] The British preoccupation with Asian, especially Indian, opinion on China policy was nothing new, of course. A leading reason Bevin had given Acheson for Britain's recognition of the People's Republic was the importance of staying in step with Asian opinion. But London's return to this theme following the outbreak of war in Korea was presumably stimulated in part by the stepped-up efforts of Peking to turn Asian opinion against the United States in the wake of UN intervention in Korea and U.S. neutralization of Formosa.

Thus Chou En-lai had claimed on June 28 that the United States had incited South Korea to attack North Korea as "a pretext for the United States to invade Taiwan, Korea, Viet-Nam and the Philippines." Chou described the United States as the enemy of "all the oppressed nations and peoples of the East," who were "undoubtedly capable of burying the vicious and hated American imperialist war-makers once and for all in the great flames of struggle for national independence."[15] Chinese media echoed Chou's accusations. The lead editorial in *People's China* for July 16, 1950, for example, accused the United States of "acts of naked, savage and utterly unprovoked aggression in Asia," and asserted that this was "the logical outcome of the long chain of half-veiled aggressive acts by which the United States has tried, but failed, to stem the rising tide of the national liberation movements in Asia, to turn Asia's lands and people into a reserve of imperialism in its plots against progressive mankind headed by the U.S.S.R."[16]

In their efforts to turn Asian opinion against the UN intervention in Korea, the Communists gave particular attention to India. In a report to the Foreign Office July 25, Hutchison commented that the People's Republic highly valued the presence of the Indian ambassador and the maintenance of friendly diplomatic relations with India. At a recent official banquet, Hutchison reported, Ambassador Panikkar had been the only foreign representative Mao toasted or shook hands with.[17] In the Foreign Office, Franklin observed that this was an "extremely important point"; the Chinese were paralleling their attacks on the Americans in Asia with an all-out effort to win the sympathy and support of the Indians.[18] Of course, this effort made the British even more anxious to maintain their influence in New Delhi.

Meanwhile, India had become the leading Asian proponent for the immediate seating of the People's Republic in the United Nations, Peking's all-out support of North Korea's defiance of the UN notwithstanding. Prime Minister Nehru believed that progress toward ending the Korean War could be made if the Soviet Union could be induced to participate once more in Security Council deliberations. Since the Soviet Union had walked out of the Security Council because the PRC was not seated, seating the PRC now (and simultaneously expelling the Nationalists) would allow the Soviet Union to return. This logic seemed impeccable; but to accept the conclusion that bringing the Soviets back would help end the Korean War required a leap of faith the U.S. government was unwilling to make. In any case it was not willing to pay the price. In a note to Nehru dated July 18, Acheson held that the issue of Chinese representation should be decided on its merits, not dictated by "unlawful aggression" or by putting the UN under "coercion and duress."[19] In the event, the Soviet representative returned to the Security Council a short time later, even though the People's Republic had not been seated, and his return did not noticeably improve prospects for ending the Korean War.

Averell Harriman, upon returning from a trip to the Far East in August, was so dismayed by India's influence on Britain's position that he complained to a correspondent of the *Times* of London that the United Kingdom would have "to choose between the United States and India." When British Ambassador Franks was told of Harriman's outburst, however, he dismissed it as based more on emotion than on reflection and as unrepresentative of the views of the State Department and the administration as a whole.[20]

The principal immediate concern of the British with respect to the new U.S. policy toward Formosa was that any new conflict in the Far East should be localized and "not be allowed to develop into general war, either with the Soviet Union or with Communist China." At the U.S.-U.K. discussions on the "present world situation" held in Washington between July 20 and 24, U.K. representatives "particularly stressed the advantages of localizing any conflict between the U.S. or the U.K. on the one hand and the Chinese Communists on the other" to avoid a general war and "in order that a *possible* drift of the Chinese communist regime away from Moscow might not be interrupted."[21] The British expressed the "strong hope" that "a Chinese communist attack on Formosa would be localized," to which the U.S. representatives replied that it was the U.S. "desire and intention that any such hostilities be localized." In view of the "character of the President's statement of June 27," they were convinced that "there would be no invasion of the mainland in connection with a Communist attack on Formosa."[22]

For their part, the British were not sanguine about the prospects for any kind of settlement of the Formosa issue. Thus Ambassador Franks wrote to Minister of State Kenneth Younger on July 26, shortly after the conclusion of the U.S.-U.K. discussions in Washington: "The explanation that Formosa has simply been sealed off pending the 'restoration of security in the Pacific, a peace settlement with Japan, or consideration by the United Nations' is perhaps not much more than a convenient formula. Whereas on a superficial view it might seem to open the way to a solution in due course, in reality it may be doubted that it offers such a prospect, since the United States has now taken up a stand from which it would be difficult to withdraw."[23] Sir Oliver's sense of the U.S.-Formosa relationship was obviously acute. At the time of the Truman announcement of January 5, he wondered whether the administration could stick to its hands-off policy, and now he was prophetically skeptical that the United States would be able to withdraw from its commitment to the defense of Formosa as easily as the Americans seemed to think. As matters turned out, the U.S. commitment, solidified by a mutual defense treaty in 1954, did not come to an end for nearly thirty years.

In a further discussion of Formosa with Rusk and Jessup on August 10, Franks revealed that the British cabinet had received Truman's June 27 statement well, but had feared at first that the Formosa part of the statement would lead to "many complications." Though the cabinet had now begun to understand the importance of military neutralization, "on which the Brit[ish] Chiefs had expressed agreement," cabinet anxieties had once more been aroused by General MacArthur's visit to Formosa and reports of Chinese Nationalist bombings of the mainland.[24] The visit had also created anger, if not anxiety, in Washington.[25] Rusk assured Franks that U.S. policy was firmly based on the President's statements of June 27 and July 19.[26] The policy was not designed as a stepping-stone for U.S. entry into the mainland or to put Chiang Kai-shek back on the mainland. When Franks speculated that there might be some possibility of reducing British and American differences on Formosa policy by finding a "proper U.N. formula along with some common understanding on the longer range development of the Chi[nese] question," Rusk and Jessup responded that they "did not wish the disposition of Formosa to be settled simply by deciding the question as to who is China."[27] In replying thus, they reflected the State Department's view that the fate of Formosa per se, rather than the fate of the Nationalist government, was the primary American concern. Reporting this conversation to the Foreign Office, Franks summed it up by saying that Jessup and Rusk had assured him that the "policy of putting Formosa on ice held without qualification."[28]

Not long after getting this assurance from Washington, the Foreign Office received some corroboration from the British consul in Tamsui, who reported on August 14 that although the Americans "for reasons of military expediency" had to cooperate with the Nationalists in defense of Formosa and to furnish them with military supplies, there was no indication that the Nationalists would succeed in maneuvering them "into co-operation in operations against the mainland."[29]

In the previous few weeks the State Department had, in fact, endeavored to make clear to the Chinese Nationalists the full implications of Truman's June 27 statement. Thus in a message to Strong in Taipei on July 21, the department noted its understanding that Nationalist air and sea operations against the mainland had been suspended as the Nationalist government had promised on June 28, but it instructed Strong to "make clear" to Foreign Minister Yeh that the Seventh Fleet had explicit orders to carry out President Truman's June 27 directive. Defiance of the directive would be considered a breach of the Chinese government's assurances.[30] In a further message to Strong on July 22, Acheson asked him to inform Foreign Minister Yeh that the president's June 27 declaration did not apply to the offshore islands, such as Quemoy and Matsu. In the event of a Communist attack, the United States would not participate in the defense of any islands under Nationalist control except Taiwan and the Pescadores; but neither would it stand in the way of Nationalist efforts to defend these islands.[31]

In view of the fact that the Nationalists still hold Quemoy and Matsu, it is interesting that Yeh told Strong that the Chinese government was considering withdrawal from Chinmen (Quemoy) despite its "great importance to both China and US."[32] Strong himself felt it was "certain that Chinese Government intends withdraw from Chinmen" and that the United States would be made the "complete scapegoat."[33] But on August 8 the British embassy in Washington informed the Foreign Office that a State Department official, noting "reports of some days ago that the Nationalists would withdraw from Quemoy, . . . surmised that as a result of MacArthur's visit they had decided against withdrawal."[34] MacArthur's visit did undoubtedly much encourage Chiang Kai-shek, but it seems unlikely that the Nationalists had seriously contemplated an early withdrawal from Quemoy, which less than a year before had been the scene of one of their rare military triumphs over the Communists.

Be this as it may, in yet another interpretation of Truman's June 27 declaration, Strong was instructed on July 24 to tell Foreign Minister Yeh that the U.S. government would "not stand in the way of air and naval reconnaissance by the Chinese Government, provided such reconnaissance did not involve armed offensive action against the mainland."[35] Washington was prepared not only to allow Chinese Nationalist reconnaissance but to supplement it with that of the United States. Thus on July 30 the JCS authorized General MacArthur "to conduct such periodic reconnaissance flights over the coastal area of China south of the 32nd Parallel of latitude as you may consider necessary to determine the imminence of any attack that may be launched against Formosa."[36] The United States was also prepared to allow the Nationalist navy to halt Chinese shipping in the area for "visit and search," but drew the line at conducting such operations against foreign vessels.[37]

In view of the responsibility it had now undertaken for the defense of Formosa, the United States was more interested than it had been before June 27 in the ability of the Nationalists to defend the island. Accordingly, it modified restrictions it had previously imposed on sales of military equipment to the Nationalists. The new policy was set out in a letter dated July 19 from Secretary of Defense Johnson to Acheson: "In order to increase the capacity and will of the Chinese Nationalist forces to fight, the Chinese Nationalist Government should be authorized to make purchases, with its own funds, of any materiel under the control of the United States, including tanks and jet aircraft. . . . Delivery and shipment of such purchases would be expedited by United States assistance."[38] Acheson concurred.[39]

It may be recalled that the United States had stopped sales of tanks and jet aircraft to the Nationalists some months earlier, at least partly to appease the British, who had feared that with the fall of Formosa (which they firmly expected) the Communists would acquire such materiel and use it against Hong Kong. In a top secret aide-mémoire dated August 23, the State Department provided the British embassy with the rationale for the change in U.S. policy. After describing various means by which the Chinese Nationalists could procure military materiel from the United States (including continuing assistance through the $125 million in grants appropriated under the China Aid Act of 1948), the Department explained: "It has been decided that the US Government cannot logically continue to prohibit the exporting to the Chinese Government of jet aircraft and medium and heavy tanks if such equipment is found to be available in excess of the needs of the U.S. defense establishment [given] recent developments in the Far East and the increased importance of Chi Govt defense requirements."[40]

27

The Effect on Trade

At the outbreak of the Korean War, U.S. policy on trade with China was governed, as it had been since February 1949, by NSC 41. Approval by the National Security Council on December 29, 1949, of NSC 48/2, "The Position of the United States with Respect to Asia," reaffirmed the policy set forth in NSC 41 and, according to Secretary of State Acheson, did away with "considerable uncertainty that had arisen regarding the implementation of NSC 41."[1] The export of so-called 1A items, materials and supplies of direct military utility, was banned to China as well as to the Soviet Union, but exports to China of so-called 1B items, multipurpose capital goods that might be of military or strategic value, were permitted "within quantitative limits of normal civilian use and under controls." No obstacle was to be placed "in the way of trade with China in non-strategic commodities."[2]

This policy continued through the early stages of the Korean War; trade between the United States and the People's Republic was not shut off. However, some actions were taken that further restricted such trade. The export of petroleum products to Communist China had been limited to the estimated minimum Chinese civilian requirements. On the basis of such estimates, the State Department arrived at quarterly quotas of permissible shipments, which it asked the two major U.S. oil companies operating in China—Standard-Vacuum Oil Company and Caltex Company—to adhere to.[3] Shortly after the UN intervention in the Korean War, however, the State Department asked these two companies "to suspend all shipments of petroleum products to Chinese Communist ports for the time being as well as discontinue all discussions of contracts or additional shipments with the Chinese Communist consignees." It also suggested to the British embassy that the British government might take similar action with respect to the Shell Oil Company, the third major foreign oil company operating in China at that time.[4]

The initial British response was equivocal. The Foreign Office did not try to persuade Shell to suspend all further shipments of petroleum products but indicated that Shell would not expand its shipments to China, which in any case amounted to "an insignificant trickle."[5] On July 13 Acheson raised the subject with Ambassador Franks. Pointing out that U.S. companies had voluntarily agreed to stop oil shipments to China, he told Franks it was "important that all shipments be stopped to China, particularly North China." Franks replied that the military in the United Kingdom might be inclined to agree with the U.S. position on oil, but the political side would probably be slower."[6] Three days later Franks informed Acheson that "the British Government had decided to requisition all oil supplies as the quickest and least troublesome way of stopping shipments" to China.[7]

In a later meeting between the British embassy and the State Department, the British spelled out the reasons for adopting the method of requisitioning oil supplies in Hong Kong as the best method for interrupting the "flow of oil to China from British sources." The British government did not wish to appear to be discriminating against the Chinese Communists; it wanted any action to be taken by the U.K. government and not by the Hong Kong authorities and to be taken in such a way as to protect Shell and its employees in China. Accordingly, the British Admirality was requisitioning all stocks of petroleum products in Hong Kong including those held by American companies.[8]

To protect itself against "the appearance of unilateral British action in cooperation with the United States with respect to China," the British government asked the U.S. government to seek the cooperation of other governments to embargo shipments of oil products to "all Soviet bloc destinations." On July 28 the governments participating in COCOM agreed to put six categories of petroleum products on "International List I," which action had the effect of embargoing the shipment of these products from all COCOM countries to the Soviet Union, eastern Europe, and North Korea, as well as to China.[9]

The British went even further to avoid the appearance of discrimination against the People's Republic by prohibiting oil exports to Formosa. On September 13 after the government of Hong Kong had refused permission to Caltex to export aviation gasoline to Formosa, the British embassy informed the State Department that "UK and Hong Kong export controls must be applied with equal severity to the Chinese mainland and to Taiwan as part of China. . . . This position is necessary in order to avoid giving the lie to prohibition of petroleum exports from Hong Kong to China on grounds of need by the British armed services."[10]

Some three weeks after the outbreak of the Korean War, a COCOM meeting in Paris noted that all participating countries "are applying presently agreed Eastern European controls to both North Korea and Red China."[11] This had been a State Department goal for some time.

On June 8, for example, Acheson had informed Secretary of Commerce Charles Sawyer that the State Department believed "the export of both 1A and 1B materials to Communist China should be governed by the same principles that now govern the export of such materials to the USSR and its eastern European satellites." Under this policy the export of 1A materials to Communist China should be "uniformly denied," instead of allowing some exceptions "on grounds of the national interest." As for 1B materials, two exceptions would be made from the "principles and criteria that now govern the export of such commodities to the USSR and its eastern European satellites." One exception would arise when a denial of licenses to American exporters would merely divert trade to alternative suppliers in the United Kingdom or western Europe. The other exception would be made when "denial of export licenses for shipment of 1B materials to Communist China would place American nationals or property in China in serious jeopardy."[12]

The United States now had agreement in COCOM that the same principles and criteria would be applied to controlling trade with Communist China as with the Soviet Union and eastern Europe, but there was nevertheless a great deal of latitude for disagreement with its allies as to the treatment of specific commodities—as to whether a commodity belonged in category 1A or 1B or whether it should be considered nonstrategic. Moreover, differences on the specifics needed to be ironed out within the U.S. government before a U.S. position could be put forward in COCOM. An example of such differences had arisen several months earlier over a proposed shipment of fifteen tons of steel rails from West Germany to the People's Republic.[13] The Pentagon wanted to prohibit the shipment on the grounds that the rails were of strategic importance to China, the 1A criterion. But the State Department argued that there would be no harm in shipping a quantity of rails commensurate with normal civilian use in China, the 1B criterion.

Such haggling within the U.S. government and within COCOM undoubtedly had an inhibiting effect on trade with the People's Republic. Even so, trade continued and in some areas even grew. Thus, for some British companies trading with China, business improved as a result of the war, because of greater interest on the part of the Chinese authorities in imports of industrial equipment.

For other British firms in China—industrial concerns and trading companies whose business was primarily *within* China—business continued to deteriorate, however, because of Chinese policies long antedating the Korean War. The most important of these, described by the secretary of the London Chamber of Commerce in a letter to the president of the Board of Trade as a matter of "grave import," was "the increasing orientation of the Chinese People's Government toward the setting up of State trading organizations and the suppression or absorption of private enterprise." The chamber suggested that the United Kingdom should make it one of the conditions for establishing diplomatic relations with China that private merchants, both British and Chinese, be allowed to operate freely in each other's countries. The chamber recognized, however, that "in practice the People's Government of China may refuse to permit its own private merchants to come here."[14]

Despite understandable frustration with trading conditions in China, the chamber's suggested solution revealed a woeful ignorance of the revolutionary changes taking place there. The chamber received a polite bureaucratic reply from an official of the Board of Trade to the effect that His Majesty's government could not appropriately make establishment of diplomatic relations with the People's Republic subject to such a condition, but the chamber could be assured that the government would do everything possible in the present emergency conditions to foster the interests of individual merchant firms.[15]

Several weeks later (August 23) a deputation from the China Association, headed by Chairman W.J. Keswick, called on Assistant Undersecretary Dening at the Foreign Office to ask if the British government was prepared to guarantee British industrial concerns in China against loss. Keswick recalled that in March, in a meeting with the China Association, Foreign Secretary Bevin had expressed the hope concerning British business in China that the "threads would hold." Keswick said the Foreign Office should know that now the threads were about to break. Traders, banks, and insurance companies "might hang on longer," but British industrialists in China were about to pack up. The China Association also wished the Foreign Office to know of its anxiety lest U.S. actions with respect to Formosa involve the United Kingdom in hostilities and of its worry about Chinese Nationalist mining and attacks on shipping.[16]

After consulting with the Board of Trade, the Foreign Office informed the China Association that His Majesty's government believed businesses "should continue to maintain a foothold in China where possible" but that the firms themselves would have to make their own decisions; the government could not guarantee British industrial concerns against loss.[17] The Board of Trade had given the Foreign Office two reasons for refusing such guarantees. One was that British firms in other countries were also at risk, and the government could not discriminate in favor of those in China. The other was that to guarantee such firms against loss might encourage maltreatment by the Chinese. The maltreatment the Board of Trade presumably had in mind was the imposition of obligations on foreign businesses operating at a loss that required them to obtain remittances from their home countries, thus providing the Chinese with needed foreign exchange and a source of tax revenue.[18]

In sum, the outbreak of the Korean War itself seems to have had little adverse effect on Chinese treatment of foreign businesses. In fact, the British consul general in Shanghai reported to the Foreign Office on September 7 that conditions had become "somewhat easier," largely because of "a reduction in taxation."[19] Meanwhile, adverse preKorean War conditions, such as the foreign firms' "inability to reduce staff" and the "Chinese Government trend to official monopolies," continued, causing industrial concerns to make shift "largely by consuming stocks" and obliging other concerns "to bring in funds," though apparently not at as high a rate as previously.

28

British Foothold Survives

The Sino-British preliminary and procedural discussions on the establishment of diplomatic relations were not resumed after the outbreak of the Korean War. The People's Republic had never seemed to be particularly interested in them anyway, and the United Kingdom had gone about as far as it could in meeting Chinese demands. In response to a letter from Assistant Undersecretary R.H. Scott in the Foreign Office asking whether the Chinese really wanted to have diplomatic relations, Hutchison wrote on September 11 that he did not believe "the Chinese think us so desperately keen that we will pay any price for diplomatic relations. . . . On the other hand, the indications seem to be that they are not desperately keen either, since our elucidations . . . have been sufficiently conciliatory in tone to have enabled the Chinese to profess themselves satisfied (if not contented) had they been anxious to do so."[1] Hutchison speculated that the reason the Sino-British negotiations had failed "to click" boiled down to the fact that the British regarded the Chinese as Soviet satellites and they regarded the British as American satellites. Thus, in view of the state of Sino-American and Soviet-American relations, "a cordial approach" was difficult both for the British and for the Chinese. Not much could be deduced, Hutchison thought, from "a polite and friendly attitude" toward himself and his staff.[2]

On the Chinese side, Chou En-lai continued to emphasize specific dissatisfactions with British policy. According to a report from Panikkar of an interview he had with Chou on September 9, Chou had said that he was not concerned with Anglo-American relations. He was not unrealistic enough to think that England would go against America for the sake of friendship with China. What bothered the Chinese, according to Chou, was that having recognized the Chinese government, England continued to "uphold the Kuomintang."[3] Speaking to Hutchison of this interview with Chou, Panikkar said he had come away with the strong impression that the Chinese government was genuinely eager to establish diplomatic relations with the United Kingdom and wanted Panikkar to facilitate the process. In the Foreign Office, Franklin commented that the Indian ambassador was "always rather apt to hope for the best and to give the Chinese Government the benefit of quite a few doubts."[4] In a later message, Hutchison acknowledged that "Panikkar in his conversation with me did not clearly distinguish between points raised by himself and those raised by Mr. Chou."[5]

Not long afterward, Chou went public with his explanation of why the Sino-British negotiations were stalled. In the course of his report to the National Committee of the People's Political Consultative Conference commemorating the first anniversary of the founding of the People's Republic, Chou alluded to "our long-drawn-out negotiations with Britain, out of which nothing has yet come." He went on: "The reason for the fruitlessness of the negotiations is that while on the one hand, the British government has made known its recognition of the People's Republic of China, on the other it agrees to permit the so-called 'representatives' of the reactionary rump of the KMT clique to continue its illegal occupation of China's seat in the United Nations.

. . . And Britain's extremely unjustifiable and unfriendly attitude towards Chinese residents in Hongkong and other places cannot fail to draw the serious attention of the Central People's Government."[6]

Chou's charges of Britain's "extremely unjustifiable and unfriendly attitude towards Chinese residents in Hong Kong" echoed the complaint Chang Han-fu had made in his last meeting with Hutchison, June 17, when he criticized Hong Kong immigration restrictions as an example of the unfriendly British attitude towards China.[7] The British had revised their immigration regulations towards the end of April in an effort to stop the huge influx of refugees from China, which was swelling Hong Kong's population at an alarming rate. Under the new procedures, Chinese who spoke southern dialects and who had business or other connections with Hong Kong were allowed to cross the border, but those speaking Shanghai or other northern dialects were assumed to be refugees and were turned back unless they could show good reason for entry.[8] The People's Republic officially protested the new "restrictions imposed on Chinese entry into Hong Kong by the British authorities" as "an act unreasonable and unfriendly to the Chinese People's Republic and its people," recalling that in more than one hundred years "Chinese entering and leaving Hong Kong have never been regarded or treated as foreign immigrants."[9]

By renewing its charges against British treatment of Chinese immigrants, by ignoring conciliatory British moves on the Chinese representation issue in the UN, and especially by failing to resume the preliminary and procedural discussions with Hutchison, the CPG seemed clearly to be signaling its disinterest in establishing diplomatic relations with the United Kingdom.

Of course, the British were not entirely cut off from the CPG. According to a Foreign Office memorandum, the office of the British chargé d'affaires (as the British, not the Chinese, called it) continued to make representations to the CPG on such questions as British commercial interests in China, exit and entry permits for British subjects, attacks on British shipping, and Chinese Nationalist refugee soldiers in Hong Kong. Though Chargé Hutchison usually did not receive replies to these representations, they occasionally produced results.[10] Lack of diplomatic relations prevented Hutchison from seeing Mao or Chou, but he had managed to have several interviews with the head of the Western European and African Department of the Foreign Ministry, and members of his staff called at the ministry about twice a week. Additionally, his office carried on frequent formal and informal correspondence with the ministry.[11] Thus, the Chinese had forced a sort of de facto, second-class diplomatic relationship on the British. But so long as London wished to maintain a foothold in China, such a relationship, though rather humiliating, seemed preferable to none at all.

The United States by this time had no relationship at all with the People's Republic. Nevertheless, since some hundreds of American citizens continued to reside in China, the United States had a certain stake in the continued British official presence there. Although most of the Americans still in China at the outbreak of the Korean War were there voluntarily, some remained against their will, either because they could not obtain exit permits or because they had been imprisoned. British officials in China continued to make representations to the Chinese authorities on behalf of these detained Americans.

At the outbreak of the Korean War four American pilots were languishing in Chinese prisons. Unlike Smith and Bender, who had finally been released May 8, these prisoners were civilians. Not only did the United States rely on the British to make representations to the Chinese on their behalf, but it was often only through the British consular officials that Washington was able to obtain any reliable information about them. For example, the first word the State Department had that American pilots Carden and MacGowan were being detained came from British Consul General Eric Shipton in Kunming. Carden and MacGowan were unlucky enough to have landed their Trans Asiatic Airways Company plane in Kunming on December 23, 1949, just after General Lu Han had staged a coup against the governor of Yunnan Province and declared his allegiance to the CPG. Although the plane was registered in the Philippines, Lu had it impounded, stranding the pilots.[12] Despite Shipton's fears of "serious consequences," Carden and MacGowan were allowed "complete local freedom" for some six months after Communist troops took over Kunming before being taken into custody "for their own protection."[13]

In Peking, Hutchison wrote to the Ministry of Foreign Affairs requesting that Carden and MacGowan be released as soon as possible. Typically, Hutchison received no reply to this communication; so on August 14 he again wrote the ministry requesting that they be released and that they meanwhile be allowed to exchange messages with their families.[14] Now Chinese authorities in Kunming took action, but whether as a consequence of British representations in Peking will probably never be known.

On August 23 the British vice-consul saw Carden and MacGowan being transported toward the west gate of the city under military escort and reported that "they did not look happy."[15] Three days later the vice-consul was summoned to police headquarters and handed a letter from Carden, saying that by the time the vice-consul read the letter the pilots would be on their way home. On September 2 he received a telegram from Carden sent from Lashio, a town in Burma not far from the Chinese border, reporting the pilots' safe arrival there.[16] Upon his return to the Philippines, Carden told U.S. embassy officers in Manila that the British consular officials in Kunming had been most cooperative in their endeavors to assist American citizens to depart from China.[17]

British efforts were much appreciated by the State Department, as well as by the Americans on whose behalf their representations were made. After the release of Smith and Bender in May, for example, Acting Secretary of State James Webb sent a letter to British Ambassador Franks in Washington expressing thanks for the assistance rendered by the British in their release, referring especially to the work of the British chargé in Peking and the consul general in Tsingtao. Webb said that their efforts "may have contributed substantially to the successful outcome of the case."[18]

Yet, though the British efforts were appreciated in Washington, and deservedly so, Anglo-American accord did not always exist on the best way to make representations to the CPG. For example, on June 20 the American embassy in London sent a memorandum to the Foreign Office regarding the longtime inability of seven American businessmen in Shanghai to obtain exit permits, "contrary to all recognized standards of international conduct." The embassy asked that the British chargé d'affaires in Peking be instructed to bring this matter to the attention of the highest Communist authorities, and in so doing to say that unless the People's Republic responded to this approach, the U.S. government would "be obliged bring this matter to attention U.N."[19] But Chargé Hutchison told the Foreign Office he thought this language "ill-judged and unwise," and "likely to irritate the Chinese Government so much that they will delay issuance of permits even longer." In Hutchison's view, experience had "amply demonstrated that the courteous and reasonable approach has the best chance of success." He requested that the State Department give him a free hand on the timing and wording of the demarche.[20] The State Department agreed that "in the first instance" Hutchison could have a free hand, but if there was no satisfactory response "within a reasonable time," he should proceed on the basis of the department's original request.[21]

In fact, no matter how they were made, British representations on behalf of detained Americans were frequently unsuccessful. In a case similar to that of Carden and MacGowan, two other commercial airline pilots also landed in Yunnan Province on the eve of General Lu Han's coup, but in Mengtze rather than in Kunming. Their Civil Air Transport plane was impounded by the authorities and they were prevented from leaving Mengtze. On January 21 the American embassy in London reported this information to the Foreign Office and asked that British officials in China urgently request the release of the two Americans. The Foreign Office immediately passed the American request to Consul General Shipton in Kunming, asking him what action he considered it possible to take to assist the pilots.[22]

Shipton's reply indicated that there were complications to this case. He had heard that Civil Air Transport had been trying to evacuate the Chinese Nationalist Twenty-sixth Army from Mengtze to Hainan. Shipton said it would be helpful to him to know the exact nature of their business in Mengtze. In the meantime he would make representations, but he could not hope to do more for them than for Carden and McGowan.[23] On March 3 Shipton reported that the pilots, Buol and Jaubert, had been brought to Kunming in custody, along with eight Chinese CAT personnel and ten political prisoners.[24] Two weeks later the American embassy in London informed the Foreign Office, "According to General Chennault, CAT was engaged in airlifting tin concentrates from Mengtse to Hainan," but Chennault had acknowledged that some Chinese Nationalist officers might have gotten aboard.[25]

The Far Eastern Department felt that "even if tin concentrates, rather than Nationalist Officials, were the main cargo, we should have been told whether they were military goods and whether Captain Buol was acting under the orders of the Nationalist Forces." Earlier, the Foreign Office Legal Department had offered the opinion that there was "a *prima facie* case to show Buol was assisting the Nationalist Forces," in which case the Foreign Office would not be justified in asking the British chargé d'affaires to take up the case in Peking, as the State Department had requested.[26] Another reason for British reluctance to press the Chinese was the fear that to do so might weaken pleas for the release of still another American pilot, Captain James McGovern, who had crash-landed in south China on December 4, 1949, and was reported to be in jail in Nanning in poor health.[27] The upshot of these deliberations was that the Foreign Office, though it did not feel justified in pressing for Buol's release, had Hutchison in Peking ask the Chinese to allow Buol local freedom of movement and to allow British Consul General Shipton in Kunming to see him.[28]

After receiving further information from the American embassy in London on Buol's activities before his detention, the Foreign Office instructed Hutchison on October 5, provided he saw no objection, to ask the Chinese to release Buol. The Foreign Office pointed out that Buol had been detained nine months "apparently without trial and in our opinion without sufficient reason."[29] Although Hutchison carried out his instructions on October 14, by the end of the year Buol had not been released from prison and the Foreign Ministry had not bothered to reply to Hutchison's letter.[30]

29
Focus on the United Nations

Shortly before the outbreak of the Korean War, the United States and the United Kingdom had drifted farther apart on the issue of Chinese representation in the United Nations. The British had decided in mid-June to vote for seating the People's Republic in UNICEF, and the decision had drawn sharp criticism from Secretary of State Acheson. Acheson was particularly disturbed, according to a British embassy report, that the United Kingdom had made such a decision just when, as a result of much administration effort, there were signs of securing a bipartisan approach in Congress on Chinese matters.[1]

Commenting on this report, A.R.K. Mackenzie, on the American desk in the Foreign Office, warned that it should not be assumed that a bipartisan policy on China would mean U.S. recognition of the Communist regime or an end to U.S.-U.K. divergences. Although he felt the U.S. administration deserved handling with sympathy and adequate consultation, since it was confronted with an aroused public opinion, he recommended that if the Foreign Office was satisfied with its present recognition policy, the United Kingdom should go ahead and vote for Peking's representation on the UN. There was no prospect of getting U.S. agreement at least until after the November elections.[2]

The outbreak of the Korean War even further dimmed any prospects of the U.S. support for Britain's position. In an "eyes only"
message to Bevin, Acheson summed up the U.S. attitude:

We do not have a closed mind on the question of Chi representation in the UN,
but we do feel strongly that the question should be taken up by the UN on its
merits. . . . We do not believe the UN can deal with the matter on its merits
under the coercion of (a) Communist aggression against Korea or (b) Russian
absence, with Peiping seating as the price of return. If the coercion were
removed, the UN could set about the matter of seating in a normal fashion,
perhaps seating no Chi representative pending full consideration of the unpre-
cendented problem of competing claimant Govts.[3]

The coercion of the Russian absence ended August 1, but that of
"Communist aggression against Korea" remained, and Acheson again
made it clear in the Anglo-French-American foreign ministers' meeting
on September 14 that the United States would do its best to defeat any
attempt to admit the PRC delegation at the opening of the General
Assembly.[4] On September 19 such an attempt was defeated.

Despite this defeat, Foreign Secretary Bevin was sanguine about
the prospects for a change in U.S. policy. Thus he cabled the Foreign
Office from New York, where he had come for the opening sessions of
the General Assembly: "There has been a noticeable trend in the press
and informed opinion towards a modification of the American attitude
to China and [sic] though would not hold out hope that there would be
any practical results until after elections. I do think there is a real
chance that Peking representative will be accepted in the U.N. before
many months have passed, provided always that Chinese Government
behaves with moderation and restraint. . . . preposterous to think
U.S. has aggressive intentions China or Korea.[5]

Meanwhile, British anxieties about the possible consequences of
U.S. policy toward Formosa had been increased when Chou En-lai on
August 24 sent a letter to Soviet UN representative Yakov Malik,
president of the Security Council for August, and to UN Secretary
General Trygve Lie, accusing the United States of "armed aggression
on the territory of China." Chou asserted that the UN Security Council
was "obliged by its inalienable duties to condemn the United States
Government for its criminal act in the invasion of the territory of China,
and to take immediate measures to bring about the complete withdrawal of all the United States armed invading forces from Taiwan and
from other territories belonging to China."[6]

In an instruction to Franks dated August 25 Bevin opined that the

United States would have to modify its policy on Formosa, since that policy would not command general support in the United Nations. The Chinese appeal to the Security Council introduced a time factor that made it urgent to "try to get the agreement of the maximum number of powers to a common line," but first it would be necessary to ensure that the line would be acceptable to the United States.[7]

Pursuant to his instructions from Bevin, Ambassador Franks had three meetings with senior State Department officials (including Acheson at the third meeting, August 31) in which ideas were exchanged about what line to take in the United Nations on the Formosa question.[8] These meetings crystallized the areas of agreement and disagreement between the United States and the United Kingdom, which were clearly delineated September 1 in a memorandum prepared for the forthcoming Tripartite Foreign Ministers' meeting. Though it was agreed that "the Cairo Declaration must be taken into consideration in any study of the ultimate status of Formosa," there was disagreement as to its relative importance; the United Kingdom thought it of fundamental importance, but the United States did not.[9] It was agreed that the problems of temporary military neutralization and of the ultimate disposition of Formosa were distinct, but there was no agreement as to the most desirable long-term alternative—consolidation with the mainland, independence (possibly after a plebiscite), or UN trusteeship. The United Kingdom questioned the feasibility of a plebiscite and believed independence to be "irreconcilable with the Cairo Declaration and unacceptable to both Chinese parties." In the U.K. view, moreover, certain actions of the Chinese Nationalists were inconsistent with Truman's June 27 declaration, and military neutralization was not truly bilateral.[10]

Both the United Kingdom and the United States entertained the idea of a UN commission to deal with the Formosa question, but they differed as to its terms of reference. Britain wanted it to determine when the "moment was ripe for the hand-over [to the PRC] and the conditions under which it should take place."[11] The United States wanted to charge the commission with the responsibility of recommending to the General Assembly "an appropriate peaceful settlement of the Formosa question."[12] In other words, the United Kingdom was ready to predetermine the solution to the Formosa question, and the United States wanted to keep the matter open, taking account of (among other things) the wishes of the inhabitants.

The British could take some comfort from the State Department's assurance that it was keeping an open mind on Formosa's future, but the Chinese Nationalists were nervous about the vagueness of American intentions. Their worries were not alleviated by President Truman's press conference statement on August 31 that it would "not be necessary to keep the 7th Fleet in the Formosa Strait if the Korea thing is settled,"[13] or by press reports of negotiations on China between the United States and India, a strong advocate of expulsion of the Nationalists from the UN and their replacement by representatives of the People's Republic.

Foreign Minister Yeh unburdened himself of such Nationalist worries to the new U.S. chargé in Taipei, Karl Rankin, on September 4, as indicated in the following excerpts from Rankin's telegraphic report of the same date:

He [Yeh] deplored unsettling effect of series of recent events and reports . . . on Chinese Government, armed forces, and Formosan population. Understands US readiness have the "aggression" against Formosa investigated by UN but fears anticipated arrival UN investigators. . . . Bulk of Formosan population would interpret UN investigations as directed against Chinese Government rather than U.S. aggression.

Yeh expressed hope that US recognized fact that Formosa today one of most peaceful and stable parts of Asia . . . [and] also that substantial progress has been made in improving effectiveness of government and economic and military conditions. . . . Believes it would be most helpful if US Government could take public cognizance these facts and contribute further to allaying uncertainty caused by recent events and rumors by stating definitely that future status of Formosa must await peace settlement with Japan. Alternative time limits involving "consideration by UN" or taking of "international action" are being freely interpreted to mean that any morning people in Formosa may wake up to learn that they have been turned over to some international authority, with reasonable certainty that in resulting confusion Chinese Communists will actually be ones to take over.[14]

Interestingly, Foreign Minister Yeh did not object to a determination of the future of Formosa connected with a Japanese peace settlement, possibly because he was confident that the Russians and the Chinese Communists would not take part in such a settlement. But it is curious that in describing this conversation with Yeh in his memoirs, Rankin includes determination of Formosa's future at a Japanese peace settlement as one of the alternatives Yeh did object to.[15]

In responding to Rankin's report of his conversation with Yeh, the State Department asserted that rumors of negotiations between India and the United States "for trusteeship Formosa with deal on Chi[nese] representation baseless." Perhaps the Nationalists were reassured by this statement and by the department's reiteration that all questions regarding Formosa should be settled by peaceful means and not by force; however, they presumably took less comfort in the department's reminder that whether the Formosa question was referred to settlement through a Japanese peace treaty or the United Nations, "negotiations would be multilateral and in regular channels."[16]

For his information only, the department advised Rankin to keep in mind in his contacts with Nationalist government officials that the "rest of the world" did not generally hold to the concept that the Nationalist government was the only legal Chinese government and should receive international treatment as such.[17] This statement, though it apparently reflected political realities as viewed from the State Department, was technically incorrect. A substantial majority of the world's countries at this time continued to recognize the Nationalist government as the sole legal government of China.

In his memoirs, Acheson remarks that exchanges between the United States and India at this time were designed to "seek evidence of Chinese intentions toward Korea."[18] But the Indians also used them as a means of conveying information to Peking as to U.S. intentions toward Formosa. U.S. views on Formosa were set forth in an informal memorandum U.S. Ambassador Loy Henderson handed to Sir Girja Bajpai, secretary general of the Ministry of External Affairs, on September 3.[19] When Bajpai asked Henderson if he would object to having excerpts of his memorandum sent to Ambassador Panikkar to be used in discussions with the Peking government, Henderson replied that Bajpai could use his own judgment but pointed out that the memorandum was not a formal document and should not be considered as a message from the United States to the "Peiping regime."

On September 4 Bajpai told the British acting high commissioner in New Delhi about the "informal communication" he had received the previous day from Henderson and said that Prime Minister Nehru had now authorized him "to send to the Indian Ambassador at Peking the more encouraging positions of the United States Government's latest communication . . . with instructions to inform Peking Government and to insist with them yet again on the importance of adopting a more helpful and less aggressive attitude as regards their policy and propaganda. He was to urge that time pressed as the Peking Government had not very long between now and the meeting of the General Assembly to remove unfortunate impressions abroad created by their recent statements."[20]

On this subject British thinking paralleled Indian. Before he had learned of the Indian action, Bevin had sent a message to Nehru describing the Peking government's communication to the UN on Formosa as "rather unfortunate" and likely to prejudice opinion against China. Bevin thought "a great deal" would depend on how the People's government delegation behaved when it arrived in New York. It would be very embarrassing if it took its cue from the Russians and behaved in an intemperate manner. Did Nehru think it might be advisable to send some kind of discreet warning to the Chinese?[21]

Nehru, of course, had already done so; but when the British acting high commissioner gave Bajpai Bevin's message, he got some of Bajpai's "personal thinking" as to Formosa. The time was not ripe for a long-term settlement of the Formosa problem, according to Bajpai, and General Assembly debate might "prejudice an eventual solution more especially having regard to the existing state of American public opinion."[22] It is interesting that at this point both New Delhi and London seemed more concerned that Peking's behavior would have an adverse affect on its chances of getting China's seat in the UN than about the consequences of the American neutralization policy, which had concerned them so much initially.

Meanwhile, Washington was concerned about how its efforts to deal with the Formosa issue in the UN would be affected by Nationalist talk of recapturing the mainland. Thus, after General Ch'en Ch'eng had talked publicly about a general counteroffensive on September 4, the State Department asked Rankin to keep in mind during his conversations with Nationalist officials that the U.S. government did not support any Chinese Nationalist program to return to the mainland but sought simply to protect Formosa. The message continued: "As you will appreciate handling of matter in UNSC and UNGA in effort to achieve pacific settlement of problems centering on island is delicate operation, with many complications posed by reasons attitudes of powerful friends US and China, particulary UK and India. Actions taken by Nat Govt prejudicial to pacific solution problem cld . . . hardly work otherwise than to detriment Nat Govt itself."[23]

While Taipei talked on the one hand of returning to the mainland by a counteroffensive, on the other it sought a long-term commitment from the United States to defend its island base of Formosa. But Washington was unwilling to give such a commitment. The State Department told Rankin that the Nationalist government could "be assured that our belief is UN offers best channel for peaceful, just solution problems centering on Formosa." Rather surprisingly, the department even envisaged that the "UN itself might find it possible and appropriate continue with concept neutralization pending final resolution of indicated problems."[24]

Three days after firing off his communication demanding U.S. withdrawal from Formosa, Premier Chou sent letters to the same addressees and to Secretary of State Acheson, strongly protesting attacks by U.S. airforce planes on Chinese territory along the Yalu River, the boundary between North Korea and Manchuria, and demanding complete withdrawal of U.S. troops from Korea. The letter to Acheson also demanded that the United States punish the air force and pay compensation to the victims. On August 30 Chou sent a second letter to Malik and Lie claiming that further U.S. air action had "killed and wounded a number of Chinese." Again Chou demanded complete U.S. withdrawal from Korea.[25]

Reporting on the Chinese protest, Hutchison (who had been given a copy of Chou's letter to Trygve Lie by the Foreign Ministry) thought it might presage an intensification of the Chinese press campaign against U.S. action in Korea and Formosa and might also be used to justify Chinese intervention in Korea.[26] At this time, it should be noted, U.S. and other UN forces were still battling defensively deep in South Korea and hardly presented a threat to China.

In the Far Eastern Department of the Foreign Office, Colin Crowe commented: "The Chinese propaganda machine is now in top gear and incidents are being played up which could justify Chinese intervention in Korea or an attack on Hong Kong. . . . [the propaganda] is in any case very dangerous, lest it commit the Chinese to positions from which they cannot retreat even if they would."[27] In Peking, however, Hutchison now took a calmer view of Peking's treatment of the U.S. air incursions. Although he reported that the air attacks had dominated the press since August 28, and that they had been described by the press as "provocative and intended to enlarge the Korean incident," he saw no change in the basic Chinese propaganda line and no indication of Chinese government intent to intervene in Korea. The reports themselves, he said, were "brief and factual and not inflammatory.[28] However, in the Foreign Office, Crowe noted: "The reports may have been noninflammatory but the use of them has been the reverse. I scarcely see how the two can be divorced."[29]

The U.S. reaction to the PRC protests of the air attacks was non-provocative, if not conciliatory. The U.S. representative in the UN Security Council, Ambassador Warren Austin, wrote to Trygve Lie August 29 welcoming an on-the-spot investigation.[30] He later proposed that a commission composed of India and Sweden investigate these and subsequent Chinese charges.[31]

The U.S. suggestion, supported by the British, was transmitted to the CPG through Indian Ambassador Panikkar, along with a U.S. offer to settle any legitimate claims arising from U.S. bombing of Chinese territory. Panikkar was also instructed to express India's willingness, if the People's Republic was willing, to appoint a representative to act with a Swedish representative in making an investigation and assessing damages. According to U.S. Ambassador Henderson in New Delhi, Bajpai told him that the Indian government considered the U.S. offer generous and could not see how Peking could continue to maintain that the United States was not doing all it could be reasonably expected to do to compensate China for any damage that U.S. planes might have inflicted on Chinese territory.[32]

Although Ambassador Panikkar reported to the Indian government in mid-October that the Chinese government was telling him it was considering the matter, the Peking press was giving indications that the Chinese reaction would be unfavorable. Peking, in fact, did reject the offer of investigation. Nevertheless, in British eyes at least, the U.S. offer and Bevin's message "served the very useful purpose of demonstrating to Indian Government that both Americans and ourselves are anxious to dispel any general misconception which the Chinese may have to deal with them on a reasonable basis."[33]

30

Chinese Intervention in Korea

The apparent miscalculation by Moscow and Peking in the late spring of 1950 of the probable U.S. response to a North Korean attack on South Korea was matched in the early fall by a U.S. miscalculation of PRC intentions and capabilities. In ordering U.S. troops north of the 38th parallel, President Truman ignored clear warnings from Peking, transmitted via Indian Ambassador Panikkar, that such action would bring Chinese intervention in the war. As Richard Neustadt, a former Truman White House staff member, explains the decision, Truman's advisers did not take the Chinese warnings seriously, and it probably would have made no difference to Truman if they had. Neustadt writes:

Moscow, not Peking, had been the Pentagon's great worry. Now that the UN was on the march, an intervention by Chinese, alone, seemed relatively easy to withstand and *therefore* most unlikely to occur. . . . In Washington no less than in MacArthur's headquarters there was some lack of readiness "to take seriously a country which up until this time had been notorious for its political and military weakness."

Even had Peking appeared more formidable, more in earnest, less a mere blackmailer; even had the British, say, not Panikkar, been chosen to transmit Chou's threat, it is improbable that Truman's chief advisers would have counseled abandoning MacArthur's broad advance or putting off the General Assembly action. It is equally improbable that Truman would have accepted such advice if offered.[1]

One of Truman's influential advisers who did not take the People's Republic seriously enough was Secretary of State Acheson, and his memoirs provide an explanation. Although Acheson says that the United States was seeking, through the Indian government, "evidence of Chinese intentions towards Korea," when he received a warning given by Chou En-lai to Indian Ambassador Panikkar on October 3 that China would enter the war if American troops crossed the 38th parallel, Acheson felt that it could be regarded as "a warning" but not as an "authoritative statement of policy."[2] Part of the problem was the mistrust American officials had of the conveyer of Chou's message. Thus John K. Emmerson, who was at the time planning adviser in the Bureau of Far Eastern Affairs, notes in his memoirs: "Pannikar [*sic*], like Krishna Menon, the long-time Indian representative at the United Nations, was so thoroughly disliked by American government officials who had had to deal with him officially, that no one had confidence in his word. As a result, we disregarded Chou's clear warning."[3] But Acheson and President Truman's other advisers had a second chance to take Peking more seriously, and their failure to do so is less understandable, perhaps, than their failure to heed the initial warnings. As UN forces for the first time entered the region of North Korea bordering China, substantial numbers of Chinese troops began to appear on the battlefront, some of whom were taken prisoner. On November 2 Peking announced that Chinese volunteers had entered

Korea to help the North Koreans. Chinese intervention was acknowledged in a report by General MacArthur to the United Nations on November 6. A lull in the fighting ensued as the UN forces halted their advance to the Yalu River.

MacArthur was confident that "his air power would stop Chinese reinforcements from crossing from Manchuria and would destroy Chinese troops already in Korea."[4] He wanted to push ahead to the Yalu, and on November 24 he renewed his offensive. The State Department had increasing misgivings about such a move and Britain and France strenuously advocated leaving a substantial buffer zone between UN forces and the Chinese border.[5] Nevertheless, Washington did not change MacArthur's orders—orders that allowed him to proceed at his discretion. In his heavily documented study of the Korean War, Joseph Goulden points out: "Even a small-scale entry of Chinese 'volunteers' in late October did not bring any change in MacArthur's orders. Truman and Acheson had convinced themselves that since the United States had no designs on Chinese territory, the Chinese could trust their motives. The Chinese did not. In sum, the Truman administration (The President, Acheson, and the JCS) made errors of magnitude comparable to those of MacArthur."[6]

Whether or not one agrees with Goulden that Truman and his advisers in Washington made "errors of magnitude comparable to those of MacArthur," it is clear that Washington had a second chance to reconsider its policy on reunification of Korea by force and did not take it. In his memoirs Acheson acknowledges that he did not serve the president well in this instance.[7] What is less clear, certainly, is whether a decision by Washington to halt MacArthur's further advance would have avoided the debacle that ensued after he renewed his offensive on November 24. A judgment on this score depends in part on one's estimate of Chinese intentions. Before turning to this, however, it is necessary to clarify U.S. intentions toward the People's Republic of China.

As indicated previously, the United States had no designs on PRC territory. Both highly classified U.S. policy documents and U.S. diplomatic actions at the time attest to Washington's desire to limit the war to Korea. This intent was spelled out again and again in NSC 73/4, "The Position and Actions of the United States with Respect to Possible Further Soviet Moves in the Light of the Korean Situation," dated August 25, 1950. For example, "in the event of a Chinese Communist attack on Formosa or the Pescadores, the United States should repel the assault in accordance with existing directives but should not permit itself to become engaged in a general war with Communist China. In any event U.S. ground forces should not be committed on Formosa." Again, "in the event of the overt use of organized Chinese Communist forces in Korea: . . . The United States should not permit itself to become engaged in a general war with China." Finally, "in the event of overt attack by organized Chinese communist forces against Indochina, the United States should not permit itself to become engaged in a general war with Communist China, but should in concert with the U.K., support France and the associated states."[8] Although the policy laid down by the NSC called for air and sea retaliation against the People's Republic if Chinese forces entered the Korean War, there is no indication that a land attack was ever contemplated in such an eventuality. As a matter of fact, even the policy of air and sea retaliation was not put into effect when the Chinese did intervene. Bombings of Chinese territory along the Yalu, to the extent that they occurred, were either accidental or against standing orders.[9] General MacArthur's recommendations for bombing and blockading China were repeatedly turned down.[10]

This policy was not forced on a reluctant military by the State Department and U.S. allies. It was a policy that the JCS itself advocated. The JCS wanted to avoid a conflict with China that might sap U.S. strength and prevent it from meeting its obligations in Europe. For this reason, the JCS not only favored halting the advance of UN forces short of the Yalu River but urged that every effort be made to settle the problem of Chinese intervention by political means through the United Nations or through negotations with the People's Republic by countries that recognized Peking. Meanwhile, the JCS advocated public reassurances that the UN did not intend to attack China.[11]

Such public assurances were given by both Truman and Acheson. At a news conference on November 16, Truman noted that the Chinese pretext for offensive action in Korea against the UN forces was their professed belief that these forces intended to carry hostilities across the border into China. He declared that no such intention had ever been entertained by the United Nations or by the United Stataes government and people.[12] The day before, Acheson had also attempted to allay Chinese fears in a speech made to a citizens conference on foreign affairs.[13]

Moreover private assurances were conveyed to the CPG by the British chargé in Peking. Thus on November 22 Foreign Secretary Bevin sent a personal message to Chou En-lai through Hutchison assuring the Chinese government that UN action in Korea was in no way aimed at China's security and that China's legitimate interests would be taken fully into account.[14]

What Peking would have done had MacArthur's forces made no further advances after the initial Chinese deployments into Korea in late October may never be known, but what actually happened on the battlefield and in the diplomatic arena suggests that the PRC intervention was intended to do far more than merely defend the Chinese border. Beginning on November 24, MacArthur's offensive was met with such an overwhelming counterattack that within twelve days the Chinese and North Koreans had retaken Pyongyang, the North Korean capital. In this way the Chinese "volunteers" gave substance to Chou's declaration to the Chinese People's Political Consultative Conference on September 30. "The Chinese people absolutely will not tolerate foreign aggression, nor will they supinely tolerate seeing their neighbors being savagely invaded by imperialists."[15]

Consistent with Chou's declaration of September 30 is the implication in Khrushchev's memoirs that the object of the PRC intervention in the Korean War was to prevent North Korea's defeat. According to Khruschev, after North Korean troops had been driven back into North Korea and the U.S. air force had taken command of the air, Mao sent Chou to see Stalin. Despite initial hesitation, Stalin agreed with Chou that "China should give active support to North Korea."[16] A buffer zone along the Sino-Korean frontier would hardly have satisfied this purpose.

The official spokesman the People's Republic sent to present its case against the United States to the United Nations, General Wu Hsiu-chuan, made it abundantly clear in a speech before the Security Council on November 26 that Peking's objectives went well beyond halting the UN advance short of China's frontiers.[17] He demanded withdrawal of U.S. and other forces from all of Korea, sanctions against the "aggressor," and withdrawal of all U.S. forces from Taiwan.[18] The general's demands were given dramatic force by the massive PRC counteroffensive against the UN, which went far beyond the needs of mere frontier defense. While this counteroffensive was being clandestinely prepared, be it noted, the PRC delegation had dawdled on its way to Lake Success, arriving ten days later than expected, but in time to permit General Wu to utter Pekings' demands just as UN forces were in full retreat before the Chinese volunteers.

Having routed UN forces in North Korea, the Chinese were confronted with a decision similar to that the UN faced after the spectacular success of its forces at Inchon in mid-September—whether to cross the 38th parallel. The Chinese decided to cross the parallel despite a request from the UN side to halt there and negotiate. After this request, made by thirteen Asian and Middle Eastern countries on December 5, was ignored, the General Assembly on December 14 adopted a resolution sponsored by the thirteen, asking the president of the General Assembly to constitute a group of three persons to determine the basis on which a satisfactory cease-fire in Korea could be arranged and to make recommendations to the General Assembly as soon as possible.[19]

The People's Republic, however, was no more interested in a cease-fire than it was in stopping at the 38th parallel; Peking ordered General Wu to return home and have nothing to do with the UN cease-fire committee. On December 22, Chou En-lai issued a statement, again making clear that the objectives of the Chinese intervention went well beyond simply protecting China's frontier. "The present issues," he said, "are definitely not confined to the Korean problem"; Peking's well-known grievances against the United States—that is, the U.S. "invasion" of "China's Taiwan" and its bombing of "Northeast China"—must be dealt with as well. Also at issue were the UN rejection of the PRC demands that foreign forces be withdrawn from Korea and U.S. forces from Taiwan and its failure to grant the PRC representatives China's UN seat. Chou went on to lay down as "a basis" for negotiation the withdrawal of all foreign troops from Korea, withdrawal of "American aggression forces" from Taiwan, and the seating of PRC representatives in the UN. "To put aside these points," Chou declared, "would make it impossible to settle peacefully the Korean problem and the important problems of Asia."[20]

Two days later in a speech celebrating "the victories of the Chinese and Korean peoples" Commander in Chief Chu Teh reiterated China's extended war aims. He declared: "We must insist that all foreign troops must swiftly withdraw from Korea, and that the domestic affairs of Korea must be settled by the Korean people themselves. U.S. aggressive forces must withdraw from Taiwan. The People's Republic of China must have her legitimate status in the United Nations. Only when these demands are implemented can Asian questions be settled peacefully."[21]

Chou's and Chu's statements were made in the euphoria of the rapid sweep of the PRC volunteers and the resuscitated Korean People's Army down to the 38th parallel and beyond. By January 4 they had captured the South Korean capital of Seoul. The Peking *People's Daily* crowed that this victory showed that "the Korean People's Army and the Chinese people's volunteers . . . can definitely wipe out U.S. land, air and naval forces, despite their bristling arms. If the Americans refuse to go, push them into the ocean."[22]

Such was the Chinese display of confidence that Swedish Ambassador Torsten Hammerstrom in Peking considered the prospect for a cease-fire in Korea hopeless. He reported to his government that either there would have to be a military demonstration that "the Chinese Communists cannot have [their] own way in Korea," or the UN would have to accept the PRC conditions.[23] Some months later, Ambassador Hammerstrom told an officer of the American consulate general in Hong Kong that Chou En-lai had refused to see him about the cease-fire because the Chinese felt they had a fair chance of driving UN troops out of Korea.[24]

Inevitably the Chinese intervention in Korea brought Anglo-American differences on China policy to a head. Unlike the United States, the United Kingdom did not oppose the PRC conditions for ending the war, since London had long been in favor of seating the People's Republic in the United Nations, wanted to see Formosa given to the People's Republic, and was constantly afraid the United States would get drawn into a war with China that would weaken it in Europe. None of these attitudes was new. It is not surprising, therefore, that in talks held early in December 1950 between Truman and Prime Minister Attlee, the latter thought (to quote Acheson) that "withdrawal from Korea and Formosa and the Chinese seat in the United Nations for the Communists would not be too high a price" to pay for a cease-fire in Korea.[25]

The Americans countered with arguments that the Chinese should not be rewarded for their aggression in Korea, that failure of the United States to stand by its commitment to South Korea would call into question the value of its defense commitments in Europe, and that U.S. withdrawal from Korea under pressure from European allies would seriously erode support for NATO in the United States. Truman and Acheson thus argued for a simple cease-fire to halt the fighting, after which political questions could be discussed. Eventually, the British supported this tactic.[26]

The Truman-Attlee talks revealed continuing Anglo-American differences about the more efficacious approach to Communist China—the carrot or the stick. Attlee claimed the support of Asian opinion in his advocacy of conceding to the People's Republic on the UN and Formosa issues in return for a cease-fire in Korea. Moreover, in the British view, such an approach might modify Peking's lean-to-one-side policy. The Americans took the opposite view. Acheson stressed. "If Formosa were turned over [to the People's Republic] as a result of aggression, this fact would be exploited in a most devastating way. . . . If we give concessions, they will become increasingly aggressive."[27]

From Hong Kong, now the chief American China-watching post, Consul General Walter McConaughy had a similar reaction to the British position. In his view, the British at the Truman-Attlee talks "overemphasized adverse effect on Asian opinion resulting from our refusal turn Formosa over to Chinese Communists and fail to give sufficient weight to effect such action on Chinese themselves."[28]

The question of China's "aggressive plans" for Southeast Asia aside, it is difficult to see how, after its smashing victories in Korea, the People's Republic could regard concessions from its enemies as anything but the fruits of its victories and the proof of the wisdom of its policies. Indeed, this seemed to be the confident tenor of the Chinese media. For example, an editorial in *People's Daily* declared: "on the one hand, the American imperialists have already suffered fiasco in Asia and will continue to suffer still more deplorable fiascos, and, on the other hand, the Chinese people . . . who are now closely united under the leadership of Mao Tse-tung and who have become the ally of the Soviet Union, have now become the master of their own country and the centre of gravity of the power of the Asian peoples."[29]

A major result of the Truman-Attlee talks was greater understanding on the part of the British of the American attitude toward Formosa. The United States emphasized Formosa's military importance in the situation then prevailing. Thus in one session, General Marshall said that Formosa must be looked at "as a wedge" in the island chain extending from Japan in the north to the Philippines and Indonesia in the south. From the military point of view if would be "very dangerous to give up Formosa. . . . if we split the island chain that would really be serious."[30]

British participants in the talks acknowledged the force of "the arguments on the military aspect of Formosa," as Robert Scott of the Foreign Office put it, although they wished that somehow the questions of safeguarding Formosa and recognition of the Nationalists could be separated.[31] In the end, the United Kingdom, though adhering to its position favoring PRC admission to the UN, backed away from its willingness to turn Formosa over to the People's Republic.

The new British position on Formosa was reflected in the joint U.S.-U.K. communiqué issued on December 9, which contained the two points the United States had been advocating since September, that is, that any settlement of the Formosa question should take into account the interests of the people of Formosa and the maintenance of peace and security in the Pacific.[32] The communiqué called for UN consideration of the Formosa problem, but when the item, "Question of Formosa," was recalled in the First Committee on February 7, the Americans supported a British move to adjourn consideration of the item "in view of the unsettled state of the situation in the Far East."[33] The motion was carried by thirty-eight votes to five, with eight abstentions.[34] This outcome, of course, pleased the Nationalists, who, according to a telegram from Rankin in Taipei, had been hoping the United States would "withdraw if possible or at least arrange indefinite postponement beyond present GA session of any discussion future of Formosa."[35]

31
The End of Flexibility

Not long after his return to London from his meetings with President Truman, Prime Minister Attlee became concerned about what U.S. intentions toward China really were. In a letter of January 8, 1951, he told Truman that he had been "left with the impression, particularly from Secretary Acheson's message to Mr. Bevin of the 5th January, that the United States Government may wish to substitute for a policy of localising the conflict in Korea, a policy aimed at developing limited action against China."[1] In this connection he mentioned his fears that the United States might be intending to urge on the UN a "campaign of subversion or guerrilla warfare against China involving the use of Chiang Kai-shek's men." Because of such fears, Attlee explained, the United Kingdom had been opposing "the introduction at this stage of a resolution in the United Nations condemning China as an aggressor and calling on the Collective Measures Committee to consider measures to be taken." He proposed as an immediate step designed to "consolidate opinion in the United Nations which is at present disarrayed" a resolution based on the latest set of principles drawn up by the Cease-Fire Committee.[2]

Truman lost no time in assuring Attlee that, as they had agreed, "resistance in Korea" would continue unless UN troops were driven out by superior forces, that it was still the desire and intention of the U.S. government "to confine hostilities to Korea," that the United States did not intend to recommend to the UN a campaign of subversion or guerrilla warfare against the mainland of China by "Chinese National forces," and that his chief concern was that UN action "appropriate to the present situation in Korea . . . should be honest and honorable and directed to preserve the great principle of collective security."[3]

In the event, both the United Kingdom and the United States got the UN resolutions they wanted. On January 13 the First Committee of the General Assembly approved the five principles embodied in the Supplementry Report of the Cease-Fire Group.[4] It then approved a Norwegian resolution calling on the chairman of the First Committee to transmit the statement of principles to the CPG.[5] In what amounted to a new UN proposal for cease-fire, the principles went beyond previous UN cease-fire proposals in meeting Peking's desiderata, since they envisaged holding a conference to discuss Far Eastern questions, including China's seat in the UN and Formosa. But from the Chinese point of view, they had a fatal flaw, namely, "the principle of cease-fire first and negotiations later." The CPG rejected this principle in much the same language the CCP negotiators had used in rejecting the Nationalist government's cease-fire proposals in April 1949—as merely a device to give "breathing space" to a beaten enemy so it could regroup. The People's Republic insisted that negotiations on the basis of its agenda get underway before a cease-fire.[6]

Peking's rejection of the latest UN cease-fire offer paved the way for the United States to introduce on January 20 a resolution that found "the Central People's Government of the People's Republic of China . . . [had] itself engaged in aggression in Korea," affirmed "the determination of the United Nations to continue its action in Korea to meet the aggression," and asked the Collective Measures Committee "as a matter of urgency to consider additional measures to be employed to meet this aggression." The U.S.-sponsored resolution also affirmed that it continued "to be the policy of the United Nations to bring about a cessation of hostilities in Korea" and asked "the President of the General Assembly to designate forthwith two persons who would meet with him at any suitable opportunity to use their good offices to bring about this end."[7]

Arguing for the U.S. resolution, Ambassador Warren Austin stressed that the People's Republic had repeatedly refused "to agree to a cease-fire followed by negotiations on Far Eastern problems" but had instead demanded "the right to continue their assault on the United Nations until negotiations are concluded." He went on to point out that Peking's terms for negotiations in effect required UN acceptance in principle of its political demands as to Formosa and Chinese representation in the UN even before negotiations began. He charged that the Chinese position was nothing more than "their masters' response, that of the Soviet ruling circles," and asked rhetorically if the Chinese Communists were trying "to break into the United Nations with mortars and grenades."[8]

The British were ready to condemn PRC aggression in Korea, but they were reluctant to support the part of the U.S. resolution that called on the Collective Measures Committee urgently to consider additional measures to meet the aggression. They preferred to wait and see what the Good Offices Committee might be able to come up with. In conversation with Assistance Secretaries Rusk and John D. Hickerson on January 26, Ambassador Franks gave his "personal views" on the fundamental causes of the British hesitation. There were three: mistrust of the UN command in Korea and of U.S. intentions, "above all U.S. impulsiveness"; the influence of Nehru at the recent meeting of commonwealth prime ministers; and the feeling in London that the latest message from Peking "contained more hope" than the United States seemed to think.[9]

The following day Acheson telephoned Franks to tell him that after talking to Rusk, Hickerson, and the president, he had authorized the addition of language to the U.S. resolution to the effect that the Collective Measures Committee could withhold its report if the "other Committee" (that is, the Good Offices Committee) was getting along well with its work. Acheson stressed that this was as far as the United States could go in meeting the British and that he had the backing of not only the president and the cabinet but the House and Senate foreign affairs committees as well.[10] The proposed amendment was transmitted the same day by the State Department to the U.S. mission at the UN, with the comment that the department would be willing to accept it "if it would be helpful in bringing UK along on our res."; the department also believed "it might induce the French and other western Europeans" to vote for the resolution.[11] The amendment did succeed in winning the British and western European votes for the resolution, which was approved by the First Committee on January 30 and by the General Assembly on February 1 by large margins.[12]

The United Kingdom may have been persuaded to vote for the amended U.S. resolution partly by Chou En-lai's negative response to a message from Prime Minister Nehru urging him to issue a statement affirming China's peaceful intentions in the Pacific. Nehru apparently hoped that such a statement would increase support for a joint resolution that had been introduced in the First Committee on January 24 by twelve Arab and Asian nations, recommending a meeting of the United States, the United Kingdom, the Soviet Union, Egypt, India, and the People's Republic "for the purpose of securing all necessary elucidations and amplifications" of Chou En-lai's reply to the UN ceasefire proposal of January 13.[13] But Chou had rejected Nehru's suggestion on the grounds that as long as a resolution was pending in the UN condemning his government as an aggressor, such a statement might look as though the People's Republic were weakening in the face of charges against it.[14]

Assistant Undersecretary Scott and others in the Far Eastern Department felt "thoroughly discouraged over Chou's response." They pointed out to the U.S. embassy that on no single occasion had the CPG itself ever taken the initiative in the negotiations with the UN, and they saw in this a striking parallel to U.K.-PRC negotiations for the establishment of diplomatic relations. Although on occasion the CPG had asked for clarification of a British position, it had never indicated any desire to regularize its relationships with Britain. In their opinion, Chou's reply to Nehru was merely a clumsy and ineffectual attempt to influence the voting on the U.S. resolution.[15] For Scott and others in the Foreign Office, Chou's rejection of Nehru's appeal for a gesture to show that the People's Replubic was earnestly striving for a peaceful settlement was the last straw. They felt, according to a U.S. embassy report, that "it should now be apparent to all that CPG (a) has never intended seriously to negotiate peaceful settlement in FE, (b) has never sincerely desired establish diplomatic relations with UK, and (c) has never made serious effort enter UN (except on terms it knew would be unacceptable); it has only wished make noises to that effect."[16] Further indication of a lack of interest in relations with Britain came the following month during Hutchison's farewell call on Vice–Foreign Minister Chang Han-fu. Chang displayed a "studious lack of cordiality," and Hutchison's efforts to get him to express an opinion on the means of reactivating negotiations for the establishment of diplomatic relations were futile.[17]

This disillusionment with the People's Republic may have encouraged the United Kingdom to support the U.S. resolution condemning PRC aggression in Korea, but it did not, at first at any rate, affect the British position on seating the People's Republic in the United Nations. In a message to Sir Oliver Franks dated February 15, Ernest Bevin specifically rejected Washington's argument that a government that had been condemned as an aggressor by the UN ought not be admitted to it. He did not regard the condemnatory resolution "as relevant to the question of representation, which should be based on recognition of facts alone and should not be connected with moral approval or condemnation."[18]

However, when Acheson some two and a half months later sent a personal message to Herbert Morrison, who had replaced the ailing Bevin in March, proposing that the Washington and London "agree to a moratorium" on their debate on the Chinese representation issue, Morrison expressed interest in the idea. Acheson argued that discussion of the possible admission of the "Chinese Communists" to the UN at a time when they were fighting UN forces "on a major scale, and denying the validity of every provision of the Charter" would have "the most divisive possible effect" and give them "the greatest encouragement in continuing their present course."[19]

In replying to Acheson on May 10, Morrison expressed interest in the moratorium idea as a means of preventing "our known differences of view . . . from developing into a source of misunderstanding between us." Morrison repeated the British position that the legal arguments for seating the People's Republic were conclusive and pointed out that he "could not act in such a way as might imply support for the fiction that Chiang Kai-shek's representative in the United Nations speaks for China." On the other hand, Morrison did not "wish to display any enthusiasm in championing the claims of the Central People's Government of China at the United Nations so long as they are set on their present course."[20]

In the circumstances the British clearly did not wish to vote for either Chinese government. The Taipei government did not represent China; the Peking government was fighting the UN. Acheson's suggestion, which Morrison agreed to, was that both the United States and the United Kingdom support a UN resolution that would simply postpone a vote on which Chinese government should represent China in the UN. There would be a moratorium on discussion of the issue, and the United Kingdom would not have to vote for either Peking or Taipei. In effect, of course, this procedure would preserve the seat for the government in Taipei.[21]

Britain, in explaining its vote in support of the postponement resolution, would make clear that it still recognized the CPG as the government of China but that it was "compelled to take notice of the fact" of the aggression of the People's Republic and its refusal "to accept a settlement of the Korean dispute on honorable terms."[22] When the Labor government was replaced in the fall by a Conservative government, the new foreign minister, Anthony Eden, was willing to adhere to the moratorium arrangement of his predecessor, but opposed any changes that might imply that Taipei was "more entitled" to China's UN seat than Peking.[23]

With the massive offensives of Chinese volunteers in late November, pressure for a complete embargo on U.S. trade with the People's Republic had built up rapidly in Washington. Interestingly, despite the long-standing appraisal in foreign circles that China under the Communists was in desperate economic circumstances, at this time it was actually exporting more to the United States than it was importing. According to the secretary of commerce, the United States was getting "important amounts of tungsten" from the People's Republic and "some wool and tin," but 85 percent of American exports to China consisted of cotton; "nothing of any military importance had been shipped" there.[24]

The Commerce Department promulgated a regulation, effective December 3, that required all persons wishing to export any commodities to mainland China, Hong Kong, or Macao to apply for an export license. This regulation would in theory have permitted goods determined not to have any strategic value to be licensed for export, but the Treasury Department called it "tantamount to a *de facto* embargo upon export trade."[25] In a memorandum to the National Security Council, Secretary John Snyder pointed out the inconsistency of applying such trade restrictions while failing to block Chinese assets. Unless assets were blocked, China could "transfer dollars so as to import similar goods from other countries."[26] Treasury wanted financial controls that would put all financial transactions with China under individual licensing.[27]

As might be expected, the JCS went further than Treasury in objecting to the State Department position that the United States "should not at this moment undertake full unilateral trade embargo and financial freezing measures against Communist China." The JCS called this position "anomalous" and said it permitted "the giving of aid and comfort to Communist China at a time when that nation is militarily attacking United States armed forces." It therefore pressed

for a "full unilateral embargo, together with financial freezing measures against Communist China" to be taken at once.[28]

On December 16 the U.S. government placed all Chinese Communist assets within U.S. jurisdiction under control and prohibited all
vessels of U.S. registry from calling at Chinese Communist ports. In a
high-level State Department meeting two days earlier Acheson had
acknowledged that such measures though they "would have no real
effect upon the Chinese" would need to be taken to appease public
opinion.[29] In a circular instruction to all diplomatic officers the State
Department said that the United States did not "desire these restrictions [to] become permanent" but continued to hope that China would
"abandon action which runs counter to interests and objectives UN in
present Far Eastern crisis."[30]

The People's Republic answered the U.S. move in kind. On December 28, the CPG ordered that all assets of the U.S. government and
American enterprises within China immediately be brought under
control of the CPG, and all government and private deposits of the
United States in banks within China immediately be frozen.[31]

How the CPG's freeze order was implemented locally is illustrated
by a communication dated December 31, 1950, from the Shanghai
manager of an American company to the company's Hong Kong office:

On the 30th instant, Mr. Mou and I were summoned to a meeting of the Trade
Section of the Military Control Commission, which was attended by representatives of all American firms, where we were informed that the matter of control
of American firms was necessitated by actions of the U.S. Government in the
States. It was pointed out that the measures about to be brought into force did
not constitute confiscation but meant control and supervision. . . . Later in the
afternoon, five delegates from the Military Control Commission came to the
office and explained their position as supervisors. . . . In addition to this, a
company (32 in number) of soldiers has been moved to our Tungku Terminal
for protection of property.[32]

A copy of this communication was sent to the State Department by
Cathay Oil Company on January 8, 1951, together with a letter stating
that the company's "operations at Shanghai remain completely out of
our jurisdiction and such sales as we make are only of merchandise,
supplies, etc. which were on hand at Shanghai prior to the occupation
of that city by the Communists."[33]

Judging by a report to the Foreign Office from the British consul
general in Shanghai dated January 30, 1951, the experience of Cathay
Oil Company was fairly typical of the treatment accorded American

companies in Shanghai, especially those with substantial assets in China. According to this account, which had been prepared for the consul general by a "responsible American," American power and telephone companies were

completely under control and management of military representatives. Former managers merely carry out instructions and are instructed not to seek or obey any instructions from the Board of Directors or New York Office.

Affairs of all other companies having considerable properties, stocks and staff are controlled by Government representatives who have desks in the companies' offices and with regard to some such companies (principally oil companies) virtually direct their affairs and with regard to all such companies at least exercise the veto power on all affairs. . . . Cheques drawn by all companies must be counter-signed by Government representatives and in many cases companies named required to transfer their accounts with local foreign and independent Chinese Banks to Government Banks"[34]

Having "instituted comprehensive controls" over all its economic relations with Communist China, which State Department officials acknowledged to be a resort to "economic warfare," the United States was now anxious to persuade other UN members to follow suit to the extent possible. Realizing that other countries might reach different conclusions about whether "comprehensive economic sanctions against the Chinese Communists" would be in their national interest, the United States did not press other UN members for a full embargo, but it made clear that it considered as an "irreducible minimum a resolution by the GA recommending the immediate imposition of an embargo on petroleum, atomic energy materials, arms, ammunition, and implements of war."[35] On May 18, 1951, the UN General Assembly adopted a resolution incorporating essentially the language proposed by the United States as the "irreducible minimum." The resolution concluded with an affirmation "that it continues to be the policy of the United Nations to bring about a cessation of hostilities in Korea, and the achievement of United Nations objectives in Korea by peaceful means, and requests the Good Offices Committee to continue its good offices."[36]

The United Kingdom had decided to support the embargo resolution only reluctantly. Considerations accounting for the British reluctance included the strong feeling of the Hong Kong and Singapore governments that, despite the fact that the measures being contemplated by the Additional Measures Committee were already being enforced by the British, the proposed UN resolution would be "dangerously provocative"; and the fear that the resolution would be the starting point for general economic and political sanctions to which the British had been and remained strongly opposed.[37] The Foreign Office had favored defering the report of the Additional Measures Committee to the General Assembly until the Good Offices Committee had "failed." But U.S. officials pointed out that the British position was in conflict with the General Assembly resolution of February 1, "which merely authorized the AMC to defer its report if GOC reported satisfactory progress"; in fact, the Good Offices Committee had made no progress whatever. It appeared to the State Department that "the British still believed that additional measures might provoke the Chinese Communists to continue the aggression." U.S. analysis "indicated that they would if anything provide an additional stimulus for the Chinese Communists to seek a peaceful settlement."[38] Once again the fundamental difference in the American and British views of economic sanctions as an instrument of policy had cropped up—a difference that had first appeared in 1949.

The British, of course, had long been applying an embargo on strategic items, including petroleum, a fact noted with disgust by a spokesman of the Ministry of Foreign Affairs in Peking. In a statement roundly condemning the "illegally adopted" UN embargo resolution, the Foreign Affairs Ministry official declared: "It should be pointed out that, long before the said resolution submitted by the United States was illegally adopted, the British Government has already taken a succession of unfriendly actions against the People's Republic of China in the field of trade, and has been determined to be the enemy of the Chinese people. All the countries that follow the lead of the United States in banning shipments to China and Korea shall be responsible for all the consequences resulting from their hostile acts."[39]

Peking's condemnation of the UN embargo resolution was only to be expected, and it did not deter the majority of UN members from complying with the resolution. According to a report to the NSC by Secretaries Acheson and Robert H. Lovett (Defense), by September 25, 1951, not only had a majority of UN members and some nonmembers reported compliance but in addition, "largely subsequent to the adoption of the Resolution, many States recently have taken measures going beyond the generally understood scope of the Resolution."[40] On the other hand, the secretaries acknowledged. "There continues to be a substantial volume of goods shipped into China. This trade still includes a certain amount of strategic commodities, but very little consists of direct war materials. . . . The United States continues day-by-day efforts to observe and bring to the attention of responsible authorities infractions of their regulations by smugglers and others who attempt to evade controls applying to trade with Communist China."[41] In a public statement about a month later, the assistant secretary of state for economic affairs, Willard Thorp, noted: "Forty-three countries have accepted the resolution and are actively applying it. And among those forty-three countries are all of the principal suppliers of strategic items to China, except of course, the Soviet bloc countries."[42]

Another manifestation of the hardening of U.S. policy after the PRC intervention in the Korean War was a restoration to the Nationalists of large-scale military assistance, accompanied by a substantial military advisory group. Thus, on January 30, 1951, U.S. Chargé Rankin in Taipei informed Foreign Minister Yeh by diplomatic note that the United States government was "prepared to make available to the Republic of China . . . certain military material for the defense of Taiwan against possible attack." This material would only be furnished "on the understanding that it will be used and disposed of pursuant to" certain "undertakings." Among these were that the material would be used by the "Chinese Government . . . to maintain its internal security or its legitimate self-defense" and that the Nationalists would agree to receive U.S. government personnel and would accord facilities "to observe the progress of the assistance furnished, to confirm that the material furnished is being used as shall be mutually agreed pursuant to this agreement." By a note dated February 9 the "Chinese Government" accepted these terms.[43]

On February 16, at the request of the State Department, President Truman allocated $50 million as grant aid to Chinese Nationalist ground forces for the defense of Formosa. The major items to be supplied under this grant included signal equipment, tanks, motor vehicles, small arms and ammunition, engineering and medical equipment.[44] The State Department's telegram informing the U.S. embassy in Taipei of this action added: "Navy and AF grant aid programs ($5.2 and $16 million respectively) complementing above also been prepared by Def and approved by Dept which requesting Pres allocate funds."[45]

On May 1, the first contingent of the Military Assistance Advisory Group arrived in Taipei under the command of Major General William Chase. Chargé Rankin welcomed this development, though he felt some concern about overexpansion of the American official presence in Taipei. Thus he comments in his memoirs: "The decision finally had been reached in Washington to reverse our earlier position that no further missions of this kind would be sent to China. I had thought that we might do well enough on an informal basis, by enlarging our staff of military attachés. But it probably was better to face the matter squarely, and General Chase made an outstanding contribution during his four years in Taiwan."[46]

It should be noted that the reversal of U.S. policy Rankin mentions took place only after the PRC entry into the Korean War. In another passage in his memoirs Rankin lists "the most significant events in the development of our policy toward Formosa" after June 27, 1950, the date President Truman announced U.S. entry in the Korean War and neutralization of Formosa. These included the military assistance allocation in February 1951 already mentioned; the notification to Taipei on April 20 that the Military Assistance Advisory Group would be established; "the allocation on June 21, 1951, of nearly forty-two million dollars in additional economic aid" to the Nationalists; and "the passage of the Mutual Security appropriations in October, 1951," which included "some three hundred million dollars in aid for Formosa in the fiscal year 1952."[47] It is significant that none of these developments took place until after the PRC entry in the war and Pekings' rejection of UN cease-fire proposals.

The effect of the Chinese intervention in Korea may be seen in NSC 48/5, dated May 17, 1951, dealing with U.S. policy on Asia. This paper reflected growing U.S. concern over the Communist threat in Asia and provided the rationale for increased military and economic aid to Formosa. Thus one of the current objectives it listed was: "Deny Formosa to any Chinese regime aligned with or dominated by the USSR and expedite the strengthening of the defensive capabilities of Formosa."[48] The courses of action toward China set forth in NSC 48/5 contrast sharply with policies the United States pursued in 1949. For example, instead of providing for a policy of flexibility among political factions in China as did NSC 34/1 in January 1949, NSC 49/5 called for expanded and intensified efforts to influence the leaders and the people of China to oppose the "Peiping regime" and for support of anti-Communist elements. Instead of providing for U.S. and Japanese trade with Communist areas of China, as did NSC 41, NSC 48/5 called for continued U.S. economic restrictions against China and the imposition of political and economic sanctions by other nations. Instead of willingness to abide by a majority vote in the UN Security Council on the seating of the People's Republic, which was the U.S. policy in 1949-1950, NSC 48/5 called for intensified efforts to persuade other nations to oppose the seating.[49] Thus, by mid-May 1951 the United States had adopted the rather rigid set of hostile policies that were to characterize its posture toward China for some two decades. As we have seen, these policies evolved largely in response to policies adopted by the CCP leadership following its military triumphs in China and the PRC's entry into the Korean War.

Even while the hard-line policies were being put in place by the United States, however, the State Department was endeavoring to establish informal contacts with the CCP leadership. Hundreds of hours were devoted to this purpose from January to June 1951 by Burton Marshall, a member of the department's policy planning staff, and others. Although these efforts came to naught, as in the case of the attempt to reply to the so-called Chou En-lai demarche, it was not for lack of desire on the part of U.S. officials to open a channel of communication with Peking.[50] Since there is no conclusive evidence that word of Marshall's efforts ever reached the highest authorities in Peking, this failure to establish communication between Washington and Peking cannot with any certainty be blamed on the CCP leadership. On the other hand, it is evidence that even while adopting tough policies toward the People's Republic, the United States was willing to discuss Sino-American differences.

32
The Imprisoned and the Detained

The Chinese intervention in the Korean War had much greater consequences for westerners, especially Americans, in China that the outbreak of the war itself had had. Despite an intensification of anti-American propaganda after the outbreak of the war and the neutralization of Formosa, the situation of westerners in China did not change markedly. Most who wanted exit permits were able to get them and depart.[1] Those who chose to stay were able to continue with their activities more or less as before the war. The situation of businessmen who had been denied exit permits remained much the same; they could leave if replaced by other "hostages."[2] The State Department continued to favor the maintenance of American missionary and humanitarian institutions in the People's Republic. Thus as late as November 2, 1950, Deputy Assistant Secretary of State Merchant wrote to Gerard Swope, Sr., chairman of the American-Chinese Committee of the Mass Education Movement. "There are at the present time no regulations of the United States Government which obstruct remittances of funds from this country for the support of such institutions in China, nor has the Department of State discouraged individuals or institutions in the country in their financial support of missionary or similar institutions operating in China. In point of fact, the continued support of such institutions and organizations has been one of the few remaining ways in which the American people could express in tangible form their traditional friendship for the Chinese people."[3] But after the Chinese intervention the atmosphere changed. There was a rush for exit permits and the numbers of westerners who were imprisoned or otherwise prevented from leaving China increased dramatically.

That Chinese intervention in Korea would have a serious impact on the nationals in China of countries represented in the UN forces was not difficult to foresee, and preliminary signs of Chinese intervention prompted the Foreign Office to instruct Hutchison in Peking on October 9, 1950, that in the event of conclusive evidence of "organised Chinese armed intervention in North Korea," he should "advise all non-essential British subjects, particularly dependents, women and children to leave China." However, the Foreign Office warned Hutchison that as regards "essential British subjects, i.e. persons representing substantial British interests," the responsibility would rest on the individuals; the Foreign Office "would not wish to see them abandon their stake prematurely."[4]

On November 3 the Foreign Office notified Hutchison that should it prove necessary to advise U.K. subjects to leave China, the U.S., Australian, and New Zealand governments would like similar advice to be given at the same time to their nationals.[5] But Hutchison himself was not yet prepared to issue a general official warning. He informed the Foreign Office that he was merely asking consuls to let it be known that in his opinion the time had come when nonessential British subjects should leave China. In his circular telegram instructing British consuls, Hutchison cautioned them not to issue written advice or call meetings. Up-country missionaries should be informed by letters from their own mission representatives, but such letters should not quote Hutchison or the consuls. American, Australian, New Zealand, Canadian, and South African nationals should be informed in a similar manner.[6]

By the time these instructions went out, the People's Republic had already publicly acknowledged the participation of Chinese volunteers in the Korean War. Their infiltration had begun early in October, and about the same time, Chinese authorities in Peking stopped issuing exit permits to Americans. Thus Hutchison reported to the Foreign Office on November 18:

In Peking at least it appears clear that the authorities present policy is not allow any Americans to leave. Last to do so went some six weeks ago. Recently several have been refused including some perfectly innocuous students who were told that their applications were "temporarily refused." . . . If a similar state of affairs exists elsewhere in China it seems doubtful whether it is worthwhile issuing an evacuation warning to the Americans. I have not so far issued one in Peking (which would in any case be very difficult to do discreetly in view of the nature of Communication) but I am having hints dropped wherever possible.[7]

In Washington, meanwhile, officials in the State Department had been wrestling with the problem of what might be done to expedite the departure of those Americans, mainly businessmen, who had long been prevented from leaving China. In a memorandum to Edmund Clubb, now director of the Office of Chinese Affairs, dated December 8 (by which time the UN forces were in full retreat before the Chinese volunteers) Robert Strong raised the question of whether all U.S. business and philanthropic institutions "having American representatives on the mainland" should order such repesentatives to attempt to leave for safe haven and to make whatever financial sacrifice was necessary to facilitate their departure. Strong opined that "the concerned companies are going to have to pay heavily to bail them out."[8]

But Clubb disagreed with the idea of a general withdrawal, noting on Strong's memorandum that "missionaries and businessmen have been 'warned' repeatedly, only 'hard core' remain, and they were recently presumably warned by British." Deputy Assistant Secretary Merchant agreed with Clubb. He felt that warning these people might only raise their hopes while the United States was in fact helpless.[9]

But American organizations did not need prompting from their government. Repercussions of the Chinese intervention in Korea both in the United States and in China ensured that American institutions would advise their members in the field to leave. Most important of these repercussions was the U.S. decision to freeze Chinese assets and cut off financial transactions with the Peoples Republic, leaving American-supported organizations without their primary source of funds. The seizure of American-owned assets in China by the CPG, which followed, put American-supported schools and universities under exclusive Chinese control.[10] These developments, coupled with an intensification of anti-American propaganda in the Chinese media, resulted in what the British consul general in Canton, describing the atmosphere in Lingnan University, called a distressing "skin-saving stampede." He reported that "Those who have had contact with foreigners" were clearly being intimidated.[11]

The difficulties faced by Chinese Christians under these circumstances was a leading cause for the decision of missionary organizations to order their missionaries out of China. In January 1950, for example, Hutchison reported from Peking that the China Inland Mission (probably the largest Protestant missionary organization) had concluded that the "purpose for which missionaries are in China is largely impossible of fulfillment in the present circumstances." For this reason, and to avoid "unfavorable repercussions" on Chinese Christians, the mission had decided to evacuate the majority of its personnel. According to Hutchison, the same decision in principle was taken by almost all American and British Protestant missions.[12]

The Protestant missionary organizations' decision to pull out of China resulted, of course, in a sudden surge of applications from their missionaries for exit permits. Some received permits in due course without excessive waiting periods. Others were kept waiting as long as two years. A good many were placed under a kind of house arrest; others were imprisoned for several months to several years. The type of treatment received by the missionaries seemed to depend on several factors, including their location, the organization with which they were connected, and the personal history of the individual missionary.

A number of missionaries were subjected to denunciation meetings. In the fall of 1951, the *China Bulletin*, published by the National Council of Churches of Christ in the U.S.A., described such meetings as follows, based on detailed accounts appearing in the Chinese magazine *Tien Feng:*

The persons accused are usually American missionaries. . . . The usual accusations against them are: 1. They place religion above politics. 2. They teach Love, Praise and Fear America poison. 3. They oppose Russia, Communism, and the People's Government. 4. They act as spies for their government. 5. They use "small favors" to gain the good will of the people for America. This last charge is laid indiscriminately against all who have really helped the Chinese people in one way or another that cannot be denied.

. . . .

It is evident that the meetings are not spontaneous, but are carried through by pressure from the ever watchful Religious Affairs Bureaus of the local governments. . . . Government officials not only start the plans for these meetings, but are active in the direction of all the charges made.

In spite of this government backing, the denunciation movement is only moderately successful. . . . This has worried the editor of *Tien Feng*, and he devotes two editorials (Aug. 18 and 25) to whipping up the flagging zeal.[13]

One reason the denunciation movement was only moderately successful was that some Chinese colleagues of missionaries refused to denounce them, despite the risks they ran by such noncooperation with an officially sponsored movement. Such was the case, for example, with Hugh and Mabel Hubbard, veteran missionaries whose service in China extended back to the twilight years of the Manchu dynasty. Their experience, and that of their neighbor Alice Huggins, provides useful insights into the inevitable conflict between the demands of the new Chinese order and the aspirations of even the liberal missionaries.

In June 1950 Hugh Hubbard, one of the rural reformers whose work is described in James Thompson's *While China Faced West*,[14] rejoined the North China Christian Rural Service Union (NCCRSU), which he had helped to found some twenty-five years earlier. He hoped to give more years of service to the villagers of China and to adjust to the new order of things.[15] In explaining to members of his family in the United States why he had decided to try to carry on his work in the People's Republic of China, Hubbard undoubtedly voiced the sentiments of many other missionaries who had chosen to remain there. On July 2, 1950, he wrote:

I come to my work in North China under the People's Government with three convictions, or principles:
1. I am going to try to trust God more fully. . . . He knows what He is doing and works in mysterious ways which are too often misunderstood by His children. . . .
2. I am going to try to see what is good in the present order and cooperate with every constructive movement. In this way only is it possible for the Christian movement to win its way. We must first of all deepen our Christian faith and then, by devoted sacrificial service, express it. . . .

3. I am going to follow and trust Chinese leadership. . . . We have given our Chinese friends essential Christianity. Let us trust them to see, perhaps more clearly than we can, what is required of Christians at this critical juncture of their national history.

Hugh Hubbard returned to work with the NCCRSU at just about the time the Korean War broke out. Nevertheless, throughout the fall, things seemed to be going quite well. On October 29 he wrote of the "decided success" of a fair in which the Service Union participated, along with "the Prefectural Office over 13 counties." Noting that the "chief governmental official in charge had some very nice things to say about our part in it." Hubbard said it "warmed our hearts with the feeling that perhaps we are accomplishing something of that for which we are working." On the other hand, he also wrote of some disturbing local manifestations of anti-Christian and antimissionary behavior.

During this period Hubbard participated in one of the political study groups that all members of Chinese organizations were expected to take part in. Some years later Hubbard described this experience as follows:

Twice a week we would have what they called study classes . . . and one man of our group who was a loyal Christian had taken a course of three months under the Communists in Peking. . . . I don't know just how it came about but we found that he was appointed to be head of our study group, which made it much easier for us than to have an outsider come in. . . . He would announce a subject for the evening meeting, and probably make a short speech, and then he would ask each one in turn in the group what their opinion was, and you had to answer. . . . You weren't allowed to keep quiet, silence.[16]

Hubbard recalled that the NCCRSU study group to which he belonged "didn't strike any serious snags." However, after Chinese intervention in the Korean War, he stopped attending, for as he put it, "That was the big divide between getting along and not getting along."[17]

Hubbard later indicated that he stopped going to the study group in December at the time he and his wife applied for exit permits. They had applied to leave only after receiving two cables from their mission board in the United States that month, the second of which read, "Definitely request complete missionary withdrawal China earliest possible." As Hubbard summed up the situation in a letter dated December 31, 1950: "Missionaries . . . must leave if possible, or else go against the advice of the Board and find some means of subsistence on the field. Even so, any connection they may have with Chinese organizations will clearly handicap the latter in establishing their independence and 'cutting off all connections with foreign countries.' "

In the fifteen months intervening between the time they applied for exit permits and the time they finally received them, the Hubbards had a comparatively easy time of it. Although they were unable to carry on any of their usual missionary activities and were not permitted, despite Hugh's increasing need for dental attention, to travel the thirteen miles from their house in Tunghsien to Peking, they took daily walks or bicycle rides, received mail (minus all magazines and newspapers) from the United States, and pursued personal hobbies without serious harassment. In a letter dated July 2, 1951, Hubbard wrote: "The bulk of my time recently has been spent in translation of our bird book into Chinese, reading, Chinese study and woodcarving, which I have taken up again."[18] In his letters home, Hubbard from time to time noted that despite the virulent anti-American propaganda, individual Chinese continued to treat him and his wife in a polite and friendly manner. Thus in the letter just quoted, he said: "We try to get in a daily bicycle ride or a walk and often have calls from friends, or from convalescing soliders, who like to drop in. They are quite friendly and all hope for peace. I hate the idea of these good-natured boys being sent back to the front to be shot up by my countrymen, or vice versa. Let's hope we'll soon see an end to it."

The mild treatment accorded the Hubbards while they were detained in China sharply contrasted with that meted out to their friend and neighbor Alice Huggins, who had devoted decades of her life to a mission-run girls' school. She was repeatedly denounced and physically harassed by girls at the school under the leadership of a woman brought in from the outside by the authorities.[19] The school girls even invented a Chinese song about "Beast Huggins," which Hubbard described as extremely degrading. According to Hubbard, students "went at will to her house, opened her trunks or suitcases, looked over her things, and . . . had demonstrations against her." At commencement exercises, Huggins was meanly denounced by a girl she had helped financially. She was finally driven out of her house all together.

Why was Huggins subjected to this ordeal? When Hubbard protested against her expulsion from her house, the school principal told him that a resolution had been passed at a mass meeting of all the teachers and all the students and workers at the school that Huggins should be forced from her house. He called this "an uprising of the people." Hubbard took this to mean that Huggins was seen, in the context of the revolution, as an oppressor, a class enemy. He also believed that the campaign against her was designed to whip up anti-American feeling, to wipe out any trace of American influence at the school.

This sort of thing was going on in 1951 all over China. A British missionary in West China who was on the whole sympathetic to the revolution but distressed by the treatment of his colleagues who were seeking to depart, was told by an official, in effect: "For too long the masses have experienced the presence of the foreigner, who always claimed to be right, to have special wisdom, and who had power to command. We have been shamed for too many years. We must show to everyone that the power of the men from across the ocean is broken."[20] The official went on to argue that even the most well meaning foreigners were unconscious agents spreading an alien culture. In other words, the revolution demanded that the power and influence of the foreigner must not only be broken but must be seen to be broken. For this reason denunciation meetings against foreign missionaries were needed, as well as against Chinese landlords and other local oppressors whose power had to be broken.

There seems to be no adequate explanation of why the Hubbards were detained for fifteen months other than that they, or at least Hugh Hubbard, had been singled out to be made an example of. Hubbard was not denounced apparently only because his Chinese colleagues in the NCCRSU refused to come forward. Indeed, one of them told him that "a great deal of pressure" was being put on NCCRSU members to accuse him, but they had held a secret meeting and decided that if anyone accused him, all would in turn accuse that person. Nevertheless, the Hubbards were detained long after all other members of their mission, except Alice Huggins, had been granted exit permits. Hugh Hubbard himself speculated about the reasons. One might have thought the Communists would consider him sympathetic, in view of his years of service in rural reconstruction and mass education, some of it carried out in areas controlled by Communist guerrillas during the early stages of the Japanese occupation of North China. But a Chinese friend had warned him that the fact that he had been engaged in rural work and had been trying to help the farmers with better seeds and so on did not stand to his credit at all with the Communists. "Because when you do it," the friend said, "it makes friends for America. Your standpoint is wrong. You're doing it as an American." The fact that Hubbard was widely known as an unusually able missionary, whose chief work had been in the very sector of society where the Communists felt themselves to be the strongest, may well have been his chief crime in their eyes, making him a particularly desirable object for discreditation. He was clearly guilty of reformism, described by one of China's new church leaders as "simply a device, under the name of the 'Social Gospel,' to stave off revolutionary zeal among oppressed people."[21] In any event, as in the case of many other missionaries who were detained for various lengths of time, no explanations were ever provided by the authorities.

Some of those detained spent periods in prison without charges ever being brought against them. Such a one was Frank Cooley, who was held in solitary confinement for fifty days in a four-by-six-foot cell.[22] An idealistic young YMCA man at Chungking University, Cooley represented a new generation of missionaries, and he too wanted to carry on under the new regime. A fellow missionary described him as "a man who lived in a simple way with his staff, talked Chinese better than any other missionary around, and gave most of his salary to try to bail out the Chungking Y.M.C.A. . . . . When the Communists came in Frank settled down to the job of educating his missionary colleagues so that they would be *en rapport* with the new government. . . . The increase in anti-American propaganda as a result of the Korean struggle finished things for Frank, and he asked for a permit to leave the country. After an unexplained delay of ten months, followed by two months in jail without trial, he was ordered out of the country.[23]

Most of the Americans imprisoned for longer periods seem to have been accused of spying, a charge to which they usually pleaded guilty, some because they considered themselves guilty, others because it was a means of gaining release. Three Americans who spent a total of more than eleven years in a Peking prison have written books about their experiences whose very titles illustrate their divergent reactions. Thus Fulbright scholars Allyn and Adele Rickett called their book *Prisoners of Liberation*, and Father Harold Rigney, the head of a Catholic university, called his *Four Years in a Red Hell*.[24] The Ricketts and Father Rigney were among those who were denied exit permits in the fall of 1950, as signs of Chinese intervention in Korea began to appear.

Allyn Rickett and Father Rigney were arrested on July 25, 1951, a day when many foreigners in Peking were rounded up. The American wife of a British diplomat living in Peking wrote at the time: "I have already heard of at least twenty foreigners who were arrested . . . on July 25. . . . No announcement was made of any of these arrests. It never is. . . . This particular sweep includes not only Americans, but Belgians and Dutch, Italians and Germans; priests, sisters, professors, merchants, doctors."[25]

On May 21 the State Department had told the press that it believed more than thirty Americans had been imprisoned, but it couldn't be sure because "in most cases, the local Chinese Communist authorities have given no explanation of the arrests or any information concerning the welfare or whereabouts of the persons arrested." Moreover, access had been denied to legal counsel and to British officials, "who have been representing American interests in Communist China since the closure of our consulates."[26]

British officials, of course, had long been familiar with the difficulties of extending aid not only to imprisoned Americans but also to British and other subjects of the commonwealth in the face of a judicial process very different from that in the West. This process had been described by the British consul general in Tientsin in a telegram to the Foreign Office the previous summer.

Legal advice is virtually unobtainable because no lawyers are allowed to practice in court. . . .

The accused is not allowed to ask any questions either before or during trial, is not allowed to cross-examine the witnesses and is, in fact, not brought before the court until he has, under duress, admitted his guilt to the satisfaction of the authorities. . . .

When "trial" takes place it appears invariably to consist merely of confirmation before a judge of records already made during interrogation and "education" of the accused by the police. . . .

I understand that the accused persons are invariably detained INCOMMUNICADO for at least 3 days pending either release or trial and conviction.[27]

Noting that these procedures were "regarded by local authorities as satisfactory and normal," the consul general commented: "I fear in no circumstances will any Communist regime in China grant to any British detainee facilities remotely approaching those accorded to detained aliens in the U.K." He also felt that until official recognition was granted to British consuls by the People's Republic, requests for communication with the detainees would likely be ignored.

Commenting on this observation, a Foreign Office official wrote that "even in communist countries where our consuls are recognised very little can be done to secure justice for British subjects." Citing experience in Poland, he indicated that legal procedures there were much like those now in effect in China. The Poles, he noted, "have not made a practice of telling us of the arrest of British subjects, but have left us to find out for ourselves." Another Foreign Office official added to the minute: "The practice in Bulgaria, Rumania and Hungary too is substantially the same as in Poland. . . . when there is even the most remote and imaginary political slant access is invariably refused."[28]

The inability of the United States to obtain information about Americans imprisoned in China or to obtain access to them through the British became a growing irritant in relations between Washington and Peking, an irritant that persisted long after the end of the Korean War and the repatriation of prisoners from that war. It also became the cause, as we shall see later, for the resumption of direct diplomatic-level contacts between the United States and the People's Republic of China.

As it explained to the press on December 8, 1951, the State Department had refrained from making public the individual names of Americans detained in the China for two major reasons: "(1) requests of relatives or associates of the person concerned that no publicity be given for fear of jeopardizing the person's welfare; and (2) warnings by countries assisting in making representations to the Chinese Communists that in their opinion official publicity, particularly during the period of their activity on our behalf, might jeopardize the success of their efforts."[29] Why relatives and associates requested no publicity is illustrated by the case of Dr. William Wallace, a Southern Baptist missionary, who died while being held incommunicado in a prison in Wuchow. In reporting Dr. Wallace's death to the State Department on February 21, 1951, Consul General McConaughy telegraphed from Hong Kong: "Mission representatives here have requested we avoid publicity for present because it might lead to reprisals against Miss Hayes at Wuchow who is not presently under arrest but has been unable to obtain exit permit and against seven American Mary Knoll [sic] priests who are reported to be under arrest there."[30] As to the warnings by countries assisting in making representations on behalf of detained Americans, in the late summer of 1951 the United States approached a number of governments having diplomatic relations with the People's Republic, requesting that their representatives in Peking bring the plight of the Americans to the attention of the CPG. Among the governments approached were the Indonesian, Burmese, Indian, Swiss, Soviet, Swedish, Norwegian, and Danish.[31] According to a series of reports from British Chargé Lionel Lamb (who had replaced Hutchison in February), there was opposition to a concerted approach by representatives of these governments in Peking, but most of them were willing to help.[32] Indian and Swiss representatives feared "injudicious publicity" on the part of the United States, however.[33]

The State Department's public explanation of why it had avoided giving out names of detainees was occasioned by Senator William F.

Knowland's release earlier on the same day of the names of thirty-two Americans imprisoned in China, names that had been furnished to him on a confidential basis by Assistant Secretary Rusk the previous October.[34] According to the *China Bulletin* of December 11, the list comprised thirteen Roman Catholic missionaries, nine Protestant missionaries, seven businessmen, and three Fulbright students.

By September 1952 the State Department was taking a harder public line on the problem of imprisoned and detained Americans, partly because the presidential campaign was then in full swing, and Democrats were being accused by Republicans of softness towards the Chinese Communists. But the harder line also reflected Chinese policies. In a press conference statement on September 10 Secretary Acheson outlined the cases of four Americans who had died as a result of ill-treatment. The following excerpts from this statement will give the flavor:

You have all heard of the death of Bishop Francis Ford in a prison in Communist China. . . . we could never be sure what had happened to the Bishop because, in the tragically familiar pattern of the Communist police state, arrest meant that he was cut off completely from outside contact, and no one in authority would divulge any information concerning him. . . . Credible reports now indicate that Bishop Ford was allowed only the most meager diet and was subjected to maltreatment. . . .

Gertrude Cone, a Methodist missionary, applied to Communist officials for an exit permit in January 1951. Her permit was refused. In the summer of 1951 she became ill with cancer. . . . she asked Communist officials for permission to telegraph Hong Kong for money to live on. Her request was refused. . . . Gertrude Cone was carried by stretcher across the border into Hong Kong February 18, 1952. She died 48 hours later. Gertrude Cone was not accused of any crime. . . .

Dr. William Wallace, an American Baptist physician . . . was arrested by the Communists on December 19, 1950. . . . [He] was grilled and tortured by his Communist jailers. He died in prison February 10, 1951.

Philip Cline, an American businessman, was arrested in April 1951, accused of spying. He was released several months later in a precarious state of health. He suffered from heart disease and diabetes. . . . he was rearrested in August 1951 and forced to stand endless questioning. . . . In October 1951 he was again released from prison. . . . In the middle of November 1951 Cline died in the city of Tsingtao. A principal cause of this American's death was the denial to him of insulin for treatment of his diabetes while in prison.[35]

Acheson concluded his press statement with the kind of sentence the State Department had cautiously avoided in earlier days. "We only know," Acheson declared, "that these Communist crimes will be forever condemned by those who believe in simple justice and fair play for human beings." Such statements appeared to have little affect on the Chinese handling of the detained, but then neither had the avoidance of such statements.

The effectiveness of diplomatic representations on behalf of detained foreign nationals was also problematical. En route to London from Peking in mid-1953 Lamb told the U.S. consulate general in Hong Kong that he had been hopeful that representations made by various diplomatic missions on behalf of imprisoned foreign nationals might be successful, but this hope had been shattered by the wholesale arrests of Catholic priests in Shanghai just before his departure. He doubted that in most cases representations had any effect at all on the Chinese authorities, who seemed to release people when they were ready and not before.[36]

Chinese treatment of Americans unquestionably hardened both public and official opinion towards the People's Republic of China, but it was not, on the whole, discriminatory. Other foreign missionaries and businessmen had been treated in the same way, and the treatment of foreigners in general merely reflected a system of "revolutionary justice" that was applied to Chinese as well as foreigners. If there was any discrimination, it was probably in favor of the foreigner. But whether or not the system was discriminatory, it could never be condoned by the West.

The rooting out of their "imperialist" cultural presence was painful enough for Americans; to have it accomplished under such a system of justice was even more galling. It soured not only such cold warriors as Acheson but even missionaries and others, such as Hugh Hubbard, who were determined to see what was constructive in the new government's policies and to cooperate with them and who were opposed to the Truman-Acheson China policy. Thus Hubbard wrote on board ship on April 1, 1952, the very day he, his wife, and Alice Huggins sailed from Tientsin, his "indictment of communism" in the "field of human rights and justice." After describing the familiar mass trial procedures and giving specific examples from his personal knowledge, Hubbard concluded that the "function of the police and so-called justice is to protect the revolution against its enemies. The outsider has no rights." Hubbard was by no means blind to the new regime's accomplishments, but he grieved for the outsiders. On that first day of his own liberation, he wrote: "This is the side of the picture we could not write about before. We told you all the good things we could. They still stand, an impressive list of constructive accomplishments in several fields. But our hearts fill with sadness with the knowledge of the reign of terror tightening around the rank and file . . . and especially our Christian friends."

33
An Aftermath of Bitterness

The Korean War left a legacy of bitterness in Sino-American relations that affected them, especially on the American side, for years to come. As Roderick MacFarquhar sums it up in his documentary study of Sino-American relations: "By the time the armistice agreement was signed on July 27, the United States had suffered more than 142,000 casualties, including 33,629 dead. The Chinese casualties were never disclosed but were estimated by the United Nations at 900,000. Mao Tse-tung's son was among those killed. The memory of all that bloodshed was another bitter barrier between China and America in the years ahead."[1] This memory ensured that the political and economic sanctions adopted by the United States against the People's Republic during the war would not be soon modified. Also working to this end was the McCarthyite hysteria spawned by the Korean War.[2]

The armistice negotiations themselves had contributed to the hardening of U.S. opinion. The drawn-out negotiations strengthened the U.S. perception that, as Dwight Eisenhower once put it, Communists "respect only force and hold fidelity to the pledged word in contempt."[3] Thus Vice–Admiral C. Turner Joy, the chief UN negotiator for the first ten months of the armistice negotiations, wrote: "Communists are not embarrassed in the least to deny an agreement already reached. It makes little difference that such agreements may be in written form. If so, the Communists simply state your interpretation is an incorrect one."[4] He added: "An agreement has no special validity of its own, no matter how solemnly ratified. An agreement is binding on Communists only if it operates to the advantage of their purpose."[5]

It was not long after the armistice agreement came into effect that perceptions of this kind were reinforced by the PRC interpretation of Paragraph 60 of the agreement, which recommended "to the governments of the countries concerned on both sides, that, within three (3) months after the Armistice Agreement is signed and becomes effective, a political conference of a higher level of both sides be held by representatives appointed respectively to settle through negotiation the questions of the withdrawal of all foreign forces from Korea, the peaceful settlement of the Korean question, etc."[6] The UN General Assembly on August 28, 1953, adopted a resolution approving the conclusion of the armistice agreement and welcoming the holding of a political conference as recommended in Paragraph 60. Part of the resolution recommended that the Soviet Union "participate in the Korean political conference provided the other side desires it." The United States was designated to "arrange with the other side for the political conference to be held as soon as possible."[7]

Pursuant to this resolution, the State Department sent a communication to the CPG and the North Korean government through the Swedish Foreign Office suggesting a time and place for the political conference. The UN secretary general had already communicated the resolution separately to Peking and Pyongyang. Peking's response was to denounce the UN resolution as illegal and to demand that the whole question of the political conference be reconsidered in the General Assembly with the participation of PRC representatives. The People's Republic also wanted certain Asian "neutral" countries to participate in the conference. In view of this impasse, the United States offered to send representatives to meet with representatives of the CPG and the North Korean government to discuss arrangements for the political conference. The latter agreed to such a meeting, suggesting that it be held at Panmunjom (the site of the armistice negotiations) on October 26, 1953, but making it clear they expected to discuss the composition of the conference as well as the time and place of its convening. These arrangements led to the first post–Korean War diplomatic-level negotiations involving the People's Republic of China and the United States.

It would be hard to conjure up a site or a scenario less conducive to productive negotiations than Panmunjom and the situation prevailing there at the time the so-called preliminary talks on the Korean political conference got under way on October 26, 1953. Tens of thousands of hostile troops were entrenched along both sides of a demilitarized zone stretching across the Korean peninsula. The negotiations took place within this zone, in one of the huts built astride the line demarcating the boundary between North and South Korea, with the north door of the hut guarded by North Korean soldiers and the south door by UN troops. The long table at which the negotiators sat was placed so that a crease down the center of the green felt cloth covering it approximately coincided with the boundary between North and South Korea. In another part of the demilitarized zone, thousands of prisoners were being held by Indian troops, in accordance with the armistice agreement, pending their decision as to whether to return to their own sides. So many Chinese prisoners had indicated that they would refuse to return to the People's Republic that Peking had stopped trying to persuade them and was loudly accusing the UN side of sabotaging the armistice agreement. In this hostile, confrontational environment it was hardly surprising that the preliminary talks on the Korean political conference failed to produce results.

The failure was not for lack of a genuine U.S. desire for success, at least on the part of the head of the small mission sent to Panmunjom to conduct the preliminary talks on behalf of the UN. He was Arthur Dean, a public-spirited citizen and a successful New York corporation lawyer, who was a member of the law firm to which Secretary of State Dulles had formerly belonged. Dean expressed optimism both publicly and privately that the negotiations would be concluded in ten days or two weeks. En route to Korea he told members of his mission that it was of great importance for the new Eisenhower administration that this negotiation succeed.[8]

Dean argued at the outset of the preliminary talks that the language of Paragraph 60 made it perfectly clear that the political conference was to be composed of countries that had fought in the Korean War, and in fact, this language had been proposed by the North Korean side in the armistice negotiations. Nevertheless, Dean eventually agreed to include the composition of the conference, as well as its time and place, on the agenda of the preliminary talks. This agreement on the agenda was the only agreement the talks produced. Although the United Nations' side modified its initial position and agreed that neutrals could be present at the Korean conference, Dean would not agree to allow the Soviet Union to participate in the Conference as a neutral, though the UN would welcome attendance by the Soviet Union as a full participant bound by whatever agreements might be reached at the conference.

Dean's flexibility was not matched on the other side of the table. At about the halfway point in the preliminary talks the North Korean and PRC representatives (respectively Ki Sok Bok and none other than

Huang Hua) devoted increasing time to extraneous matters, primarily the POW issue. They repeatedly charged the UN side with delaying the preliminary talks in order to carry out its "nefarious schemes" with respect to the POWs from the Communist side who had refused repatriation. They constantly attacked U.S. motives and finally even questioned Dean's authority to negotiate. In short, they had ceased to negotiate. When, during a long session on December 10, they accused the United States of perfidy in connection with Syngman Rhee's unilateral release in June 1953 of North Korean POWs, Dean walked out. The preliminary talks had become a farce.

Returning to the United States, Dean explained the failure of the talks in a radio broadcast to the nation on December 21. He told the country: "Except for the other side's insistence on the U.S.S.R. participating as a neutral, and except for ironing out the particular neutrals to participate, which really constitutes no fundamental difficulty, we have fully met the other side on this question as to the participation of nonvoting observers, their right at the conference and the voting procedure.[9] As for the chances of a "true Korean peace," Dean judged the outlook "discouraging but by no means hopeless." Stressing that the "Communists are in no hurry," Dean warned that to come up with a solution would "take all the brains, energy, resolution and patience at our command."[10]

But the State Department apparently wished that Dean had displayed more patience at Panmunjom. Rather taken aback by his sudden walkout, it sought to get the preliminary talks restarted. To save face it demanded that objectionable parts of the record of the December 10 session be expunged. Five meetings ensued between so-called liaison secretaries of the two sides in January 1954, ending when the Chinese and North Korean liaison secretaries walked out after repeatedly refusing to change the record to delete the charge of perfidy.[11]

In early December 1953, while the preliminary talks at Panmunjom were still in progress, a summit meeting of the United States, the United Kingdom and France was held in Bermuda. China policy was not a major topic of the conference, but the State Department was worried that Britain's support for the moratorium procedure might weaken in light of the cessation of hostilities in Korea. In a position paper on this subject written the previous June in anticipation of the armistice agreement, Ruth Bacon, the adviser on United Nations affairs in the State Department's Bureau of Far Eastern Affairs, warned that the United Kingdom was contemplating "early abandonment" of the moratorium procedure and "active support for seating of Chinese

Communists soon after the armistice is signed." Bacon was also fearful that France might change its stance if there were a prospect of successful negotiations on Indo-China. Thus she urged that "agreement should be reached, in principle, that the three governments will continue, in all UN bodies, jointly to support some procedural action by which votes on the substance [of Chinese representation] can be postponed."[12]

Bacon's worries undoubtedly sprang from her conversations with her opposite numbers in the British embassy and the British UN delegation, but this was a matter on which Prime Minister Winston Churchill wished to support his American ally. Thus, President Eisenhower reports in his memoirs that Churchill told him that though the United Kingdom had no intention of breaking relations with the People's Republic, it would always vote with the United States to bar China from the UN. Eisenhower quotes him as saying, "We do prefer the U.S. over Red China as an ally."[13] The United Kingdom did in fact adhere to the moratorium for the remainder of Churchill's tenure of prime minister and beyond.

The United States and the United Kingdom were closer together tactically on China policy than they had been before Chinese intervention in the Korean War, but there continued to be a wide gulf between them as to the best strategy for splitting Peking from Moscow. This divergence was basically the same as it had been in 1950 when different political parties had been in power both in Washington and in London. A top secret memorandum reported Dulles's presentation on the subject at a restricted session of the tripartite summit meeting December 7 thus:

In the question of relations between Communist China and the USSR, it was difficult to come to a clear conclusion but he thought we were justified in believing that there was strain . . . . The fact that this relationship exists is important and may eventually give us an opportunity for promoting division between the Soviet Union and Communist China in our our common interest.

There were major differences between the three powers in their approach to this problem, especially between the United Kingdom and the United States . . . . There were two theories for dealing with this problem. One was that by being nice to the Communist Chinese we would wean them away from the Soviets, and the other was that pressure and strain would compel them to make more demands on the USSR which the latter would be unable to meet and the strain would consequently increase.[14]

Dulles went on to stress that the United States adhered to the view "that pressure should be maintained on Communist China both politically and economically and to the extent possible without war, military pressure should likewise be maintained." In the American view this course was preferable to seeking "to divide the Chinese and Soviets by a sort of competition with Russia." Acknowledging that the United Kingdom had recognized the People's Republic, Dulles said recognition "did not mean that you had to give them aid of a political, moral or economic nature."[15]

The practical point of Dulles's exposition on China policy was to persuade the British to hold the line on the moratorium. On this point he was successful, as already noted, but Eden made it clear in response to Dulles's presentation that the United Kingdom still believed in the wisdom of the contacts with the People's Republic that British recognition afforded. He pointed out that the Russians and Chinese were trying to divide the three allies, "just as we were trying to divide them, and that in itself was in a measure an excuse for not thinking it wise to break off all contacts, however unsatisfactory our relationship with the Chinese Communists might be at present."[16]

What the preliminary talks at Panmunjom failed to accomplish, a four-power conference held in Berlin several weeks later succeeded in doing. The United States, Britain, France, and the Soviet Union, meeting at the foreign minister level, agreed to convene a Korean political conference composed of the nations that fought in Korea plus the Soviet Union.[17] There would be no neutrals present. In his memoirs, Eden recalls that in a message to London he pointed out: "Mr. Dulles admits that non-recognition is no obstacle to meeting the Chinese and, in fact, the Americans are meeting them at Panmunjom."[18]

The United States, after all, had agreed as early as 1952 to the language of Paragraph 60 of the armistice agreement calling for a conference with the People's Republic and had been trying at Panmunjom to persuade China to follow through on it. Despite this long-standing commitment, Dulles and the Eisenhower administration had come in for heavy criticism from hard-liners in Congress, as well as from Taipei and Seoul, for agreeing to take part in a conference with the People's Republic not only on Korea but on Indo-China as well. As Robert Randle has pointed out in his study of the Geneva Conference, there were

differences between negotiating with the Chinese at the forthcoming Geneva Conference and negotiating at the earlier conferences at Panmunjom. Geneva was to be a conference of the great powers, called to discuss East Asian problems . . . . It would meet in the famous Swiss city that had served as the meeting place of the League of Nations and had hosted other international conferences. Panmunjom had been a conference of Korean War belligerents, almost on the field of battle . . . . Geneva, which would bring a modicum of international prestige to the Chinese, might open abundant opportunities to a government intent upon demonstrating to the world that it was reasonable and fully capable of behaving like a great power. It was this "semblance of recognition" by participation—prestige by the mere fact of China's presence—to which Senator Knowland and others objected.[19]

Although pressures from the congressional China lobby did not deflect the Eisenhower administration from its decision to participate in the Geneva Conference, the administration went to some lengths to assure the American public that participation did not mean U.S. recognition of Communist China; on the contrary, it was being called to account for its aggression. The People's Republic, on the other hand, stressed that China would participate in the conference as one of the big powers.[20]

34
A PRC Policy Reversal

The armistice in Korea did not result in any significant improvement in U.K.-PRC relations. The Chinese did nothing to revive negotiations on the establishment of diplomatic relations, which they had allowed to die following the Hutchison-Chang meeting of June 17, 1950; the British chargé was still called by the CPG the "head of the British delegation for negotiation of the establishment of diplomatic relations." In his memoirs Humphrey Trevelyan, who took over as chargé shortly after the armistice agreement was signed, describes his relations with the Ministry of Foreign Affairs thus: "After my first formal call, I could get no more interviews. They made it quite clear that I was not to be treated as a *de facto* chargé d'affaires. The Vice-Minister only answered my letters when he wanted to be particularly offensive and to publish his reply; my requests for interviews were simply ignored."[1]

A subject of special British concern was the treatment of British businessmen in China. Three weeks before the armistice signing, Lionel Lamb, whom Trevelyan replaced as chargé, told the American consulate general in Hong Kong that British firms had made little progress toward liquidation and withdrawal and that foreign businessmen were being used as hostages to squeeze more money out of the firms.[2]

This was an old story, of course, dating back to before the outbreak of the Korean War, and it is not surprising that the practice continued during the War, but Trevelyan might have been expected to witness some amelioration of the situation following the armistice. Instead, he saw only its refinement. Thus, he reports in his memoirs that the "method now used was to put every form of pressure on a firm to induce it voluntarily to surrender all its assets to the Chinese Government, so that there could be no claim to compensation." One form of pressure (a familiar one) was the refusal of exit permits, making the "British managers and their assistants . . . virtual prisoners, unable to do business, unable to leave."[3]

Although the Korean armistice did not bring about an improvement in Sino–British relations, the Geneva Conference did. Attending the conference as a member of the British delegation, Trevelyan was able to do there what he had been unable to do in Peking; PRC policies towards the British in China suddenly relaxed. He recalls: "I held regular meetings with Huan Hsiang, the head of the West European Department of the Chinese Foreign Ministry and with Lei Jen-min, one of the Vice-Ministers of Foreign Trade . . . . Many of the troubles of the British community in China were now resolved. Exit permits were granted, negotiations for the closure of British firms began to move forward."[4] At Geneva, too, came the first sign that the People's Republic was prepared to reverse its policy of refusing to establish diplomatic relations with the United Kingdom. The signal was almost casual. When at a dinner party he gave for Chou En-lai, British Foreign Secretary Anthony Eden "twitted him with not having a representative in London, he expressed a willingness to send one."[5] It is possible that Chou spoke off the cuff on this occasion, since a Chinese official later explained to Trevelyan that the official who would eventually be sent to London would, "like Trevelyan be a negotiating representative."[6]

Upon his return to Peking, however, Trevelyan was treated like a real chargé d'affaires. He was not only accorded the title for the first time by the Chinese, but he was received by Chou En-lai, who told

Trevelyan that he wanted to pick an especially good man for the London posting. The Ministry of Foreign Affairs now arranged for him to call on Chinese officials he had never been able to meet with before, such as Chu Teh, Kuo Mo-jou, the minister and vice-minister of culture, the president of the People's Bank, and the minister of trade.[7] A Foreign office memorandum tells the rest of the story:

> In a Note dated 2 September, 1954, the Chinese responded to the British Note of 6 January, 1950, by nominating a Chargé d'Affaires to the United Kingdom having the same position and duties as the British Chargé d'Affaires in Peking. The Embassy in Peking was henceforth designated by the Chinese the "Office of the British Chargé d'Affaires." It is evident that the Chinese had by this time decided to accept the establishment of formal relations and acknowledged that the Chargés were no longer "negotiating representatives." H.M. Chargé d'Affaires in Peking has subsequently been shown in the Chinese Diplomatic List, ranking below Chargés d'Affaires *ad interim.*[8]

Thus Britain achieved an objective it had been striving for since January 1950 in its relations with China, but this objective was achieved only when Peking was ready to let it be achieved. The ostensible reasons for the PRC refusal to grant diplomatic relations in 1950 were still there in 1954. Britain's policy on the Chinese representation issue in the UN, the "persecution" of Chinese in Malaya, the unsatisfactory immigration policies of the Hong Kong government had not changed. It had been the British contention all along that such problems could be dealt with more effectively if diplomatic relations were established between London and Peking, but until now Peking had preferred to make their existence an excuse for the denial of such relations.[9]

Although the shift in PRC policy toward the United Kingdom was evidently welcomed by the British, a change in policy toward the United States was only accepted reluctantly and in a limited way by the Americans. In fact, the positions taken by Peking and Washington represented almost a reversal of their pre–Korean War stances. When Trevelyan, in response to an American request, raised the problem of Americans detained in China with Chinese officials in Geneva, the latter responded that if the United States was concerned about its citizens, it should take up the matter directly with them. If, on the other hand, the Americans insisted that Peking recognize the right of the United Kingdom to protect American interests in China, the People's Republic would insist that the United States grant the same right to a power designated by Peking to protect Chinese interests in the America.

Already under political attack for participating in an international conference at which Peking but not Taipei was represented, the Eisenhower administration was in a dilemma. On the one hand, it did not want to take part in direct bilateral negotiations with the People's Republic; on the other, it could not allow a protecting power to look after Chinese interests in the United States, since that was the job of the embassy and consulates representing the Nationalist government. However, on humanitarian grounds, the United States could not refuse to discuss with the People's Republic the plight of American citizens held in China.

Washington therefore agreed to direct negotiations with the Chinese at Geneva, at which the secretary generals of the U.S. and PRC delegations were designated to represent their respective governments. The American government, which had negotiated at Panmunjom under the UN banner and was participating with the People's Republic in multilateral negotiations at the concurrent conferences on Korea and Indo-China at Geneva, was unhappy at the thought of U.S. and PRC representatives sitting alone at the negotiating table wearing their own hats. It insisted on the presence of Trevelyan at the table. In fact, Trevelyan recalls, the Americans "tried to maintain the fiction that I was convening a meeting at which they and the Chinese happened to be present."[10] Indeed, this was the impression the State Department conveyed in its press release of June 5 announcing the first meeting: "In an effort to secure the release of United States citizens at present imprisoned or otherwise detained in Communist China, U. Alexis Johnson, American Ambassador to Czechoslovakia and a member of the U.S. delegation at the Geneva Conference, today accompanied Humphrey Trevelyan, British Chargé d'Affaires at Peiping, to a meeting with a member of the Chinese Communist delegation."[11] The State Department announcement did not mention that the PRC representative at the meeting would be Ambassador Wang Ping-nan, although the United States had carefully specified that the Chinese representative should be of no lower rank than Wang Ping-nan, secretary general of the PRC delegation.[12]

The fiction that a U.S. representative was merely attending a meeting conducted by the British did not last long, for the Chinese were not willing to put up with it. Trevelyan describes the denouement thus: "I introduced the contestants and umpired for two rounds. The Americans tried to keep me in the ring, but at the beginning of the third round the Chinese, with elaborate politeness, delicately indicated that the talks should be between the two principals. I withdrew."[13]

This meeting was the conception, if not the birth, of the series of diplomatic-level bilateral negotiations between the United States and the People's Republic known more familiarly as the Warsaw talks. When the 1954 talks were revived at the ambassadorial level in August 1955, the principals were again Alexis Johnson and Wang Ping-nan, and the site was again the Palais des Nations in Geneva, where the talks "umpired" by Trevelyan had been held. The negotiations continued to be held there until December 1957; they did not become the Warsaw talks until September 1958.[14]

By offering to hold discussions with U.S. officials on the subject of Americans detained in China, Peking reversed the policy it had pursued in 1949 and early 1950 when the United States still had diplomatic and consular officers in China. Then, Communist authorities had time and time again refused to discuss such problems as the Ward case on the grounds that the two countries had no diplomatic relations or that the United States was supporting the Chinese Nationalists. In his final interview with an official of the Ministry of Foreign Affairs in April 1950, it may be recalled, Clubb's efforts to discuss American grievances were rebuffed as "worthless talk" so long as the United States did not break with the Nationalists. This was at a time when Truman had publicly declared that the United States would not defend Formosa and when economic aid to the Nationalists was minimal and further military assistance denied. At Geneva, however, Peking was willing to discuss such problems even though the United States was now publicly committed to defend Formosa and was supporting the Nationalists with hundreds of millions of dollars' worth of military and economic aid and, of course, still did not recognize the People's Republic.

Five meetings were held between Ambassadors Johnson and Wang during June 1954, in which the U.S. representative urged the release of Americans imprisoned or otherwise detained in China, and the PRC representative pressed the issue of Chinese in the United States who had been prevented from returning to their homeland. On May 29 the U.S. delegation to the Geneva Conference, in response to allegations by the Chinese delegation's press spokesman, had issued a statement giving the "facts" on this subject. Of the several thousand Chinese students in the United States at the time of the Communist conquest of China, "the overwhelming majority chose, of their own free will, not to return to their homeland." The statement acknowledged that since the outbreak of the Korean War, exit permits had been "temporarily denied" to 120 "students," but 314 had been permitted to depart. It also "emphasized that none of the Chinese in the United

States has been imprisoned, detained, or mistreated. All have enjoyed, and enjoy, complete freedom of movement; they are free to communicate with anyone and free to accept any employment they choose."[15]

The United States and the People's Republic agreed to review the cases of the detained nationals of the other. Before the end of the Geneva Conference six Americans who had been denied permission to leave China were granted exit permits, and Ambassador Johnson notified Ambassador Wang that fifteen Chinese who had been refused permission to leave the United States were now free to leave. In the final Wang-Johnson meeting, arrangements were made to continue the talks on detained Americans and Chinese at the consular level in Geneva, but within a few months they petered out without producing further results.[16]

It is clear that the People's Republic did not make these significant changes in its policies toward Britain and the United States in response to changes in their China policies. British policy toward the People's Republic had actually toughened somewhat under the Conservative government of Winston Churchill, but it remained fundamentally the same as it had been since British recognition in January 1950. American policy had become much harder, but there is no evidence that this hard line accounted for Peking's greater willingness to discuss American grievances in 1954 than in 1949-50.

The answer to Peking's change of heart seems to lie in its changing world view and in the fulfillment of its immediate domestic goals. In the words of A. Doak Barnett: "From about 1952 on, China moved gradually to abandon the dichotomous world view that had shaped its policy since 1948; it returned to a united-front strategy, designed to 'ally' China 'with all the forces that can be allied with' in order to struggle against 'American imperialism.' "[17] Edmund Clubb, writing a history of twentieth-century China rather than dispatches to the State Department, has speculated that this major change in course "was presumably decided upon at Moscow in August-September, 1952, during the month-long negotiations between Soviet leaders and the Chinese delegation headed by Premier Chou En-lai and Deputy Chief of Staff Su Yu."[18] The new strategy was further developed after the death of Stalin in March 1953.

Be this as it may, the Korean War must have demonstrated to Peking the bankruptcy of the two-camp view of the world and the futility of formulating policy in the expectation of a new world war pitting the Soviet Union against the United States. Non-Communist Arab and Asian countries, Mao's despised "third-roaders," proved to be friends who had tried hard at the UN to end the Korean War on terms much more favorable than those China managed to salvage after rejecting them. At the same time, the Korean War did not develop into the world war so widely anticipated in China. Both the Soviet Union and the United States saw to that.

The establishment of diplomatic relations with the United Kingdom fitted well into China's new international strategy. Although China can hardly have expected to ally itself with Britain, the formalization of PRC-U.K. relations was a step in the direction of isolating the United States from its friends on the question of China policy. At the same time, willingness to discuss American grievances gave the People's Republic an appearance of reasonableness in the eyes of non-Communist powers, something Peking had not valued much in its two-camp posture. Moreover, it forced the United States to deal with the People's Republic on a one-to-one basis, lending credence to the PRC claim that it was at Geneva as one of the five powers. This claim was also reinforced by the establishment of diplomatic relations with Britain.

Another factor contributing to Peking's new flexibility towards America and Britain was undoubtedly the elimination of British and American power in China. As Clubb has pointed out: "By 1952 the privileged position of 'imperialism' in China had been completely wiped out. . . . The position of foreign investment capital in China had been destroyed. And the treaty ports that had been the center of foreign activities suffered corresponding shock."[19] By 1954 the CPG had not only crushed "imperialist" economic and cultural institutions but had extended its authority throughout continental China, including Tibet, and had further consolidated its domestic power through the "3- and 5-anti" campaigns, which dealt blows to its putative enemies within and outside of the party and government apparatus.[20] Thus by the time of the Geneva Conference, the People's Republic of China had reached a new stage in its evolution—one that allowed it to take a more flexible stance vis-à-vis the "imperialist" nations.

Part IV
SUMMING UP

The NSC characterized U.S. policy toward China in early 1949 as flexible. On the one hand, the Nationalist cause seemed doomed; on the other, the Communist cause was hostile. In this situation the United States would avoid commitment to either side but would stay put in China and hope to develop some kind of working relationship with China's new masters. The British posture toward China at this period was very much the same. Moreover, both the United States and the United Kingdom had a common purpose of trying to keep China from becoming an adjunct of Soviet power. It soon became apparent, however, that despite the similarity of their objectives, the United States and the United Kingdom would seek to achieve their purposes by quite different means.

As matters turned out, it didn't make much difference which means were used; so long as Western purposes conflicted with CCP purposes, they would not, for the most part, be achieved. After its string of crushing military victories in Manchuria and North China, the CCP was in the driver's seat in China; it was up to the West to adjust. A British consul in Tientsin summed up the implications of the Communist triumph succinctly in April 1949, three months after the "liberation" of that city: "The Communists in China are real. Power is in their grasp. They have come to stay. They have their policy, programme and doctrine. They intend to revolutionize the social, political and economic structure of China. They are unlikely to be deterred by tradition, vested interests or even international complications. They are confident they can succeed."[1]

In their dealings with the United States and the United Kingdom, Mao and the CCP knew where their priorities lay: achievement of revolutionary goals took precedence over Western goodwill, over obtaining recognition and getting into the United Nations, and even over trade with the West—regarded by both British and American officials as a trump card in their hands. Among the CCP's revolutionary goals was the liquidation of Western "imperialism" and all its cultural and economic institutions in China. This process was fundamentally incompatible with normalization of relations with the United Kingdom and the United States, as Mao was realistically aware. Therefore, he was in "no hurry" for diplomatic relations with these "imperialist" powers.[2]

By contrast, there was a good deal of unrealism among many in the foreign community in China as to the significance for them of the Communist triumph, particularly among that group sometimes called old China hands epitomized by the commercial community in Shanghai. Their view was aptly summarized in a Foreign Office memorandum in mid-1950. "For a long time they held the view that this was *just* another Chinese Government; that John Chinaman will always trade; that China was too big for any one Government; that the Chinese character and Communism were mutually exclusive; that it was only a question of time and of making the necessary contacts and then everything would go swimmingly and we would carry on with our trade where we had left off."[3] Although this memorandum was describing attitudes in the British commercial community, similar views could be found in the smaller, and on the whole less sanguine, American business community in Shanghai. Thus U.S. Consul General Cabot noted in his diary on May 17, 1948: "After dinner various businessmen opined that they would probably do business after a communist takeover. I was finally constrained to dissent vigorously—I said I believed they would be slowly throttled. Maybe I'm wrong because I don't know my China—but I think I know communism."[4] Cabot's prediction of the fate of the Shanghai foreign business community was duly fulfilled. His understanding of Communist methods stood him in better stead at this juncture of Chinese history than the generations of China experience represented in that community.

An obvious ingredient in the outlook of the business community was wishful thinking; it is difficult to face facts that spell doom for one's means of livelihood. A natural reaction is to find a scapegoat and the British business community found one in American China policy. For example, in a memorandum dated July 31, 1950, British Consul General R.W. Urquhart wrote that it was "a fact that their [America's] mistakes in the Far East have already cost us a great deal and must cost a great deal more."[5] Urquhart was not entirely wrong. There were mistakes in American policy, and the costliest one—the decision to send U.S. troops north of the 38th parallel in Korea—was yet to come. But blaming the plight of British businessmen in Shanghai on the United States was to wish away the realities of the Communist revolution.

By and large, the Foreign Office and the State Department saw eye to eye on the realities of the Communist revolution in China; their differences lay in how to cope with it, how to influence CCP/PRC policy in a way favorable to their interests in China and elsewhere. At first their methods did not differ markedly. In fact, as Urquhart himself pointed out in a message to the Foreign Office in July 1949, the United States initially tried harder than the United Kingdom to communicate with the Communist authorities. There was no British equivalent of the Stuart-Huang talks, of Stuart's effort to present U.S. views to CCP leaders through third-force intermediaries, of the U.S. reply to the Chou demarche—none of which met with a positive or encouraging response. On the other hand, the British experienced no official humiliations comparable to the incarceration of U.S. Consul General Ward and his staff in Mukden and the harassment of the U.S. consulate general in Shanghai. It was only after a combination of failed American attempts at communicating with CCP authorities, the unconscionable treatment of the Mukden staff, and the harassment in Shanghai that marked differences in the American and British approaches to the CCP emerged.

One thing British and American officials continued to share, however, was an exaggerated sense of the importance of British and American policy as a means of influencing CCP behavior, particularly in the area of trade. Both U.S. and U.K. officials thought that China's serious economic plight would give them leverage on CCP/PRC policies, but they sought to apply this leverage in nearly opposite ways. The British took the line that the way to capitalize on the Communists' economic difficulties was to entice their goodwill by offering them as much trade as possible. The American approach was to restrict trade so the Chinese would be willing to make concessions to avoid catastrophe. Thus President Truman thought the Nationalist blockade would have a salutary effect on CCP/PRC policies. However, neither of these approaches was effective. Peking made do with the trade it could get without allowing either trade inducements or penalties to affect its political policies.

Chinese treatment of foreign firms seemed to depend more on how particular firms fitted into their economic plans than on the policies the firms' countries were pursuing toward China. Humphrey Trevelyan illustrated this point when he told members of the U.S. delegation at the Geneva Conference that he had been unable to find any evidence that British firms were treated less favorably than those of Western countries that had established formal diplomatic relations with the People's Republic.[6] Earlier, shortly after U.K. recognition, Hutchison had noted that the Communist authorities were doing business with some banks of countries that had not recognized the People's Republic, rather than with British banks.

British and American officials also overestimated the leverage PRC interest in recognition and admission to the UN would give them. Here again they diverged on the use of that leverage. The United Kingdom thought recognition would provide an opportunity for Peking to distance itself somewhat from Moscow and to pursue a more independent foreign policy. There was a good deal of logic to this position, but it did not produce the desired result and Chinese propaganda organs heaped scorn on it. Meanwhile, the United States took the position that withholding recognition from Peking and keeping it out of the UN might force the People's Republic to improve its international behavior. This theory didn't work either.

Even with the more flexible policies adopted by the People's Republic at the Geneva Conference, there was no basic shift in its anti-West, pro-Soviet posture. The Chinese and Soviet delegations worked in close coordination, and both maintained a tough line with respect to the West and the UN. As Trevelyan observed, the Chinese were speaking primarily to an Asian audience and cared little about the impression they made in the United States and western Europe. At a time when some westerners hoped, and others feared, that Peking would offer tempting concessions in order to gain entry to the UN, Trevelyan correctly predicted that the People's Republic would not bargain for admission to the UN but would continue to demand it as a right and wait indefinitely rather than make concessions.[7]

Though the United Kingdom and the United States had neither the political nor the economic leverage (whether in the carrot or the stick mode) to modify PRC policies inimical to their interests, they were successful in achieving two of their objectives: the British succeeded in holding on to Hong Kong and the Americans were able to deny Formosa to the Communists. Britain's policy of recognizing the People's Republic and stressing the importance of economic ties probably helped to preserve the status quo in Hong Kong. On the other hand, the United States, abandoning its initial policy of denying Formosa to the Communists by diplomatic means only, used the threat of force to keep that island out of Peking's power.

It is highly doubtful, however, if either the United Kingdom or the United States would, or could, have pursued these policies if a substantial number of the inhabitants of Hong Kong or Formosa had wished to embrace Peking. From one point of view it appears that both the United Kingdom and the United States pursued imperialistic policies toward these two Chinese territories: in the case of Hong Kong, Britain was preserving a relic of the old imperialism; in the case of Formosa, the United States was arguably creating a new imperialism. From another viewpoint, however, it is clear that both were safeguarding havens for millions of Chinese who had fled in fear of the Communist-led revolution. Moreover, in the case of Formosa, the native-born population never showed any signs of wanting that revolution to spread to their island, despite Nationalist political repression.

President Truman's order to the U.S. Seventh Fleet to neutralize Formosa was a major turning point in U.S. policy toward China, but it did not constitute complete abandonment of flexibility. The United States was not yet prepared, for example, to guarantee Formosa to the Nationalists; other possible futures were still envisioned for the island. American and Japanese trade, though restricted, was maintained with the People's Republic; financial transactions were not blocked or assets frozen. In addition, the continued presence of substantial numbers of Americans in the People's Republic was not prohibited. Although by the fall of 1950 the flexibility policy was ailing, it was not yet dead. Once combat was joined with the Chinese, however, flexibility expired on the battlefields of Korea.

British diplomats at times implied, if they did not assert, that U.S. policy would have been closer to British had it not been for a group of strongly pro-Nationalist conservatives in Congress. But the documentary evidence tends to support Secretary Acheson's contention that what he called the "attack of the primitives" had little effect on China policy during his tenure.[8] Thus by September 1949, months before Senator Joe McCarthy made his notorious accusations about Communists in the State Department, significant American differences with Britain on recognition of the People's Republic and its admission to the UN, on attitudes toward trade and blockade and toward Formosa had already appeared. These views were developed by career and noncareer officials in the Foreign Service and State Department, many with long China experience, including Philip Sprouse and Leighton Stuart, to name a representative of each category. Their differences with their British opposite numbers reflected different assessments of American and British strategic and economic interests in China, Hong Kong, and Formosa; different perceptions of Chinese Communist vulnerabilities; and different traditional approaches to diplomacy (for example, over the moral ingredient in U.S. policy).

It was not pro-Nationalist influence that was responsible for lessening flexibility in U.S. policy towards the People's Republic after June 1949 but a growing official U.S. perception of the latter's antithetical policies. The basic reasons advanced by Acheson in September 1949 for not recognizing the People's Republic were its refusal to accept China's international obligations (a position the British agreed with at the time) and its treatment of American citizens, notably the consular staff in Mukden. There was no indication that the United States was acting out of pro-Nationalist sentiment, which in fact did not abound in the State Department or the White House.

Thus the U.S. decision in January 1950 to pull American officials out of China was not followed by an improvement in U.S. relations with the Nationalists or a change in the no-defense-of-Formosa policy. The Dulles memorandum in mid-May advocating drawing the line against Communist expansion at Formosa was not a reflection of pro-Nationalist sentiment but an assessment that Formosa was a piece of real estate, long judged by the JCS to be strategically important to the United States, where it would be advantageous to draw the line. Dulles, in fact, gave vent to the lack of confidence U.S. officials and the public had in the Taipei government in an interview with a Nationalist official at the time he was advocating Formosa's defense.

The U.S. public's lack of confidence in the Nationalist government in Taipei seemed to be exceeded only by its opposition to recognition of the Communist government in Peking. According to the report of a Minnesota poll Senator Hubert Humphrey sent to Secretary Acheson on April 7, 1950, 58 percent opposed sending troops or warships to help defend Formosa, and 59 percent opposed recognition of the Peking government.[9] A *New York Times* survey some three months earlier on the "state of opinion on China" revealed, on the one hand, that "recognition of the Communists now would be resented" and, on the other, a "widespread indifference to the fate of Chiang."[10]

Even after drawing the line at Formosa, the United States made clear both to the Nationalists and to other governments that Washington continued to make a distinction between Formosa and the nationalist government. It strictly limited military assistance to the Nationalists, and it limited their military operations as well. It held to the view that the future of Formosa had not yet been decided and would be determined by international consultations, taking into account the wishes of the inhabitants of the island, among other things. Only after the PRC intervention in Korea and Peking's rejection of the UN cease-fire offers did the United States in effect become committed to preserving the status quo on Formosa, more because it was at war with the People's Republic than out of pro-Nationalist sentiments.

As noted in the last chapter, the rigidities built into the Communists' policy toward the United States and Britain by their dichotomous world view and their need to liquidate British and American "imperialist" influence in China presumably prevented them from taking the more flexible positions in 1949-1950 that they took at Geneva in 1954. It is quite possible too that the CCP leadership was subjected to restraints by the Soviet Union under Stalin's leadership that limited its flexibility. Moreover, in view of the severe impact the treatment of the staff of the Mukden consulate had on U.S.-PRC relations and of the close cooperation in Manchuria between PRC and Soviet officials, Soviet responsibility for deliberately exacerbating U.S.-PRC relations seems probable.[11] On the other hand, the CCP/PRC seemed to throw away opportunities to exercise leverage against Moscow by being so unbending and unimaginative in its handling of relations with the United Kingdom and the United States. If it is argued that Peking was genuinely afraid of a hostile U.S. imperialism,[12] it can also be argued that PRC policies directly contributed to the growth of such hostility[13] and failed to take advantage of opportunities to diminish it.

There were a number of opportunities to lessen hostility in 1949-1950. To begin with, if American consular officers had been allowed to discuss U.S. grievances with CCP/PRC officials on a day-to-day basis, instead of being rebuffed whenever they attempted to do so, some sort of working relationship might have been established. If such contacts had not brought about the release of the long-suffering staff of the Mukden consulate by October 1, 1949, then at least the CPG need not have responded to Clubb's plea for their release by clapping Consul General Ward and others of the staff into solitary confinement. In fact, if the CPG had been genuinely interested in the establishment of relations with the United States, it could have promptly released Ward and his staff, Smith and Bender, and other detained Americans. Such a gesture would have removed a major U.S. grievance and generated support for recognition within the United States. Moreover, by taking advantage of (instead of ignoring) requests from Consul General Clubb to call on him in connection with the Ward case, Chou En-lai would have been able to put conciliatory views directly to Washington if he had been so minded. Support for U.S. recognition would have been reinforced if the People's Republic had reciprocated British recognition in January 1950 and quickly established diplomatic relations with the United Kingdom. At the same time, if the CPG had accepted the U.S. offer of other American consular property in Peking in lieu of the property it requisitioned, all American consular officers would not have been withdrawn from the People's Republic. Whether such actions would have produced early U.S. recognition is problematic, but they would have cut the ground from under many of the arguments of those in the United States who opposed it and provided the kind of modus vivendi the United States had sought since the capture of Mukden by the People's Liberation Army.

Notes

1. Responses to a Parade of Victories

1. Mao Tse-tung, *Selected Works of Mao Tse-tung*, 4 vols. (Peking: Foreign Language Press, 1961-1965) 4:280n.   2. Ibid., 301-3.   3. Ibid., 158-59.   4. FO371/69547 F17714 (Foreign Office document, piece no. 69547, paper no. F17714).   5. FR, 1949, 9:821-22 (Foreign Relations of the United States, 1949, vol. 9, pages 821-22).
6. Ibid.:474-75.   7. FR, 1948, 7:674-77.   8. FR, 1949, 8:65-66.   9. Ibid.:86.

2. Consulates Carry On

1. FR, 1948, 8:901-3, 907-10.   2. FR, 1949, 8:663.   3. J. Leighton Stuart, *Fifty Years in China: The Memoirs of John Leighton Stuart, Missionary and Ambassador* (New York: Random House, 1954), 215.   4. FR, 1948, 7:850-55.   5. FR, 1949, 8:659.
6. FR, 1948, 8:859.   7. Though not a China specialist, Butterworth, a brilliant officer with over twenty years' experience in the foreign service, had served as deputy chief of mission at the U.S. embassy in Nanking just prior to assuming his duties in the State Department in the fall of 1947.   8. FR, 1949, 8:665. 9. Ibid.:665-66. 10. Ibid.:667-68.
11. FR, 1948, 7:829. See also FO371/69541 F15560.   12. Angus Ward, "The Mukden Affair", *Foreign Service Journal*, February 1950, 15. See also FR, 1948, 7:829-30. 13. Ibid., 8:892-93, 911.   14. William N. Stokes, "The Future between America and China", *Foreign Service Journal*, January 1968, 15.   15. In a conversation with me on September 29, 1985, Stokes described Ward as "at his best" in his dealings with Communist officials in Mukden prior to the placement of the consulate staff under incommunicado house arrest.
16. FR, 1948, 7:841, 842-45.   17. FR, 1948, 8:933-34.   18. Ibid., 943-44. 19. Ibid.:944.   20. Ibid.:944-46.
21. FO371/75810 F4351.   22. Ibid.   23. FO371/75745 F3886. Whether or not Angus Ward had been deliberately chosen because he could weather a siege, he had obviusly been selected because of his familiarity both with the area and with the Soviet Union. Thus at the time of his assignment as consul general in Mukden in 1946, Ward had been a foreign service officer for some twenty-one years, of which he had served more than nine in China, starting at Mukden in 1925, followed by ten in the Soviet Union, ending with three years as consul general at Vladivostok. See Department of State, *Biographic Register* (1954), 82.   24. FO371/75745 F4062   25. Ibid. F3886.
26. FR, 1949, 8:949-50. Edmund Clubb, an extremely conscientious, scholarly, Chinese-speaking foreign service officer with long experience in China, had himself served in Manchuria and in the Soviet Union at Vladivostok.   27. FO371/75747 F4793. Consul General Graham had served twenty years in China at a variety of consular posts. 28. Ibid. 29. See for example the reports of British and American consular officers in Tientsin, FO371/75754 F7100 and FR, 1949, 8:1057.   30. FR, 1949, 8:1077-78.
31. Ibid.:1090.   32. FO371/75747 F4653. According to the *Peiping Digest* of 30 March, Mao, Chu Teh, "and other leaders of the CCP arrived in Peiping at 4 p.m. Mar. 25" and were welcomed at the airfield by "about one thousand workers, farmers, youths, women and democratic personalities."   33. FO371/75749 F5972.   34. Stuart, *Fifty Years*, 234.   35. New China News Agency, *Daily News Release*, 25 April 1949, 1–2.

British naval pride was partially assuaged some three months later when *Amethyst* escaped Chinese captivity.

36. In the same debate, after telling Communist M.P. Willie Gallacher that the Chinese Communist authorities "have refused to speak to us," Bevin suggested that Gallacher "send word to his friends and tell them to be more sensible." FO371/75761 F9683.   37. See, for example, FR, 1949, 8: 727.

3. The Soviet Union and the CCP

1. FO371/75754 F7099. See also FR, 1949, 8:1291.   2. See, for example, Alan Lawrence, *China's Foreign Relations Since 1949* (London: Routledge and Kegan Paul, 1975), 22.   3. FR, 1949, 8:105-6.   4. FO371/75746 F4291.   5. Mao's essay appears in *Selected Works* 4:283-86. Liu Shao-ch'i's essay, first published in Nov. 1948, is reproduced in Liu Shao-ch'i, *Collected Works, 1945-57* (Hong Kong: Union Research Institute, 1969), 123-51, from a version published in Peking by Foreign Language Press, 1951.
6. FR, 1949, 8:192-94.   7. See *John Leighton Stuart's Diary (Mainly of the Critical Year 1949)* (Palo Alto, Calif.: Yenching Univ. Alumni Association of USA, 1980), 29.
8. London *Daily Worker*, 5 April 1949.   9. FO371/75747 F4723. See also FO371/74759 F5496. Guy Burgess was the Far Eastern Department's resident expert on the Soviet Union and Sino-Soviet relations. In the spring of 1951 he disappeared in Europe, finally surfacing in Moscow in 1956. In view of his close Soviet connections, the value of Burgess's Foreign Office minutes may be questioned; nevertheless, they are part of the official Foreign Office record. Moreover, Burgess's views on China appear to have been generally accepted at the time by his colleagues in the Far Eastern Department, "most of whom were, like himself, Old Etonians." See John Fisher, *Burgess and Maclean* (London: Robert Hale, 1977), 56-57; and Douglas Sutherland, *The Fourth Man* (London: Secker and Warburg, 1980), 75-76.   10. FO371/75749 F5826.
11. FO371/75745 F4062. This is the same article, actually published 1 Nov. 1948, cited by the American embassy in Nanking to illustrate the CCP's adherence to the Moscow foreign policy line. For Mao's report to the Central Committee, see Mao, *Selected Works*, 4:157-73.   12. Paul E. Paddock, *China Diary: Crisis Diplomacy in Dairen* (Ames: Iowa State Univ. Press, 1977), 148. See also FO371/75807 F14700, and FR, 1949, 8:875. Paul Ezekiel "Zeke" Paddock, Jr., a forty-one-year-old Foreign Service officer, had served in several Asian posts and for a year in Moscow during World War II but had had no previous China experience.   13. Paddock, *China Diary*, 152-53.   14. FO371/75807 F16173.   15. Ibid. F17879; *People's China*, 16 March 1950, 7.
16. FO371/75746 F4220.

4. British and American Policies

1. See National Security Council Paper, NSC 41, dated 28 Feb. 1949, in FR, 1949, 9:826-34.   2. Ibid.   3. Ibid.   4. Ibid.:834.   5. Ibid.:835.
6. Ibid.:837-40.   7. Ibid.:841-42.   8. FO371/75749 F5523.   9. FR, 1949. 9:906-7.   A veteran of some twenty-three years in the Foreign Service, John Moors Cabot had spent the bulk of his career in Latin America. Shanghai was his first, and last, Asian post.   10. Ibid.:843-44.
11. Ibid.:282.   12. Ibid.:284-86.   13. Ibid.:291-92.   14. Ibid.:295-96. 15. Ibid., 8:20-22.
16. F0371/75747 F4595.   17. Ibid.

5. Ambassador Stuart's Initiative

1. FR, 1949, 8:676.   2. Ibid.:676, 677-78.   3. *Stuart's Diary*, 33.   4. FR, 1949, 8:665. See also Butterworth's testimony at an executive session of the Senate Committee on Foreign Relations, 18 March 1949 in *Executive Sessions of the Senate Foreign Relations Committee* (Washington: Government Printing Office, 1976), 45.   5. K.M. Panikkar, *In Two Chinas: Memoirs of a Diplomat* (London: George Allen and Unwin, 1955), 48.
6. FO371/75752 F6681.   7. FR, 1949, 8:174.   8. Ibid.:176.   9. Ibid.:174-75.
10. Ibid.:175-76.
11. Ibid.:230-31.   12. FO371/75747 F4804. For the American version of this conversation see FR, 1949. 7:1138-41.

6. The Stuart-Huang Discussions

1. See FR, 1949, 8:255, 263-64.   2. Ibid.:259-60.   3. *Stuart's Diary*, 36.
4. Ibid., 37.   5. FR, 1949, 8:739.
6. Stuart, *Fifty Years*, 292.   7. Ibid., 293. For other views on Fugh's role see Brian Crozier, *The Man Who Lost China* (New York: Charles Scribner's Sons, 1976), 334; John F. Melby, *The Mandate of Heaven: Record of a Civil War* (Toronto: Univ. of Toronto Press, 1968), 181.   8. Mao Tse-tung, *Selected Works*, 4:370.   9. FR, 1949, 8:741-42.
10. Ibid.:745-47.
11. Ibid.,:952.   12. Ibid.:956.   13. Ibid.:957.   14. Ibid.:962.
15. Ibid.:752.
16. Ibid.:753.

7. The Chou Demarche

1. FR, 1949, 8:357-60.   2. For Barrett's opinion of Chou, see his *Dixie Mission: The U.S. Army Group in Yenan, 1944,* China Research Monograph no. 8 (Berkeley: Univ. of California Press, 1970), 64-65.   3. FR, 1949, 8:363-64.   4. Ibid.:364.   5. *Stuart's Diary*, 40.
6. FR, 1949, 8:372-73.   7. Ibid.:388.   8. Ibid.:384.   9. Ibid.:397-98.
10. In the Foreign Office, Burgess called the Preparatory Committee of the PPCC "an assembly of puppets with a hard core of string pullers," e.g., Mao, Chou, Li Li-san, Chu Teh, and Coates commented that the "Standing Committee consists chiefly of died-in-the-wool Communists and misguided but perfectly genuine left-wing intellectuals," in which category he included his friend Chang Hsi-jou. FO371/75760 F9105.
11. FR, 1949, 8:394-95.   12. Quotations taken from the NCNA English language version of Mao's speech, highlights of which were telegraphed to the State Department by Clubb on 20 June. FR, 1949, 8:392-93. A slightly different English version is contained in Mao Tse-tung, *Selected Works*, 4:40-47.   13. FR, 1949, 8:398-99. Barrett thought this explanation was "unlikely in view of Chou's character." For Keon's intriguing, though rather implausible, explanation see Edwin W. Martin, "The Chou Demarche: Did the U.S. and Britain Miss a Chance to Change Postwar History in Asia?" *Foreign Service Journal*, Nov. 1981:16.   14. FR, 1949, 8:385.   15. FO371/75766 F12075/G.
16. Ibid.   17. Ibid. F12075   18. Ibid.   19. Ibid.   20. Ibid.
21. FO371/75768 F12952.   22. Ibid.   23. Several American contemporaries of Keon's have expressed such doubts to me.   24. Philip Fugh interview, 3 April 1984.
25. FR, 1949, 8:377–78, 753.

26. For a different view of the American reply and an implication that somehow the United States was to blame that "nothing came of Chou's demarche," see Warren I. Cohen, "Acheson, His Advisers, and China, 1949-1950," in Dorothy Borg and Waldo Heinrichs, eds., *Uncertain Years: Chinese-American Relations, 1947-1950* (New York: Columbia Univ. Press, 1980), 36. See also Michael Schaller, *The United States and China in the Twentieth Century* (New York: Oxford Univ. Press, 1979), 120-21.   27. See Stuart, *Fifty Years*, 248.

8. The Shanghai Blues

1. Richard Hughes, *Hong Kong: Borrowed Place—Borrowed Time* (London: André Deutsch, 1968), 113-15.   2. FO371/75811 F7235.   3. Ibid.   4. John M. Cabot, *First Line of Defense: 40 Years' Experience of a Diplomat* (Washington: School of Foreign Service, Georgetown Univ., 1979), 67.   5. FR, 1949, 8:1184-86.

6. Cabot, *First Line of Defense*, 67.   7. FR, 1949, 8:1189-90.   8. Cabot, *First Line of Defense*, 67.   9. FR, 1949, 8:1199-1200.   10. Ibid.:1202-5.

11. Ibid.:1201, and for Olive's account of his beating, a version corroborated by a non-American eyewitness, see 8:1221.   12. New China News Agency, *Daily News Release*, no. 73, 13 July 1949, 2; FR, 1949, 8:1213–14.   13. FR, 1949, 8:1222.

9. An Invitation from Mao

1. FR, 1949, 8:766.   2. *Stuart's Diary*, 42-43.   3. FR, 1949, 8:766-67.
4. Cabot, *First Line of Defense*, 68. See also FR, 1949, 8:769.   5. FR, 1949, 8:769.

6. Ibid.:766-67.   7. Mao Tse-tung, *Selected Works*, 4:415-17.   8. FR, 1949, 8:405-7.   9. *Mao Tse-tung* (Peking: Foreign Language Press, 1967), 37. As Tang Tsou points out, in the original version of "On New Democracy," Great Britain and the United States were specifically named as the imperialist powers in question. Tang Tsou, *America's Failure in China, 1949-50*, 2 vols. (Chicago: Univ. of Chicago Press, 1963), 1:210 n. 120.
10. This sentence does not appear in the version of the article published in Mao's *Selected Works*. See John Gittings, *The Role of the Chinese Army* (London: Oxford Univ. Press, 1967), 21n.

11. See FO371/75764 F11127; also Paddock, *China Diary*, p. 113. Thirty days before Mao's 30 June 1949 reiteration of his 'lean-to-one-side' views, the Cominform journal published an article by Liu Shao-ch'i on the same theme. See FO371/75760 F8903.
12. See Warren I. Cohen, "Acheson, His Advisers, and China," in Borg and Heinrichs, *Uncertain Years*, 36.   13. FR, 1949, 8:756-57.   14. Ibid.:764.   15. FO371/75764 F9316.

16. FR, 1949. 8:782-83.   17. Ibid.:801-2.   18. Ibid.:781.   19. Ibid.:782-83. 20. Ibid.:791.

21. Ibid.   22. Ibid.:779-81.

10. Fewer Stay Put

1. Stuart, *Fifty Years*, 257.   2. FR, 1949, 8:1232.   3. Ibid.:1095.
4. Ibid.:1240.   5. New China News Agency, *Daily News Release*, no. 80, 20 July 1949, 3.

6. Stuart, *Fifty Years*, 255-56.   7. FR, 1949, 8:784-85. See also *Stuart's Diary*, 45-46.
8. FO371/75763 F10513; *Stuart's Diary*, 44.   9. F0371/75763 F10513.   10. FR, 1949, 8:1308-9. Lewis Clark began his Foreign Service career as a Chinese language officer in 1925 and served for the next ten years at various posts in China, but when he replaced

Walton Butterworth in Nanking in 1947, he had been away from China for twelve years.
    11. FR, 1949, 8:1276-79. Prior to his assignment to Shanghai in the fall of 1948,
McConaughy had had only one other China post in his eighteen years in the foreign
service—at Peiping in 1941. However, much of his subsequent career was concerned with
Sino-American relations; it culminated in a long tour as ambassador to China stationed in
Taipei.   12. FR, 1949, 8:1316-17.   13. Ibid.:1303.   14. Ibid.:1136.
15. FO371/75949 F12104. A Chinese-speaking officer of considerable experience, Tyrrell
had also served in Tientsin, Chungking, and Shanghai.
    16. FO371/75949 F12104.   17. Ibid.   18. Ibid. F12190.   19. Ibid. F12392.
20. Ibid.
    21. Ibid. F12876.

11. Blockade

    1. FR, 1949, 9:1103-4.   2. Ibid.:1104-5.   3. FO371/75900 F9198.
4. FO371/75762 F9820, FO371/75900 F9209. See also FR, 1949, 9:1111-12.
5. FO371/75762 F9792.
    6. FO371/75760 F9121.   7. FR, 1949, 9:1110.   8. Ibid.:1129-30.
9. FO371/75900 F9310.   10. F0371/75903 F10739.
    11. FO371/75904 F11601.   12. Ibid.   13. Mao Tse-tung, *Selected Works*, 4:374.
14. FO371/75903 F10816. American officials in Shanghai also had a good opinion of Han
Ming. They described him as a leader of the Democratic League who seemed "clearly
belong to League's pro-American moderate wing"; at the same time, they thought he had
a "good understanding" of the Communists' "present line of thinking." See FR, 1949,
8:1193-95.   15. FO371/75903 F10816. Robert Urquhart was a newcomer to China,
having served the bulk of his career in the British Levant Consular Service. He was
knighted during his tenure as consul general in Shanghai, a perquisite that had become
virtually automatic with this prestigious assignment.
    16. FR, 1949, 9:1122.   17. Ibid.:1122-23.   18. F0371/75903 F10861.
19. FO371/75904 F11295.   20. FO371/75765 F11304.
    21. For an example of such propaganda, see FR, 1949, 8:457-58.   22. FR, 1949,
9:1278-81.   23. Ibid.:1282-83.   24. Ibid.:1274.   25. Ibid.:1123-24. Since his assignment to Peiping as a Chinese language officer in 1938, Sprouse had served at
consecutive posts in China until his transfer to Washington in 1947.
    26. FO371/75904 F11338.   27. FO371/75949 F12919.   28. Ibid.
29. FO371/75768 F12960.   30. Ibid. F12961. See also FR, 1949, 8:1289-90.
    31. FO371/75765 F12961.   32. FO371/75763 F10603.   33. FO371/75762 F10110.
34. FO371/75769.   35. FR, 1949, 8:1292. Despite this reported discrimination against
Americans, conditions for American businessmen evidently improved sufficiently by
September so that the number who chose to leave by the evacuation ship SS *General
Gordon* was "far smaller" than might have been anticipated earlier. See Nancy Bernkopf
Tucker, *Patterns in the Dust: Chinese-American Relations and the Recognition Controversy,
1949-50* (New York: Columbia Univ. Press, 1983), 123-25.
    36. FO371/75769.

12. Anglo-American Policy Differences

    1. FR, 1949, 9:50-52.   2. FO371/75813 F10976.   3. FR, 1949, 9:56.
4. FO371/75813 F11653.   5. Ibid. F12748.
    6. Ibid.   7. FO371/75814 F12843.   8. FR, 1949, 9:867-69.   9. Ibid.:875-78.
10. Ibid.:872.

11. Ibid.:369-71.   12. Ibid.:376-78.   13. Ibid.:388-89.   14. Ibid.:389-90.
15. Ibid.:81.
    16. Ibid., 8:519-21.   17. Ibid., 9:83-84.   18. FO371/75816 F14701.   19. FR,
1949, 9:82. The CCP position on treaties had been set forth on October 10, 1947, in the so-
called October 10th Manifesto, drafted by Mao Tse-tung, announcing "eight basic
policies." The eighth one stated: "Repudiate the traitorous foreign policy of Chiang Kai-
shek's dictatorial government, abrogate all treasonable treaties and repudiate all foreign
debts contracted by Chiang Kai-shek during the civil war period." Mao Tse-tung, *Selected
Works* 4:148,150.   20. FO371/75818 F16417.
    21. FO371/75814 F12843.

13. The People's Republic Proclaimed

    1. FR, 1949. 8:544-45.   2. Ibid., 9:93.   3. For an English text of the Common
Program see *Current Background* no. 9, 21 Sept. 1950, issued by the American consulate
general, Hong Kong.   4. New China News Agency, *Daily News Release*, no. 155, 4 Oct.
1949, 16. According to Guy Burgess, Pravda's important editorial of 5 Oct. stressed "as
we have done . . . exact orthodoxy with which Chinese Communist leaders can be said to
have fulfilled the Revolutionary recipies of Lenin and Stalin long ago" and the dependency on the Soviet Union and its Red Army of the Chinese Revolution for success.
FO371/75833 F15233.   5. *Daily News Release*, no. 155, 4 Oct. 1949, 6.
    6. Ibid., no. 119, 28 Aug. 1949, 4.   7. See ibid., no. 78, 18 July 1949, 3, no. 100, 9
Aug., 1949, 2-3.   8. Ibid., no. 78, 18 July, 1949, 1.   9. FO371/75833 F16091.
10. See O. Edmund Clubb, *China and Russia: The "Great Game"* (New York: Columbia
Univ. Press, 1971), 379; FO371/75758 F7879.
    11. See Hong Kong U.S. consulate general despatch, dated 31 March 1950,
793.0193A/31-3150,RG59, DSNA (Decimal File 793.0193A/31-3150, Record Group 59,
U.S. Department of State, National Archives).   12. *Daily News Release* no. 93, 1949, 1.
See also FR, 1949, 9:955.   13. FO371/75816 F14782.   14. Ibid.   15. Ibid. F14878
    16. An account of United States–United Kingdom exchanges on the question of de
facto recognition of the PRC is contained in a despatch from the American Embassy in
London dated 31 March, 1952, 793.02/3-3152, RG59, DSNA.   17. See Department of
State *Foreign Service List* for 1 Oct. 1949, and for 1 Jan. 1950.   18. FR, 1949, 9:976-78.
19. Ibid.:985-86.   20. Ibid.:994-95.
    21. See despatch from the acting political adviser to the SCAP dated 9 Dec. 1949,
Ibid., 9:1000–1001. See also Nancy Bernkopf Tucker, "American Policy toward Sino-
Japanese Trade in the Postwar Years: Politics and Prosperity," *Diplomatic History*, vol. 8,
no. 3 (Summer 1984):183-208, for an informative discussion of this subject.   22. FR,
1949, 9:964 and 969-74.   23. See Ibid., 8:971, and FO371/75764 F9316, for example.
24. For another view of the significance of the U.S. response to the Chou letter, see
William Whitney Stueck, Jr., *The Road to Confrontation: American Policy toward China and
Korea, 1947-1950* (Chapel Hill: Univ. of North Carolina Press, 1981), 132.   25. FR, 1949.
9:117-18.
    26. Ibid. 8:979.

14. The Mukden Ordeal

    1. FR, 1949, 8:984-85.   2. Ibid.:1032.   3. See Ibid.:1026-28.   4. 8:988-89.
5. Ibid.:1000-1002.
    6. FO371/75951 F17381.   7. FR, 1949, 8:1000.   8. Ibid., 9:996-98.
9. Ibid.:998-99.   10. Ibid., 8:1008.

11. Ibid., 9:1355.   12. *Stuart's Diary*, 57.   13. FR, 1949, 8:1011-13.
14. Ibid.:1015-16.   15. See FO371/75951 F17388.
    16. FO371/75950 F16872.   17. Ibid.   18. FO371/75951 F17206.   19. Ibid.
20. Ibid. F17359.
    21. FR, 1949, 8:1010.   22. FO371/75951 F17683.   23. Ibid. F17917, and see
F17557.   24. FR, 1949, 8:1021. According to Stokes, Ward's report to Clubb was
misleading. With the full approval of Ward, Stokes voluntarily complied with a request
from the Communist authorities that he attend the trial of alleged American espionage
agents who were sentenced on November 26. Interview with Stokes, 29 September,
1985.   25. Ibid.:1022.
    26. Ibid.   27. FO371/75952 F18155.   28. Ibid.   29. Ibid.
30. FO371/75952 F18155.
    31. Ibid. F18898.   32. FR, 1949, 8:970.   33. Ibid.:1005.   34. Ibid.:634.
35. Another quarter in Shanghai that deplored the adverse impact of the Mukden affair
on Sino-American relations was the British Chamber of Commerce. A secret memorandum of 7 Nov. entitled "The Case for Speedy Recognition," distributed by the chamber
expressed fear that American "distrust and hate" of "anything Communist" would now
be "greatly accentuated by Ward incident in Mukden" and would "likely add strength to
those who wish to delay American recognition as long as possible." See 793.02/1-450,
RG59, DSNA.
    36. FR, 1949. 8:1044-46.   37. Personal interview with Manhard, 11 Dec. 1981. In
contrast to the statements of Chinese officials to Manhard exonerating the Central
Peoples Government, Stokes is convinced that the forthcoming treatment accorded the
American, British, and French consulates initially by Mayor Chu of Mukden represented
policy at the time, and the orders reversing that policy came from Peking. Interview with
Stokes 29 Sept., 1985. See also Stokes, "The Future", 15-16.

15. Britain Ponders Recognition

    1. FO371/75818 F16028.   2. FO371/83284 FC1022/176.   3. FO371/75818
F16390.   4. FR, 1949, 9:151-54.   5. Ibid.:149-51.
    6. FO371/75818 F16417.   7. FO371/75819 F16589.   8. FR, 1949, 9:184-87.
9. FO371/75814 F13405, and see FO371/75821 F17093, F17095.   10. FO371/75826
F18695.
    11. FO371/75827 F18766.   12. FO371/75828 F19237, and see FO371/75825 F18103.
13. Stephen FitzGerald, "China and the Overseas Chinese: Perceptions and Policies,"
China Quarterly, Oct.–Dec. 1970:8. See also Edwin W. Martin, *Southeast Asia and China: The
End of Containment* (Boulder: Westview Press, 1977), 46.   14. Reported in a despatch to
the State Department from the American consulate general in Kuala Lumpur, dated 17
Jan. 1951. 783.02/1–1751, RG59, DSNA.   15. FO371/75826 F18695.
    16. F0371/75819 F16589.   17. FO371/75825 F18073.   18. FO371/75823 F17467.
19. For commonwealth views, see FR, 1949. 9:200-201; FO371/75821 F17052, F17163,
F17204; FO371/75823 F17462, F17471; FO371/75826 F18322. For views of Brussels Treaty
allies, see FO371/75828 F19217.   20. Judging by a Gallup Poll taken towards the end of
November, the cabinet decision was supported by less than a third of the British public.
According to the poll only 29 percent of the public favored recognition, and 45 percent
opposed it. See Brian E. Porter, *Britain and the Rise of Communist China* (New York: Oxford
Univ. Press, 1967), 162.
    21. FO371/75827 F18907. On this point see also D. C. Watt, "Britain and the Cold

War in the Far East, 1945-58," in Yanosuke Nagai and Akire Iriye, eds., *The Origins of the Cold War in Asia* (New York: Columbia Univ. Press, 1977), 97.   22. FR, 1949. 9:224-26. 23. Ibid.:219-20.   24. In reiterating the U.S. government's opposition to acting hastily on recognition, Acheson was reflecting the prevailing American press opinion as seen by State Department analysts. See Tucker, *Patterns in the Dust*, 123-25.   25. FR, 1949. 9:224-25, 219-20.

26. FO371/75823 F17484.   27. FR, 1949, 8:640.   28. See FO371/83313 FC10338/9; FO371/75835 F19234.   29. New China News Agency, *Daily News Release*, no. 235, 23 Dec. 1949, 171.   30. FO371/75835 F19153.

31. As J. H. Kalicki has aptly pointed out, "The winter of 1949-50, which Mao and a high-level CCP delegation spent in Moscow negotiating a Sino-Soviet treaty, . . . was a time of tightening bipolarity in the international system." J. H. Kalicki, *The Pattern of Sino-American Crises* (New York: Cambridge Univ. Press, 1975), 16.

16. The United States Ponders Formosa Policy

1. See for example FR, 1949. 9:590-93, and 8:604-5.   2. FR, 1949, 8:593-94. Though not a China specialist, the thirty-four-year-old Strong had been in China more than two years, serving as consul at Tsingtao and then as first secretary at the embassy office in Canton.   3. FO371/83246 FC1019/76.   4. FO371/75817 F15732.   5. FR, 1949, 8:696.

6. Ibid.:593-94.   7. Ibid.:718.   8. See ibid.:603-4, 606-11, 619-20. 9. Ibid.:719.   10. Ibid.:721.

11. Ibid., 9:437-38.   12. Ibid.:442.   13. Ibid.:443.   14. The document is reproduced in Hungdah Chiu, *China and the Taiwan Issue* (New York: Praeger, 1979), 215-18. See also FR, 1949, 9:460. A news story on this guidance paper appeared in the *New York Times*, 4 Jan. 1950, causing an uproar in pro-Nationalist circles in the United States. The British embassy learned from Fulton Freeman on the China desk at the State Department that the leak had occurred in Tokyo; however, Freeman thought the publicity might increase public sympathy for the department's position on China. See FO371/83280 FC1022/53.   15. FR, 1949, 9:460-61.

16. Ibid.:463-67.   17. Ibid.   18. Ibid.   19. See State Department memoranda of 21 and 24 Oct., ibid.:568-76. See also Robert M. Blum, *Drawing the Line: The Origin of the American Policy in East Asia* (New York: W.W. Norton, 1982), chap. 8, for the legislative history of this fund.   20. FR, 1949, 7:1215.

21. Department of State Bulletin, 16 Jan. 1950, 79.   22. For the text of the speech, see ibid., 23 Jan. 1950, 111-18.   23. FR, 1950, 6:256-57. For more on British views, see FO371/83279 FC1022/30.   24. I was one of those who was transferred to another post (Rangoon) as part of this reduction though I had been in Taipei only four months. I recall many discussions as to when and where the PLA would invade Formosa; there was never any question that the invasion would take place.   25. New China News Agency, *Daily News Release*, no. 128, 6 Sept. 1949, 21.

26. FO371/83243 FC1019/16.

17. Britain Recognizes the People's Republic

1. FO371/83282 FC1022/108, and see FO371/83280 FC1022/67.   2. Even that Republican champion of bipartisanship, Senator Vandenbrg, was concerned. He had written Secretary Acheson on 3 Jan., three days before the British announcement, "I *do* wish

that our major partners in the United Nations could be persuaded to at least postpone any 'recognition' of the Chinese Communist Government until there can be a degree of agreement among us regarding eventualities." Letter dated 3 Jan. 1950, 793.02/1-350, RG59, DSNA.   3. FO371/83279 FC1022/26.   4. FO371/83282 FC1022/135. MacArthur took less kindly to Truman's pronouncement on Formosa than to British recognition of the Communist government. Gascoigne reported that MacArthur repeated arguments he had used several times before with him "concerning the vital importance of keeping Formosa out of the hands of the Reds." He told Gascoigne that his suggestions had been accepted by service authorities in Washington and that President Truman's declaration had "come as a bolt from the blue both to him and to Ambassador Jessup." FO371/83297 FC1024/18.   5. FO371/83280 FC1022/46.

6. FO371/75827 F18900, FO371/75829 F19434.   7. FO371/75829 F19434. Before his assignment to the Far Eastern Department, Franklin had served for two years as consul in Tientsin, the last eight months after it had come under Communist control; he thus had experience none of his colleagues had had. Previously he had served at four other China posts.   8. FO371/75830 F19473.   9. On India, see FO371/83280 FC1022/44. 10. Ibid. FC1022/57.

11. Ibid. FC1022/58.   12. India took the same position. See FO371/83282, FC1022/102.   13. FO371/83280 FC1022/58.   14. FO371/83285 FC1022/215. 15. FO371/83280 FC1022/89.

16. FO371/83283 FC1022/175.   17. FO371/83285 FC1022/224. 18. FO371/83246 FC1019/81.   19. Ibid., FC1019/82.   20. FO371/83499 FC1582/10.

21. FO371/83286 FC1022/255.   22. FO371/83327 FC1051/3.   23. FO371/83297 FC1024/1.   24. Ibid., FC1024/3, FC1024/5.   25. Ibid., FC1024/9.

26. Ibid., FC1024/24.   27. FO371/83244 FC1019/28.

18. American Consular Properties Seized

1. See New China News Agency, *Daily News Release*, no. 261, 19 Jan. 1950, 77, for the text of the proclamation.   2. See FR, 1950, 6:33.   3. FR, 1949, 9:1104. 4. Ibid., 8:1110.   5. FO371/83479 FC1463/26.

6. See telegram to the British embassy, Nanking, 3 Jan. 1950, ibid. FC1463/1. 7. For the U.S. legal position, see FR, 1949, 8:1121.   8. Department of State Bulletin, 23 Jan. 1950, 119-23.   9. Ibid.   10. Ibid. See also FR, 1950, 6:270-72.

11. FO371/83479 FC1463/12. On Tihwa, see F0371/83480 FC1463/30.   12. Ibid. 13. FR, 1950, 6:275, 276-77.   14. FO371/83479 FC1463/16.   15. New China News Agency, *Daily News Release*, no. 261, 19 Jan. 1950, 77-78.

16. On China's recognition of Ho Chi-minh's government, see *Daily News Release*, no. 261, 19 Jan. 1950.   17. FO371/83480 FC1463/41.   18. Ibid.   19. FO371/83282 FC1022/115.   20. *Executive Sessions of the Senate Foreign Relations Committee*, 205-6.

21. Ibid., 206.   22. Department of State Bulletin, 20 Feb. 1950, 302. 23. FO371/83564 FC1931/5.   24. Ibid. FC1931/6.   25. FO371/83497 FC1581/11. According to State Department estimates, there were at the end of 1949 some three thousand Americans residing in Communist China, but a substantial number were persons of Chinese or mixed race "whose permanent home is China and to whom American citizenship is largely a matter of convenience." See FR, 1949, 8:647-50.

26. FO371/83283 FC1022/163.   27. FO371/83285 FC1022/212. The agreements with Bao Dai (for the State of Vietnam), and with the Kingdoms of Laos and Cambodia, were ratified by the French government on 2 Feb.

19. Sino-Soviet Accord

1. For the texts of the treaty and agreements, see New China News Agency, *Daily News Release*, no. 289, 16 Feb. 1950, 80-84.   2. FO371/83315 FC10338/88, F10338/89. For an American comparison of the Sino-Soviet Treaty with those between the USSR and eastern European countries, see telegram of 16 Feb. 1950 from U.S. embassy, Moscow, to the State Department, which found that "with exception Article 2" the treaty followed "closely 1948 friendship treaties USSR with Bulgaria, Rumania and Hungary." 661.931/2-1650. RG59, DSNA.   3. FO371/83315 FC10338/80. A few days before the signing of the Sino-Soviet Treaty, Coates had written a minute agreeing with the British embassy in Nanking that "the principal attraction of Communist China to the Soviet Union is the glittering vision of a Communist Southeast Asia" and that a forward policy there suited both countries, but he also foresaw the possibility that Southeast Asia would eventually become a bone of contention between them. FO371/83314 FC10338/50. On 21 Feb., the U.S. embassy in London reported that "the informal view" in the Foreign Office remained that the CPG could "be expected near future attempt penetrate SEA by every means at its disposal short of open military hostilities." 661.93/2-2150. RG59, DSNA.
4. FO371/83314 FC10338/47.   5. Ibid., FC10338/59.
   6. Department of State Bulletin, 6 Feb. 1950, 218.   7. 661.93/1-2550. RG59, DSNA.   8. FR, 1950, 6:308-11.   9. Department of State Bulletin, 27 March 1950, 468. 10. See 661.93/3-1650. RG59, DSNA, for this material.
   11. *People's China*, 1 March 1950, 29. These themes were echoed and elaborated 15 Feb. in an NCNA editorial captioned "New Era in Sino-Soviet Friendship." Ibid., 30-32. 12. See U.S. embassy, Moscow, telegram to the State Department, 14 Feb. 1950, 661.93/2-1450, RG59, DSNA.   13. New China News Agency, *Daily News Release*, no. 290, 17 Feb. 1950, 94.   14. FO371/83314 FC10338/55.   15. *Daily News Release*, no. 305, 6 March 1950, 24. This message, together with one from Chou to Vyshinsky, was spread across the front pages of *Pravda* and other Soviet newspapers. FO371/83315 FC10338/83.
   16. *People's China*, 1 March 1950, 3-4.   17. *People's China*, 16 April 1950, 3.

20. British Frustrations

1. FO371/83285 FC1022/215.   2. Ibid. FC1022/221.   3. See U.S. embassy, New Delhi, telegrams, 21 Jan. 793.02/1-2150, 27 Jan. 793.02/1-2750, RG59, DSNA.
4. FO371/83285 FC1022/218.   5. Ibid. FC1022/228, and see FO371/75827 F18896.
   6. New China News Agency, *Daily News Release*, no. 262, 20 Jan. 1950, 83.
7. Department of State Bulletin, 16 Jan. 1950, 105.   8. Ibid., 23 Jan. 1950, 145. Tang Tsou, and others, have speculated that the Soviet Union's "crude attempt" to oust the Chinese Nationalist delegation from the Security Council may have been "a Machiavellian maneuver to isolate Communist China from the West." See *America's Failure in China*, 523-34.   9. FO371/83285 FC1022/228.   10. Ibid.
   11. Ibid. FC1022/242.   12. Ibid. FC1022/228.   13. Ibid. FC1022/235. India had voted in the Security Council for the expulsion of the Nationalist representative, but it had abstained in the Economic and Social Council because, in its view, that was not the appropriate body to make political decision.   14. FO371/83285 FC1022/235. 15. FO371/83286 FC1022/246.
   16. FO371/83287 FC1022/279.   17. FO371/83286 FC1022/246.   18. Ibid. FC1022/254.   19. Ibid. FC1022/265.   20. FO371/83345 FC1106/34.

21. Ibid. FC1106/40.   22. FO371/83350 FC1106/179.   23. FO371/83345 FC1106/40.   24. Ibid.   25. FO371/83480 FC1463/30.

26. Ibid. FC1463/47.   27. *People's China*, 1 March 1950, 29.   28. See telegram to the State Department, 18 Jan. 1951, 661.93/1-1851, RG59, DSNA.   29. FO371/83480 FC1463/47.   30. FO371/83481 FC1463/64.

31. Ibid. FC1463/65.   32. Ibid. FC1463/69.   33. FO371/83482 FC1463/98. 34. FO371/83481 FC1463/72.

21. The Hazards of Departure

1. FR, 1949, 9:1183-84.   2. FO371/83499 FC1582/1.   3. Ibid. FC1582/3. 4. Ibid. FC1582/5.   5. Department of State Bulletin, 3 April 1950, 525.

6. FO371/83499 FC1582/27.   7. Ibid. FC1582/28.   8. FO371/83500 FC1582/37. 9. FO371/83499 FC1582/35.   10. Ibid.

11. Ibid. FC1582/28.   12. FO371/83500 FC1582/37.   13. Ibid. FC1582/49. 14. Department of State Bulletin, 3 April 1950, 525.   15. FO371/83500 FC1582/60.

16. Ibid. FC1582/61.   17. Ibid.   18. FO371/83501 FC1582/70.   19. Ibid. FC1582/74.   20. Ibid. FC1582/87.

21. FO371/83502 FC1582/107.   22. Department of State Bulletin, 24 April 1950, 636.   23. FO371/83501 FC1582/67.   24. FO371/83502 FC1582/117. 25. FO371/83503 FC1582/143A.

26. FO371/83502 FC1582/127.   27. Department of State Bulletin, 24 April 1950, 630.   28. See FO371/83502 FC1582/123,128, and FO371/83503 FC1582/129. 29. FO371/83503 FC1582/141.   30. Ibid. FC1582/123.

31. See memoranda of conversations with Paul Hopkins of Shanghai Power Co., 6 and 7 Feb., 893.2614/2-650, 893.2614/2-750, RG59, DSNA.   32. FO371/83244 FC1019/41. 33. Ibid. FC1019/39.   34. See Department of State Bulletin, 20 Feb. 1950, 296.   35. 893.2614/2-750, RG59, DSNA.

36. Ibid.   37. FR, 1950, 6:314.   38. Ibid.:313.   39. New China News Agency, *Daily News Release*, no. 300, 1 March 1950, 1. No evidence was ever produced to support charges that U.S. and Japanese pilots were manning the Nationalist bombers. 40. FO371/83244 FC1019/43.

41. See FR, 1949, 9:1141.   42. 693.0022/3-2750, RG59, DSNA. I have found no evidence that the British ambassador ever requested U.S. intervention with the Nationalists at this time to break the blockade.   43. The degree to which the Communists were able to turn the tables on the Nationalists was demonstrated in early May, when the latter ordered the evacuation of the Chusans, an important base for their sea and air blockade of Shanghai, without a fight. FR, 1950, 6:340 n.1.   44. Department of State Bulletin, 15 May 1950, 755. The CPG's sensitivity to charges that it had prevented the departure of foreigners from China is indicated by the following item from *People's China*: "The S.S. 'General Gordon' sailed from Tientsin on April 30 with 690 foreign nationals on board. This completed the exposure of American lies that the Chinese Government was delaying the departure of U.S. nationals." Issue of 16 May 1950, 23.   45. Department of State Bulletin, 27 March 1950, 469.

46. Letter to Rowland M. Cross, secretary, China Committee, Foreign Missions Conference of North America. This letter responded to one dated 26 April from Cross to Sprouse informing him of the safe arrival in Peking of two American Board missionaries, "one of the first instances of missionaries who have been permitted to return." 893.181/4-2650, RG59, DSNA.

22. An American Probe

1. FR, 1950, 6:322.   2. Ibid.:286-89.   3. Ibid.:306.   4. 661.931/2-2050, RG59, DSNA.   5. FR, 1950, 6:321 n. 1.

6. Stuart is reported to have remarked during a meeting in Secretary Acheson's office on 13 Sept. 1949 that "the top Communist leaders are quite aware that they cannot get economic help from the Soviets and must obtain it from us in order to survive." FR, 1949, 7:1205.   7. FR, 1950, 6:327-28.   8. The Communist authorities had continued to ignore repeated requests for the release of Smith and Bender, whom they had held incommunicado since Oct. 1948. The British had taken up the case in Peking on behalf of the United States as recently as 24 March 1950, but there had been no response from the Chinese. FO371/83497 FC1581/23.   9. FR, 1950. 6:329.   10. See FR, 1949, 8:377-78.

11. Memorandum of conversation with W.R. Herod, president, International General Electric Co., and Paul Hopkins, Shanghai Power Co., 893.181/3-2450, RG59, DSNA.   12. 793.02/3-150, RG59, DSNA.   13. FO371/83295 FC1022/528. Canadian correspondent John Fraser provides a distant echo of Franklin's observation in his account of an "intriguing" speech made at the Democracy Wall in Peking in the fall of 1978 by a "distinguished-looking gray-haired man who knew a great deal about foreign policy." According to Fraser, this speaker said: "Because the American imperialists were our enemies, we understood clearly their national self-interest; but because the Soviet Union was supposed to be our friend, we failed to make a proper examination of things when we were first liberated. We should have normalized relations with the United States right away. It could have been done despite the American Government's resistance had we only thought things out properly and made certain concessions." John Fraser, *The Chinese: Portrait of a People* (New York: Summit Books, 1980), 251-52.

23. Mutual Sino-British Dissatisfaction

1. FR, 1950, 3:1023.   2. FO371/83288 FC1022/319.   3. New China News Agency, *Daily News Release*, no. 193, 11 Nov. 1949, 45.   4. Ibid., no. 196, 14 Nov. 1949, 57.   5. For background on the relationship between CAT and the CIA see William L. Leary and William Stueck, "The Chennault Plan and the CIA: U.S. Containment in Asia and the Origins of the CIA's Aerial Empire, 1949-50," *Diplomatic History*, vol. 8, no. 4 (Fall 1984):349-64.

6. *Executive Sessions of the Senate Foreign Relations Committee* 212-13.   7. Anna Chennault, *A Thousand Springs: The Biography of a Marriage* (New York: Paul S. Erikson, 1962), 322, in *Best-in-Books* (Garden City: Nelson, Doubleday, 1963)   8. FO371/83288 FC1022/319.   9. Ibid.   10. Ibid.

11. As the Foreign Office had explained its position to the British Liaison Mission with the SCAP: "If the Chinese insist on introducing questions of substance, the negotiations are liable to drag on over a considerable period of time and we have accordingly instructed Mr. Hutchison not to enter into official discussion of non-procedural questions. These could clearly only satisfactorily be dealt with after not before the establishment of diplomatic relations." FO371/83279 FC1022/30.   12. FO371/83289 FC1022/350.   13. Ibid. FC1022/325.   14. Ibid. FC1022/336.   15. FO371/83290 FC1022/368.

16. Ibid. FC1022/369.   17. Ibid. FC1022/368.   18. Coincidentally, on the same day that Bevin was making this point to Hutchison, Counselor Graves in the British embassy in Washington wrote to the Foreign Office that he had been "keeping watch" on the American press on the subject of British recognition of the PRC and that "the more

responsible papers take the line that, since we have reaped no benefit from our gesture, America could not expect to get anything other than a severe snub, were she to make the same gesture." FO371/83291 FC1022/396.   19. FO371/83291 FC1022/381.   20. Ibid. FC1022/372. For the text of the Chinese statement see *People's China*, 1 June 1950, 26.
       21. FO371/83291 FC1022/381.   22. Ibid.   23. See, for example, an editorial on the Sino-British negotiations in *People's China*, 1 June 1950, 4.   24. FO371/83291 FC1022/383.   25. FO371/83292 FC1022/403.
       26. FO371/83291 FC1022/390.   27. Ibid. FC1022/401.

24. Foreign Business in a Squeeze

       1. FO371/83346 FC1106/69; FO371/83347 FC1106/115.   2. Ibid.   3. Ibid. FC1106/91.   4. Ibid.   5. Ibid. FC1106/110.
       6. Ibid. FC1106/119.   7. FO371/83348 FC1106/125.   8. Ibid. FC1106/160. 9. Ibid. FC1106/134.   10. Ibid., and see FC1106/149.
       11. Ibid. FC1106/153, FC1106/167.   12. FO371/83350 FC1106/182.   13. See, for example, Butterworth's memorandum of 27 March, 693.0022/3-2750, RGA59, DSNA. 14. 893.06/1-2550, RG59, DSNA.   15. See Shanghai consulate general telegram to State Department, 14 Feb. 1950, 893.053/2-1450, RG59, DSNA.
       16. 893.2614/2-650, RG59, DSNA.   17. Ibid.   18. Memorandum of conversation, dated 14 March 1950, 893.181/3-2450, RG59, DSNA.   19. 893.181/5-350, RG59, DSNA.   20. FR, 1950, 6:91.

25. The Neutralization of Formosa

       1. FR, 1950, 6:335-36.   2. Ibid.:340.   3. Ibid.:341.   4. Ibid.:345. 5. FO371/83565 FC1931/36.
       6. Karl Rankin, *China Assignment* (Seattle: Univ. of Washington Press, 1964), 124. 7. See FR, 1950, 1:314-16.   8. Robert M. Blum (*Drawing the Line*, 195-96) contends that since the end of March, when he replaced Walton Butterworth as assistant secretary of state for Far Eastern affairs, Dean Rusk had been trying to change existing policy towards Formosa. See also Cohen, "Acheson, His Advisers, and China," in Borg and Heinrichs, *Uncertain Years*, 31.   9. FR, 1950, 6:347 n. 1.   10. FO371/83320 FC10345/2.
       11. Ibid. FC10345/12.   12. See FR, 1950, 6:347.   13. Sprouse had told Graves, in a discussion of newspaper reports that Dulles was urging a strong U.S. stand "to prevent Formosa falling to the Chinese Communists," that he did not know anything that would indicate a reversal of Truman's statement of 5 Jan. 1950. See Sprouse's memorandum of conversation, dated 6 May 1950, 611.93/5-650, RG59, DSNA. 14. FO371/83320 FC10345/12.   15. FR, 1950, 6:366-67.
       16. *American Foreign Policy, 1950-1955: Basic Documents*, 2 vols. (Washington: Government Printing Office, 1957), 2:2468.   17. FR, 1950, 7:157-58.   18. Ibid., 6:367-68. 19. Ibid.:343.   20. Monte M. Poen, ed., *Strictly Personal and Confidential: The Letters Harry Truman Never Mailed* (Boston: Little, Brown, 1982), 58. See also FR, 1950, 7:180.
       21. FR, 1950, 7:262-63.   22. Dean G. Acheson, *Present at the Creation: My Years in the State Department* (New York: W.W. Norton, 1969), 412.   23. Merle Miller, *Plain Speaking: An Oral Biography of Harry S. Truman* (New York: Berkeley, 1973), 304. 24. Joseph C. Goulden, *Korea: The Untold Story of the War* (New York: New York Times Books, 1982), 152. According to Acheson, MacArthur had suggested, "as some Republican senators had, using Chiang's refugee army in the Korean fighting," but was "sharply

rapped over the knuckles." Acheson, *Present at the Creation*, 369.   25. FR, 1950, 7:277.

26. Reactions to Neutralization

1. For the complete text of Chou's statement see *People's China*, 16 July 1950, 4.
2. Ibid., 16 Jan. 1950, 4.   3. Nikita Sergeevich Khrushchev, *Krushchev Remembers: The Last Testament*, trans. Strobe Talbot (Boston: Little, Brown, 1974), 368.   4. *People's China*, 16 Feb. 1950, 8-9. See also Gittings, *Role of the Chinese Army*, 41.   5. Quoted by Allen S. Whiting, "Chinese Policy and the Korean War," in Allen Guttermann, ed., *Korea: Cold War and Limited War* (Lexington, Mass.: D.C. Heath, 1972), 137.

6. See Richard C. Thornton, *China: A Political History, 1917-1980* (Boulder: Westview Press, 1982), 229, for a brief account of the invasion buildup and subsequent redeployment.   7. FR, 1950, 1:363-64.   8. Ibid., 6:429.   9. Ibid.:530-31.   10. Acheson, *Present at the Creation*, 418.

11. FR, 1950, 7:329-31.   12. Ibid.:376-77.   13. Ibid.:349-51.
14. FO371/83293 FC1022/431.   15. *People's China*, 16 July 1950, 4.

16. Ibid., 3-4.   17. FO371/83293 FC1022/439.   18. Ibid.   19. For the texts of Nehru's and Acheson's notes see Department of State Bulletin, 31 July 1950, 170-71. For Acheson's rather sarcastic treatment of these exchanges see Acheson, *Present at the Creation*, 419-20. For a different view, see Stueck, *Road to Confrontation*, 198-202.
20. FO371/83320 FC10345/23.

21. FR, 1950, 3:1061-62 (my italics).   22. Ibid.:1663.   23. FO371/83320 FC10345/17.   24. FR, 1950, 6:431.   25. See Acheson, *Present at the Creation*, 422-23.

26. In the latter, contained in a "Special Message to Congress," Truman restated the U.S. desire to settle the Formosa question by peaceful means. See *Public Papers of the Presidents of the United States: Harry S. Truman, 1950* (Washington, 1965), 531-32.
27. FR, 1950, 6:432.   28. FO371/83320 FC10345/26. 29. Ibid. FC10345/27.   30. FR, 1950, 6:385.

31. Ibid.:387. This policy was in line with a recommendation of the JCS. See ibid.:379-80.   32. Ibid.:388.   33. Ibid.:390.   34. FO371/83320 FC10345/18F.
35. FR, 1950, 6:391.

36. Ibid.:395 n. 1.   37. See ibid.:523.   38. Ibid.:383.   39. Ibid.:383 n. 1.
40. Ibid.:444-46.

27. The Effect on Trade

1. FR, 1950, 6:621.   2. Ibid.:619-20.   3. See, for example, ibid.:622-25.
4. Ibid.:640.   5. Ibid.:642-43.

6. Ibid.:647.   7. Ibid.:650.   8. Ibid.:651   9. Ibid.:658.   10. Ibid.:660.

11. Ibid.:650.   12. Ibid.:639.   13. See ibid.:625-35.   14. FO371/83351 FC1106/197.   15. Ibid.

16. Ibid. FC1106/206.   17. FO371/83352 FC1106/215.   18. A Chinese political rationale for this policy had been to repatriate "profits illegally wrung from the blood of the Chinese people." See ibid. FC1106/210.   19. Ibid. FC1106/213.

28. British Foothold Survives

1. FO371/83294 FO1022/466. Robert Scott, recently promoted to assistant under-secretary from head of the Southeast Asia Department, had served extensively in China

since 1930.   2. Ibid. These observations represented some change in Hutchison's views. As late as May, he had been inclined to give some weight to the friendly treatment Chinese Foreign Ministry officials had given him and his staff.   3. FO371/83294 FC1022/480.   4. Ibid. FC1022/470.   5. Ibid. FC1022/481.

6. *People's China*, 16 Oct. 1950, 6.   7. FO371/83294 FC1022/404.   8. See Hong Kong American consulate general telegram to the State Department, dated 2 May 1950, 893.181/5-250, RG59, DSNA.   9. Consulate general telegram, dated 10 May 1950, to the State Department, 893.1846G/5-1050, RG59, DSNA.   10. FO371/83295 FC1022/504.

11. Ibid. FC1022/507.   12. FO371/83497 FC1581/1.   13. FO371/83498 FC1581/47.   14. Ibid. FC1581/57.   15. Ibid. FC1581/60.

16. Ibid. FC1581/61.   17. Ibid. FC1581/69.   18. Ibid. FC1581/45.   19. Ibid. FC1581/51.   20. Ibid. FC1581/52.

21. Ibid.   22. FO371/83497 FC1581/6.   23. Ibid. FC1581/5.   24. Ibid. FC1581/16. Jaubert turned out to be a Costa Rican, not an American.   25. FO371/83497 FC1581/24.

26. Ibid. FC1581/35.   27. Ibid. FC1581/25.   28. Ibid. FC1581/36.   29. Ibid. FC1581/67.   30. FC1581/73. Buol spent another five years in prison. Weighing only a hundred pounds on his release (in September 1955), he died three months later. James McGovern, known as "Earthquake McGoon" to his fellow CAT pilots, was released years earlier but was shot down by Vietminh antiaircraft fire the day before the fall of Dien Bien Phu. See Chennault, *A Thousand Springs*, 333.

29. Focus on the United Nations

1. FO371/83292 FC1022/423.   2. Ibid.   3. FR, 1950, 7:349-50. 4. FO371/83322 FC10345/69. See also FR, 1950, 3:224-26.   5. FO371/83294 FC1022/489.

6. For the full text of Chou's letter see *People's China*, 1 Sept. 1950, 4. 7. FO371/83320 FC10345/26.   8. See FR, 1950, 6:464-68, 473-76.   9. For U.S. views on the point, see ibid.:398.   10. Ibid.:478.

11. Ibid.:467.   12. Ibid.:475.   13. *Public Papers of the Presidents of the United States: Harry S. Truman, 1950*, 607.   14. FR, 1950, 6:484.   15. Rankin, *China Assignment*, 55.

16. FR, 1950, 6:485.   17. Ibid.   18. Acheson, *Present at the Creation*, 452. 19. See FR, 1950, 6:446-49, 478-80.   20. FO371/83294 FC1022/462.

21. Ibid. FC1022/465.   22. Ibid.   23. FR, 1950, 6:514.   24. Ibid.:514-15. 25. *People's China*, 16 Sept. 1950, 26-27.

26. FO371/83321 FC10345/28.   27. Ibid.   28. Ibid. FC10345/30.   29. Ibid. 30. Department of State Bulletin, 11 Sept. 1950, 41.

31. Ibid., 439. For a summary of these charges, see State Department memorandum, dated 26 Sept. 1950, 611.932/9-2650, RG59, DSNA.   32. U.S. embassy, New Delhi, telegram to State Department, 30 Sept. 1950, 611.9326/9-3050, RG59, DSNA. 33. FO371/83321 FC10345/55. When the U.S. proposal to investigate the air attacks on Manchuria eventually came up for consideration in the Security Council, it was vetoed by the Soviet Union. See Department of State Bulletin, 26 Feb. 1951, 356.

30. Chinese Intervention in Korea

1. Richard E. Neustadt, *Presidential Power* (New York: John Wiley and Sons, 1960).

This quote taken from softcover edition, a Signet Book, (New York: New American Library of World Literature, 1964), 131.   2. Acheson, *Present at the Creation*, 452.
3. John K. Emmerson, *The Japanese Thread: A Life in the Foreign Service* (New York: Holt, Rinehart, and Winston, 1978), 310. The State Department had received information from Hong Kong as early as 12 September that "China will provide 250,000 troops to aid North Korea." Six days later the source of this information claimed that "Chinese Communist troops will enter Korea as volunteers but will bring weapons." However, the consulate general officer reporting the information was inclined to doubt the story, and the State Department considered the source "very unreliable." See Hong Kong telegrams 12 and 18 Sept. 1950, 661.93/9–1250 and 66193/9–1850, and State Department airgram of 26 Sept. 661.93/9–2650, RG59, DSNA.   4. Goulden, *Korea*, 312.   5. See, for example, Bevin's message to Franks, dated 13 November 1950, FR, 1950, 9:1138–40. See also Stueck, *Road to Confrontation*, 249–50.

6. Goulden, *Korea*, 244.   7. Acheson, *Present at the Creation*, 466. See also Stueck, *Road to Confrontation*, 243-46, on the question of responsibility.   8. FR, 1950, 1:388-89. 9. See State Department telegram 338, 28 Sept. 1950, to the U.S. Mission to the United Nations concerning Chou En-lai's 28 and 29 Aug. charges of U.S. bombings. 611/9326/9-2850, RG59, DSNA.   10. Acheson, *Present at the Creation*, 514-17.

11. Goulden, *Korea*, 313. A similar advocacy came from the American consulate general in Hong Kong, based on reports from non-Communist Chinese there that the Chinese Communists genuinely feared that the United States intended to invade Manchuria and that this was an important reason for their intervention in Korea. See telegram of 9 Nov. to the State Department, 611.93/11-950, RG59, DSNA.   12. Department of State Bulletin, 27 Nov. 1950, 852-53.   13. Ibid., 853. Rusk also spoke along the same lines to this group. See ibid., 4 Dec. 1950, 889.   14. FO371/83327 FC1051/14. Earlier the United States had sought through the Swedish government to reassure the Chinese that it had "no hostile intentions toward the China mainland" and no "interest in any military position or bases in Korea for U.S. forces." See memorandum of conversation between Assistant Secretary Rusk and Swedish Ambassador Boheman, 13 Nov. 1950, FR, 1950, 7:1141-42.   15. *People's China*, 16 Oct. 1950, 7. See also Roderick MacFarquhar, ed., *Sino-American Relations, 1949-1970* (New York: Praeger, 1972), 84-85.

16. Khrushchev, *Khrushchev Remembers*, 372.   17. General Wu, formerly chief of staff under Lin Piao, was currently head of the Soviet and Far East Department in the Ministry of Foreign Affairs. He was accompanied by two other MFA officials, Chiao Kuan-hua, head of the Asian Department, and Kung Pu-sheng, wife of Vice-Minister Chang Han-fu. FO371/8322 FC10345/59.   18. For the text of General Wu's speech see supplement to *People's China*, 16 Dec. 1950.   19. Department of State Bulletin, 15 Dec. 1950, 100-105.   20. For the full text of Chou's statement see *People's China*, 1 Jan. 1951, 4-5, 29.

21. *People's China*, 16 Jan. 1951, supplement, 8.   22. As reported in *People's China*, 16 Jan. 1951, 28.   23. See Rusk's memorandum of conversation, dated 2 Jan. 1951, FR, 1951, 7:3-4.   24. Hong Kong despatch 386, 8 Aug. 1951, 693.00/8-851, RG59, DSNA. 25. Acheson, *Present at the Creation*, 480.

26. See documentation of Truman-Attlee meetings, 4-8 Dec. in FR, 1950, 3:1706-88. 27. Ibid.: 1712.   28. Ibid., 6:605.   29. See the "condensed translation" of this editorial in *People's China*, 1 Jan. 1951, supplement, 14.   30. FR, 1950, 3:1736.

31. Ibid.:1737.   32. For the text of the communiqué, see Department of State Bulletin, 18 Dec. 1950, 960.   33. Chiu, *China and the Taiwan Issue*, 153.   34. See FR, 1951, 7:1569.   35. FR, 1950, 6:586-87.

31. The End of Flexibility

1. For Achesons message, see FR, 1951, 7:27.   2. Ibid.:37-38.   3. Ibid.:39.
4. For the text, see Department of State Bulletin, 29 Jan. 1951, 164.   5. For the text of
the resolution, see ibid., 163.

6. See *People's China*, 1 Feb. 1951, 30, for the text of the PRC reply to the UN. Even
after Peking's rejection of the five principles, the United States was still prepared to
"agree to principle of negot[iations] with Chi Commies on other FE matters" to get a
satisfactory cease-fire agreement. See Rusk's "eyes only" telegram to Ambassador John
Muccio, 7 Feb. 1951, FR, 1951, 7:159.   7. For the text of the resolution, see Department
of State Bulletin, 29 Jan. 1951, 167.   8. See ibid., 166-68.   9. FR, 1951, 7:134-36.
10. Ibid.:136-37.

11. Ibid.:137.   12. See ibid.:148-51, for the text of the amended resolution and the
votes.   13. For the text of the Arab-Asian joint resolution see ibid.:130-131. The United
States opposed the resolution on the grounds that it constituted a "basic deviation" from
the five principles contained in the cease-fire resolution of 13 January, which the United
States considered a minimum basis" for an honorable peaceful settlement in Korea.
Ibid.:127-29.   14. Ibid.:149.   15. Ibid.:1545-46.

16. Ibid.:1546.   17. U.S. embassy, London, telegram, 27 Feb. 1951, 641.93/2-275,
RG59, DSNA.   18. FR, 1951, 2:228-29.   19. Ibid.:245-46.   20. Ibid.:246-47.
21. Ibid.:247-48.   22. Ibid.:251-52.   23. Ibid.:271.   24. FR, 1950, 6:666-67.
25. Ibid.:674.

26. Ibid.   27. Ibid.:667-68.   28. Ibid.:680-81.   29. Ibid.:681.
30. Ibid.:682-83.

31. *People's China*, 15 Jan. 1951, 28.   32. 893.2553/1-851, RG59, DSNA.
33. Ibid.   34. See American embassy, London, despatch no. 3725, 9 Feb. 1951,
611.93231/2-951, RG59, DSNA.   35. FR, 1951, 7:1926-27, and see 1953-54.

36. For the full text of the resolution see ibid.:1988-89 or Department of State
Bulletin, 28 May 1951, 849.   37. FR, 1951, 7:1686.   38. Ibid.:1952-53. For an expert
Dutch opinion contradicting the American analysis, see Hong Kong consulate general
despatch, 13 Feb. 1951, "Comments by Jan Vixseboxse, secretary of Netherlands embassy, Peiping, on Chinese Communist Policy," 693.00/2-1351, RG59, DSNA.   39. *People's
China*, 1 June 1951, 33. See also FR, 1951, 7:1898, for a report of Panikkar's conversation on
this subject with Vice-Foreign Minister Chang on 22 May.   40. FR, 1951, 7:2025.

41. Ibid.:2025-26.   42. Department of State Bulletin, 12 Nov. 1951, 762-63.
43. See ibid., 7 May 1951, 747, for texts. See also FR, 1951, 7:1521-22.   44. FR, 1951,
7:1584-85.   45. Ibid.:1585.

46. Rankin, *China Assignment*, 105.   47. Ibid., 123.   48. FR, 1951, 6:35.
49. Ibid.:35-37.   50. Marshall's efforts are extensively documented in FR, 1951, 7:pt. 2.

32. The Imprisoned and the Detained

1. See, for example, a British consulate report from Shanghai dated 28 July 1950,
FO371/83504 FC1582/159.   2. See, for example, memorandum for the files, dated 29
Aug. 1950, 893.181/7-1950, and Caltex memo, 31 Oct. 893.181/10-3150. RG59, DSNA.
3. 893.10/11-250, RG59, DSNA. Dr. James Yen, at whose request Merchant wrote to
Swope, told Merchant that the Mass Education Movement was receiving cooperation
from the Communist authorities after an initial period of suspicion.   4. FO371/83504
FC1582/160.   5. Ibid. FC1582/178.

6. FO371/83505 FC1582/195, 199. 7. FO371/83506 FC1582/208. 8. FR, 1950, 6:597-98. 9. Ibid.:598 n. 3. 10. For a sympathetic, firsthand account of this process, see William G. Sewell, *I Stayed in China* (London: George Allen and Unwin, 1966), chap. 5.

11. FO371/83506 FC1582/226. 12. Ibid. FC1582/218. 13. *China Bulletin*, 31 Oct. 1951. 14. James Thompson, *While China Faced West: American Reformers in Nationalist China, 1928-1937* (Cambridge: Harvard Univ. Press, 1969). 15. This information, and all that follows on Hubbard's experiences, is taken from his unpublished personal papers, except where indicated.

16. Hubbard oral history tape, 13-366. The Hubbard oral history tapes are in the possession of Hugh Hubbard's daughter, Gladys Hubbard Swift, but transcripts of the tapes are located at the Oral History Research Office, Butler Library, Columbia University, New York, N.Y. 10027. 17. Ibid., 13-365. 18. Hubbard, who was virtually bilingual in Chinese, was coauthor of a substantial volume on the birds of North China. 19. Huggins has written a fictionalized account of events at the school in the fall of 1950. See Alice Huggins, *Day of the False Dragon* (Philadelphia: Westminster Press, 1953). 20. Sewell, *I Stayed in China*, 126-27.

21. See article by Wu Yao-tsung in *People's China*, 1 Dec. 1951, 16. 22. *China Bulletin*, 11 Dec. 1951, 2. 23. F. Olin Stockwell, *With God in Red China: The Story of Two Years in Chinese Communist Prisons* (New York: Harper and Brothers, 1953), 64.

24. Allyn Rickett and Adele Rickett, *Prisoners of Liberation* (New York: Cameron Associates, 1957); Father Harold Rigney, *Four Years in a Red Hell* (Chicago: Henry Regnery, 1956). 25. Peter Lum, *Peking, 1950-1953* (London: Robert Hale, 1958), 71.

26. Department of State Bulletin, 11 June 1951, 947. 27. FO371/83504 FC1582/163. 28. Ibid. 29. Department of State Bulletin, 12 Dec. 1951, 1014. 30. FR, 1951, 7:1581-82.

31. Ibid.:1797. 32. Lamb was, after Hutchison, the Foreign Office's most experienced China specialist; he had spent nearly all of his thirty-year career at Chinese posts. 33. See FR, 1951, 7:1808-10. For action taken by various Asian and European diplomats in Peking on this matter, see ibid.:1827-29, 1836-37, 1845-46. 34. See "Editorial Note," Ibid.:1864. 35. Department of State Bulletin, 22 Sept. 1952, 400.

36. Telegram to the Department of State, 2 July 1953, 693.00/7-253, RG59, DSNA.

33. An Aftermath of Bitterness

1. MacFarquhar, *Sino-American Relations*, 82. 2. See Russell D. Buhite, *Soviet-American Relations in Asia, 1945-1954* (Norman: Univ. of Oklahoma Press, 1981), 185. 3. Dwight D. Eisenhower, *Mandate for Change* (New York: Doubleday, 1963), p. 123. 4. C. Turner Joy, *How Communists Negotiate* (New York: Macmillan, 1955), 130. See also Allen E. Goodman, *Negotiating While Fighting: The Diary of Admiral C. Turner Joy at the Korean Armistice Conference* (Stanford: Hoover Institution Press, 1978). 5. Joy, *How Communists Negotiate*, 134.

6. A full text of the armistice agreement may be found in Department of State Bulletin, 3 Aug. 1953, 132-40. 7. See *The Korean Problem at the Geneva Conference*, Department of State publication 5609, Oct. 1954, 4. 8. Based on my personal recollection as a member of the Dean mission. When informed, on very short notice, that I would be accompanying Dean, I was told that the negotiations were expected to take about two weeks and to pack accordingly. 9. For the text of Dean's radio report, see *New York Times*, 22 Dec. 1953. 10. Ibid.

11. I was the UN liaison secretary in this rather ridiculous series of meetings, described by a Swedish newspaper as "talks on talks on talks."   12. FR, 1952-54, 3:673-74. Dr. Bacon was one of the highest ranking women in the State Department, which she had joined in 1939.   13. Eisenhower, *Mandate for Change*, 249. One who knew Churchill intimately at this time has written that Churchill had "always been sceptical of China as a great power" and that he had "scarcely moved an inch from his attitude towards China since the day of the Boxer rebellion." See Charles McMoran Wilson Moran, *Churchill: The Struggle for Survival, 1940-1965, Taken from the Diaries of Lord Moran* (Boston: Houghton, Mifflin, 1966), 594.   14. FR, 1952-54, 3:711.   15. Ibid.   16. Ibid.:712-13.   17. See "Quadripartite Communiqué," issued at Berlin, 19 Feb. 1954, in *Korean Problem at the Geneva Conference*, 33-34.   18. Anthony Eden, *Full Circle* (Boston: Houghton Mifflin, 1960), 97.   19. Robert F. Randle, *Geneva, 1954: The Settlement of the Indochina War* (Princeton: Princeton Univ. Press, 1969), 47.   20. See John Gittings, *The World and China, 1922-1972* (New York: Harper and Row, 1974), 194. See also Kalicki, *The Pattern of Sino-American Crises* 100-101.

34. A PRC Policy Reversal

1. Humphrey Trevelyan, *Living with the Communists* (Boston: Gambit, 1971), 51. A veteran of the Indian Civil Service, Trevelyan had been appointed to the foreign service in the fall of 1947 and had served in Iraq and Germany before his posting to Peking. After two years there, he was knighted and appointed ambassador to Egypt. Later he held ambassadorial appointments in Baghdad and Moscow.   2. Hong Kong telegram to Department of State 2 July 1953, 693.00/7-253, RG59, DSNA.   2. Trevelyan, *Living with the Communists*, 53-54.   4. Ibid., 82.   5. Anthony Eden, *Full Circle* (Boston: Houghton Mifflin, 1960), 138.   6. FO371/75827 F18896.   7. U.S. embassy telegrams from London to State Department 8 and 21 July 1954, 641.93/7-2154, RG59, DSNA.   8. FO371/75827 F18896. 9. For years the People's Republic continued to give the British attitude toward the Chinese representation issue and the United Kingdom's consular relations with the Nationalists as reasons for refusing to exchange ambassadors with the United Kingdom. See ibid.   10. Trevelyan, *Living with the Communists*, 84.   11. Department of State Bulletin, 21 June 1954, 950.   12. See Trevelyan, *Living with the Communists*, 85.   13. Ibid.   14. I took part with Ambassador Johnson in the talks in June 1954, August 1955, and June to December 1957. 15. Department of State Bulletin, 21 June 1954, 949-50.   16. For Ambassador Johnson's treatment of these talks, see U. Alexis Johnson with Jef Olivarius McAllister, *The Right Hand of Power* (Englewood Cliffs, N.J.: Prentice-Hall, 1984), 233-36.   17. A. Doak Barnett, *China and the Major Powers in East Asia* (Washington: Brookings Institution, 1977), 181.   18. O. Edmund Clubb, *Twentieth Century China* (New York: Columbia Univ. Press, 1964), 343. For another view on this point, see Ishwer C. Ojha, *Chinese Foreign Policy in an Age of Transition* (Boston: Beacon Press, 1971), 180-81.   19. Clubb, *Twentieth Century China*, 322.   20. For a succinct evaluation of these San-fan and Wu-fan campaigns, see Maurice Meisner, *Mao's China: A History of the People's Republic* (New York: Free Press, 1977), 96-97.

Summing Up

1. FO371/75754 F7099.   2. In his report to the Central Committee of the CCP on 5 March 1949, Mao said, "As for the question of recognition of our country by the

imperialist countries, we should not be in a hurry to solve it now and need not be in a hurry to solve it even for a fairly long period after country-wide victory." Mao Tse-tung, *Selected Works* 4:370-71. As Goldstein puts it, "The CCP simply did not believe existing domestic or international conditions permitted the establishment of positive relations with the United States." Steven M. Goldstein, "Chinese Communist Policy toward the United States: Opportunities and Constraints, 1944-1950," in Borg and Heinrichs, *Uncertain Years,* 275. A similar view is expressed by Robert G. Sutter, *China Watch: Sino-American Reconciliation* (Baltimore: Johns Hopkins Univ. Press, 1978), 32. See also Okahe Tatsumi, "The Cold War and China," in Nagai and Iriye, *Origins of the Cold War in Asia,* 241-44. For a different point of view, see Tucker, *Patterns in the Dust,* 43; Michael H. Hunt, "Mao Tse-tung and the Issue of Accommodation with the United States, 1948-1950," in Borg and Heinrichs, *Uncertain Years.* 3. FO371/83295 FC1022/528. 4. Cabot, *First Line of Defense,* 42. An American diplomat stationed in Nanking wrote in his diary at about this same time, "Surprisingly, American businessmen here are fairly unanimous that it matters little who is in power; they can continue to do business." Melby, *The Mandate of Heaven,* 267. 5. FO371/83295 FC1022/528.

6. FR, 1952-54, 16:804. 7. Ibid. 8. Acheson, *Present at the Creation,* 369. See also Tucker's conclusions in *Patterns in the Dust,* 99. As McGeorge Bundy has aptly pointed out, "If the Peking government had changed its tactics, and behaved in a reasonable way, there might have developed a real and bitter issue between the Administration and its opponents . . . but this situation did not develop, and the battle over recognition in 1949 and early 1950 was in reality a sham battle." McGeorge Bundy, ed., *The Pattern of Responsibility* (Boston: Houghton Mifflin, 1951), 190. 9. 793.02/4-750, RG59, DSNA. 10. See memorandum dated 6 Jan. 1950, from David Eichler, deputy secretary general, Far Eastern Commission, to Assistant Secretary of State Butterworth, 793.02/1-650, RG59, DSNA. For similar information on the results of polls, see Tucker, *Patterns in the Dust,* 161, esp. n. 31.

11. Indeed, Russell D. Buhite goes so far as to assert that "pressure emanating from the Soviet Union" was "the main obstacle to some sort of CCP-American detente in 1949." Buhite, *Soviet–American Relations,* 83. In January 1950 it was the Foreign Office view that "it would probably be the policy of the Kremlin to try to seal Communist China off from the rest of the world, and to try to prevent the establishment of diplomatic relations with the Western Powers." FO371/83313 FC10338/23. 12. See, for example, John Gittings, "The Statesman," in Dick Wilson, ed., *Mao Tse-tung in the Scales of History: A Preliminary Assessment* (New York: Cambridge Univ. Press, 1977), 257. 13. As J.D. Armstrong points out, the People's Republic may have actually decreased its security by its alliance with the Soviet Union. J.D. Armstrong, *Revolutionary Diplomacy: Chinese Foreign Policy and the United Front Doctrine* (Berkeley: Univ. of California Press, 1977), 68-69.

Index